THE
BOOK
OF
MARVELS

AN EXPLORER'S MISCELLANY

MARK COLLINS JENKINS

NATIONAL GEOGRAPHIC

WASHINGTON, D.C.

Founded in 1888, the National Geographic Society is one of the largest nonprofit scientific and educational organizations in the world. It reaches more than 285 million people worldwide each month through its official journal, *National Geographic,* and its four other magazines; the National Geographic Channel; television documentaries; radio programs; films; books; videos and DVDs; maps; and interactive media. National Geographic has funded more than 8,000 scientific research projects and supports an education program combating geographic illiteracy.

For more information, please call 1-800-NGS LINE (647-5463) or write to the following address:

National Geographic Society
1145 17th Street N.W.
Washington, DC 20036-4688 U.S.A.

Visit us online at www.nationalgeographic.com

For information about special discounts for bulk purchases, please contact
National Geographic Books Special Sales: ngspecsales@ngs.org

For rights or permissions inquiries, please contact
National Geographic Books Subsidiary Rights: ngbookrights@ngs.org

Library of Congress Cataloging-in-Publication Data

Jenkins, Mark, 1960 July 12-
Book of marvels / by Mark Jenkins.
     p. cm.
ISBN 978-1-4262-0409-8 (trade)
 1. Natural areas--Pictorial works. 2. Explorers--Quotations. 3. Discoveries in geography.
4. Voyages and travels. I. Title.
QH75.J46 2009
508--dc22
                                    2008050980

Printed in China

CONTENTS

INTRODUCTION

I<small>T IS SCARCELY SURPRISING THAT AS A DREAMY YOUTH</small> Józef Teodor Konrad Korzeniowski—better known as the novelist Joseph Conrad—found the wintry levels of his native Poland, then subject to the tyranny of the Russian tsar, to be so bleak that he sought solace in dreams of the tropics and tales of adventure. When later he came to write his masterpiece, *Heart of Darkness,* he put the memory of his own boyhood into the words of his fictional alter ego, the steamboat captain he called Marlow:

> Now when I was a little chap I had a passion for maps. I would look for hours at South America, or Africa, or Australia, and lose myself in all the glories of exploration. At that time there were many blank spaces on the earth, and when I saw one that looked particularly inviting on a map (but they all look that) I would put my finger on it and say, When I grow up I will go there. The North Pole was one of these places I remember. Well, I haven't been there yet, and shall not try now. The glamour's off. Other places were scattered about the Equator, and in every sort of latitude all over the two hemispheres. I have been in some of them and, well, we won't talk about that. But there was one yet—the biggest—the most blank, so to speak—that I had a hankering after.

OPPOSITE: *Trochilidae, or Hummingbirds, by Ernst Haeckel, 1904*

PAGE 1: *Frontispiece: Antillean ghost-faced bat* (Mormoops blainvilli), *by Ernst Haeckel, 1904*

True, by this time it was not a blank space any more. It had got filled since my boyhood with rivers and lakes and names. It had ceased to be a blank space of delightful mystery...

That biggest, blankest spot of all, of course, was the interior of what was then called the Belgian Congo, and Conrad did manage to get there on the journey that inspired his story. What he saw there, of course, was the dark underside of the impulse toward exploration: the impetus toward exploitation that followed hard on its heels. The undeniable evils of colonialism aside, however, it is Marlow's comment about the North Pole that interests us here.

"The glamour's off"—a strange comment, considering that in the late 1890s, when Conrad wrote *Heart of Darkness,* nearly a decade had still to elapse before any human being would ever set foot on the Pole (if even then, for Robert E. Peary's claim to have been the first to do so in April 1909 has never ceased being controversial). Perhaps it was the international rivalries for bragging rights that tainted the "Race for the Pole." More likely, for Conrad/Marlow, it involved the loss of "delightful mystery."

Those blank spaces of delightful mystery had once encompassed most of the Earth—those deserts and oceans and forests, that is, surrounding Europe and the Mediterranean. The farther one strayed from these hearths of the age of exploration, and the closer one approached its mysterious margins, the more unusual and wonderful things naturally appeared. It is telling that in the illuminated manuscripts and bestiaries of the era the depictions of rabbits and foxes, for instance, are accurately and lovingly rendered, while those of griffins and dragons and unicorns are stylized and fantastical. Few people had actually seen them, of course, for they dwelt somewhere in "the East," where such marvels were always to be found.

Books of marvels are at least as old as Herodotus, the fifth-century B.C. Greek historian whose Histories veer from the accurate to the credulous the farther away from home his circuit of travels took him. Such books flourished in the Middle Ages, when fanciful tales of Alexander the Great described his visit to the ends of the Earth and the prophetic Trees of the Sun and the Moon. Similar fables would be enshrined in the *Travels of Marco Polo* and those of Sir John Mandeville, a charming rascal who was either the greatest travel liar of them all or the most brilliant satirist of an already established genre. The outward journey; the encounter with dog-headed people, or twin-headed tribes, or men with their faces in their chests, or mountains of lapis lazuli, and so on; followed by the return and the telling of the tale—this was the fundamental pattern that, shorn of its more dubious elements, would persist well into the age of exploration and still lurks beneath the surface of travel narratives today.

This faith that wonders might be found at the geographical margins animated Christopher Columbus, who seems to have truly believed he had approached the Earthly Paradise upon first arriving in "the Indies." Those who sailed in his wake, like Sir Walter Raleigh, may have been more interested in actual gold but nevertheless still chased rumors of an El Dorado somewhere up the jungles of the Orinoco. And even if some explorers weren't as credulous as others, the need to impress their audiences—and patrons—back home might have bent them in such a direction. For the natural tendency of the traveler remains, as the 16th-century French physician Guillaume Rondelet put it, to "make the thing seem more marvellous."

A century later the new science was still closely interwoven with the old marvels. The Oxford don Robert Burton, collecting reports of volcanoes encountered by explorers, still concluded (perhaps with his tongue in his cheek) that such volcanoes such as Hekla in Iceland and Etna in Sicily really might be the "mouths of Hell," for "Terra del Fuego, and those frequent Volcanoes in America...[are] an especial argument to prove it, where lamentable screeches & howlings are continually heard, which strike a terror to the auditors." His contemporary and fellow country-man Thomas Gage, however, appealed to a more recognizably modern sensibility when describing the terrors of the Central American jungles: "...to be lost in wildernesses where no tongue could give directions; to be devoured by wolves, lions, tigers, or crocodiles, which there so much abound; to fall from steepy rocks and mountains, which seem to dwell in the aerial region, and threaten with fearful spectacles of deep and pro-found precipices." No dragons or griffins there; though it is clearly cast as being an extraordinary place.

Though marvels gave way before science, the need for "delightful mys-tery" often found a new home—in science itself. Matthew Fontaine Maury was a pioneering 19th-century oceanographer, and his *The Physical Geogra-phy of the Sea* is literally steeped in wonder (and often gorgeously written). Alexander von Humboldt was an enormously influential German explorer and geographer who cast his influence over most of the 1800s, and the express purpose of his *Aspects of Nature* was to stimulate interest in nature by the use of "vivid representations" of its phenomena—volcanoes, earth-quakes, immense trees, and the like—making this eminently geographical work, which was very widely read in its day, something of a modern book of marvels.

If it did not find a home in science, the unfulfilled need for marvels was sometimes channeled into a language of descriptive awe, cloaked in the grandiloquence of "the sublime" that was seemingly invoked from every mountain peak throughout the 18th and 19th centuries. That same unfulfilled need also informed the "pleasure of ruins" soliloquies that encounters with ancient temples half buried in sand or abandoned cities engulfed in tropical vegetation always seemed to arouse. And then there was the mania for description, nurtured by the rage for natural scenery and channeled by those complementary idioms, the sublime and pictur-esque, which reached its height in descriptions of leaves or waves or stars that are, well, just marvels in themselves.

The 19th century was a pivotal era: More travel books than ever before were being published, and they were eagerly devoured by an ever more literate public—including the most literate, such as Henry David Thoreau, who never managed to go very far but whose imagination was so imbued with tales of exploration that he could not go to his woodpile at Walden without thinking it a journey into the heart of Borneo. "Give me the ocean, the desert, or the wilderness," he exclaimed, even though the picket fences of Concord, Massachusetts, were never long out of his sight. Something in that appealed to him—"on this side the city, on that the wilderness"—on the one hand the civilized delights of hearth and home, on the other a world still boasting unexplored primeval forests, encircled by an unfathomable sea, and capped by icy Poles whose labyrinthine approaches no man had yet to negotiate. It was a world was still rounded by that "delightful mystery."

That is what propelled Henry Bates and Alfred Russel Wallace, to take but one example, together to venture, with little more than youth and a shared passion for beetles, into the forests of the Amazon. Theirs would rank among the most famous of Victorian scientific odysseys, largely because, like Charles Darwin did before them with *The Voyage of the Beagle,* they returned from their epic journeys and wrote now classic books: Bates's *The Naturalist on the River Amazons* and Wallace's *Travels on the Amazon and Rio Negro*. Such volumes were also very widely read. The vivid descriptions of the South American forests that thrilled readers of Sir Arthur Conan Doyle's *The Lost World* or W. H. Hudson's *Green Mansions,* two of the most popular escapist novels of the early 20th century, came straight from the pages of Bates and Wallace.

Vivid representations, of course, included pictures as well as words. Gorgeous hand-colored plates depicting birds, animals, seashells, and the like appeared in sumptuously bound folios that complemented the "cabinets of curiosities" found in the libraries of wealthy patrons and scientific societies. Here again it was the 19th century that saw a burgeoning of natural history illustration as popular encyclopedias and travelogue portfolios poured off the presses. Engravings in wood or steel or copper; aquatints, mezzotints, lithographs, chromolithographs—one after another, such mass-production techniques produced a wealth of fine prints now avidly sought by collectors today.

By 1900, however, the era of the natural history artist was drawing to a close. The half-tone photoengraving, which first appeared in the 1880s, would soon sweep the field, and the published photograph would become the primary medium by which most 20th-century readers would view the world. At the same time, with the attainment of the Poles in the years just preceding the First World War, an era in the history of exploration was also coming to an end. Motor vehicles and airplanes were ushering in a more mechanized, more technological age. Be that as it may—and barely half a century after the close of that war, men were preparing to land on the moon—we still recall that for Conrad's Marlow the "glamour" had anyway fallen off long before that. The blank spaces of delightful mystery had vanished.

Perhaps it is a matter of temperament. Certainly some people still perceive marvels every day. Or perhaps we know too much. We know that the seas are not unfathomable, the forests not inexhaustible. We know that the polar ice is on the retreat—indeed, that most things are on the retreat, save the deserts, which seem ever to be on the march. Moreover, we live in a more skeptical age. Advertising and promotional copy aside, it doesn't do to marvel too openly. Most writers today know the value of understatement, carefully hedging their statements with irony.

This is a book of descriptions, in both words and art, of things once beheld as wonders or observed and rendered with a wondering if exacting eye. Imagination drove both pen and brush—imagination as it was before a little too much knowledge banished the enchantment. It is a book about journeys and returns and the telling of tales. And it is a book about Elsewhere, that place found on every map, that place where, as Sir Francis Head once described America, the heavens "appear infinitely higher—the sky is bluer—the clouds are whiter—the air is fresher—the cold is intenser—the moon looks larger—the stars are brighter—the thunder is louder—the lightning is vivider—the wind is stronger—the rain is heavier—the mountains are higher—the rivers larger—the forests bigger—the plains broader"—the only place, we may conclude, where such marvels can always be found.

WILD AND UNFATHOMABLE ALWAYS

THE SEA

"We do not associate the idea of antiquity with the ocean,
nor wonder how it looked a thousand years ago, as we do of the land,
for it was equally wild and unfathomable always."
—HENRY DAVID THOREAU

OU ARE ABOUT TO ENTER THE LAND OF MARVELS," announced Captain Nemo to his guests on the submarine *Nautilus* in Jules Verne's *Twenty Thousand Leagues under the Sea.* And in 1870, when that novel was published, science could not contradict his descriptions of underwater forests, singing fishes, sunken cities, and monstrous squids, because science had only just begun to explore the sea.

The sea—ceaselessly ebbing and flowing, rolling and heaving, foaming and thundering—had guarded its secrets since time immemorial. Men, of course, had sailed over its surface, harnessed its winds, and hauled up nets brimming with its squirming, glistening, vacant-eyed creatures. But the sea itself remained almost totally unknown, still a realm of terrors and marvels.

The terror came of old. Those brave enough to peer beneath the surface of the sea had often recoiled with horror. French novelist Victor Hugo, who spent 15 years on the island of Guernsey in the storm-tossed English Channel, saw in the abyss a teeming well of nightmares:

OPPOSITE: *Giant squid and sperm whale, 1914*

To gaze into the depths of the sea is, in the imagination, like beholding the vast unknown, and from its most terrible point of view. The submarine gulf is analogous to the realm of night and dreams. There also is sleep—unconsciousness, or at least apparent unconsciousness, of creation.

Hugo shuddered with the atavistic terror of tooth and claw—or tooth and maw, for claws were comparatively few in those "caverns, haunts, and dusky mazes, where monstrous creatures multiply and destroy each other":

> Huge crabs devour fish and are devoured in their turn. Hideous shapes of living things, not created to be seen by human eyes, wander in this twilight. Vague forms of antennae, tentacles, fins, open jaws, scales, and claws, float about there, quivering, growing larger, or decomposing and perishing in the gloom, while horrible swarms of swimming things prowl about seeking their prey….There, in the awful silence and darkness, the rude first forms of life, phantom-like, demoniacal, pursue their horrible instincts.
>
> VICTOR HUGO, *The Toilers of the Sea*

On beaches everywhere wave and tide tossed up endlessly the detritus of that pullulating life—broken shells, sea wrack, whale skeletons, twirled whelks, whorled tritons—"A vast *morgue*," as Henry David Thoreau observed of the beach at Cape Cod, Massachusetts, in the 1850s. "The carcasses of men and beasts together lie stately up upon its shelf, rotting and bleaching in the sun and waves, and each tide turns them in their beds, and tucks fresh sand under them. There is naked Nature—inhumanly sincere, wasting no thought on man, nibbling at the cliffy shore where gulls wheel amid the spray."

Like many another visitor to many another beach, Thoreau found in the seashore what he called the "Wonder-Strand," that margin between worlds. Behind him burned the hearths and whale-oil lamps of civilization, before him lay the great immensity. The Wonder-Strand was therefore "neutral ground," the "most advantageous point from which to contemplate this world." And the only one, he seems to imply, from which to begin exploring it.

While Thoreau mused, Victor Hugo brooded, and Jules Verne dreamed, great clipper ships, under clouds of sail, were making record passages around Cape Horn, bearing goods from the China Trade to Baltimore and New York. They followed tracks in the sea laid down by Lt. Matthew Fontaine Maury, first chief of the U.S. Naval Observatory, who had scoured the logbooks of numerous sea captains to compile the first accurate charts of winds and currents for the benefit of mariners. A small man with a mighty pen, whose stately cadences captured the billow and heave of the sea, Maury was also writing the first treatise on oceanography, laying the foundations for the scientific investigation of the deep. Meanwhile, steamships, heedless of wind and current, were plowing straight furrows across the sea, and soon would carry a telegraph cable across the bed of the Atlantic, a "thread across the ocean," a slender bridge to unite the hemispheres.

The sea, from where it lapped the European shingle to where it broke against American dunes, was being tamed. Or was it? Thoreau thought not:

> I think that it was never more wild than now. We do not associate the idea of antiquity with the ocean, nor wonder how it looked a thousand years ago, as we do of the land, for it was equally wild and unfathomable always. The Indians have left no traces on its surface, but it is the same to the civilized man and the savage.

Moorish idol, 1903

Ships driven against a dangerous shore, 1772

The aspect of the shore only has changed. The ocean is a wilderness reaching round the globe, wilder than a Bengal jungle, and fuller of monsters, washing the very wharves of our cities and the gardens of our sea–side residences. Serpents, bears, hyenas, tigers, rapidly vanish as civilization advances, but the most populous and civilized city cannot scare a shark far from its wharves....To go to sea! Why, it is to have the experience of Noah,—to realize the deluge. Every vessel is an ark.

HENRY DAVID THOREAU, *Cape Cod*

Thoreau, however, had never really been to sea. But Herman Melville had spent the better part of three years aboard whalers and naval frigates or in idylls on South Pacific isles, and his imagination had stretched to its utmost to unflinchingly embrace the mystery of the deep. While Thoreau visited Cape Cod, Melville was holed up in the Berkshire Hills of Massachusetts, penning his masterpiece, *Moby Dick*. And in that he issued a prophetic warning:

> [W]e know the sea to be an everlasting terra incognita, so that Columbus sailed over numberless unknown worlds to discover his one superficial western one; though, by vast odds, the most terrific of all mortal disasters have immemorially and indiscriminately befallen tens and hundreds of thousands of those who have gone upon the waters; though but a moment's consideration will teach, that however baby man may brag of his science and skill, and however much, in a flattering future, that science and skill may augment; yet for ever and for ever, to the crack of doom, the sea will insult and murder him, and pulverise the stateliest, stiffest frigate he can make; nevertheless, by the continual repetition of these very impressions, man has lost that sense of the full awfulness of the sea which aboriginally belongs to it....
>
> Like a savage tigress that tossing in the jungle overlays her own cubs, so the sea dashes even the mightiest whales against the rocks, and leaves them there side by side with the split wrecks of ships. No mercy, no power but its own controls it. Panting and snorting like a mad battle steed that has lost its rider, the masterless ocean overruns the globe.
>
> HERMAN MELVILLE, *Moby Dick*

Shakespeare's "vasty deep" was still unfathomed and perhaps unfathomable; it was increasingly enclosed yet still enclosing. It was an era when a young science was commingling with an ancient sense of awe and terror and marvel, a time when scientist, poet, and explorer could still stand castaways together on the Wonder-Strand.

Thunders of the Upper Deep

WHEN THOREAU WATCHED STORM WAVES, ONE AFTER ANOTHER, roll and boom onto the sands of Cape Cod, he could not help but see them mythically: "The breakers looked like droves of a thousand wild horses of Neptune, rushing to the shore, with their white manes streaming far behind; and when at length the sun shone for a moment, their manes were rainbow-tinted."

Waves, he understood, are the outriders of ocean. And whether lapping gently at sand or shingle or exploding in thunder and foam, waves are so obviously manifestations of ocean's eternal restlessness that they really *are* the sea to most people. They are mesmerizing, and for those who habitually reached for pen or brush, inspiring as well. In the summer of 1873, while visiting the Isle of Man in the turbulent Irish Sea, the Jesuit poet Gerard Manley Hopkins was moved to take up his writing instrument:

> We rose at four, when it was stormy and I saw dun-coloured waves leaving trailing hoods of white breaking on the beach. Before going I took a last look at the breakers, wanting to make out how the comb is morselled so fine into string and tassel, as I have lately noticed it to be. I saw big smooth flinty waves, carved and scuppled in shallow grooves, much swelling when the wind freshened, burst on the rocky spurs of the cliff at the little cove and break into bushes of foam. In an enclosure of rocks the peaks of the water romped and wandered and a light crown of tufty scum standing high on the surface kept slowly turning round: chips of it blew off and gadded about without weight in the air. At eight we sailed for Liverpool in wind and rain. ...I did not look much at the sea: the crests I saw ravelled up by the wind into the air in arching whips and straps of glassy spray and higher broken into clouds of white and blown away. Under the curl shone a bright juice of beautiful green. The foam exploding and smouldering under water makes a chrysoprase green...
>
> GERARD MANLEY HOPKINS, JOURNAL ENTRY, AUGUST 16, 1873

A quarter century later and 200 miles away, yet a third writer, the playwright and naturalist John Millington Synge, was spending summers in the Aran Islands, in the mouth of Galway Bay on Ireland's storm-lashed western coast. The waves he saw there, with 3,000 miles of ocean behind them, were terrific and sublime:

> There has been a storm for the last twenty-four hours, and I have been wandering on the cliffs till my hair is stiff with salt. Immense masses of spray were flying up from the base of the cliff, and were caught at times by the wind and whirled away to fall at some distance from the shore. When one of these happened to fall on me, I had to crouch down for an instant, wrapped and blinded by a white hail of foam.
>
> The waves were so enormous that when I saw one more than usually large coming towards me, I turned instinctively to hide myself, as one blinks when struck upon the eyes....
>
> About the sunset the clouds broke and the storm turned to a hurricane. Bars of purple cloud stretched across the sound where immense waves were rolling from the west, wreathed with snowy phantasies of spray. Then there was the bay full of green delirium, and the Twelve Pins touched with mauve and scarlet in the east.
>
> The suggestion from this world of inarticulate power was immense, and now at midnight, when the wind is abating, I am still trembling and flushed with exultation.
>
> JOHN MILLINGTON SYNGE, *The Aran Islands*

There was little need for poetic exaggeration, for the breakers on those Celtic shores could be tremendous. A little to the north of Galway Bay, on the coast of County Mayo, stood the Eagle Island Lighthouse, perched on a towering cliff. Yet on March 11, 1861, it was struck by a wave so gigantic that it smashed the glass in its lantern—over 200 feet above mean sea level.

Lighthouses, those lonely sentinels of the coast, always attract the fury of the sea. In 1911, Douglas Wilson Johnson, a geologist whose "trenchant pen," according to colleagues, was matched by his scientific rigor, undertook a study of the North Atlantic coastline, and soon found himself swept away by stories of the eternal war between lighthouses and waves:

The keeper of Trinidad Head light station, on the Pacific Coast, reports that during the storm of December 28, 1913, the waves repeatedly washed over Pilot Rock, 103 feet high. One unusually large wave struck the cliffs below the light and rose as a solid sea apparently to the same level at which he was standing in the lantern, 196 feet above mean high water, the spray rising 25 feet or more higher. The shock of the impact against the cliffs and tower was terrific, and stopped the revolving of the light....

They run high and fast, tossing their white caps aloft in the air, looking like the green hills of a rolling prairie capped with snow, and chasing each other in sport. Still, their march is stately and their roll majestic.

—MATTHEW FONTAINE MAURY

The destructive power of the masses of water hurled to remarkable heights by breaking waves is greater than one might suppose. At the Bell Rock lighthouse in the North Sea a ground-swell, without the aid of wind, drove water to the summit of the tower 106 feet above high tide, and broke off a ladder at an elevation of 86 feet. A bell weighing 3 cwt. was broken from its place in the Bishop Rock lighthouse, 100 feet above high water mark, during a gale in 1860; and at Unst, in the Shetland Islands, a door was broken open at a height of 195 feet above the sea. The keeper of Tillamook Rock lighthouse, on the coast of Oregon, reports that in the winter of 1902 the water of waves was thrown more than 200 feet above the level of the sea, descending upon the roof of his house in apparently solid masses. In October 1912, and again in November 1913, the panes of plate glass in the lantern of this same light, 132 feet above mean high water, were broken in by storm waves....

Douglas Wilson Johnson, *Shore Processes and Shoreline Development*

The shudder of waves hitting the coast at Dunkirk, France, could be felt a mile inland, and Charles Darwin, in Chile, could still hear the roar of the surf some 20 miles into the hills.

Tremendous waves were characteristic of certain seas. The great Southern Ocean, lying beneath westerly winds that sweep around the globe with hardly a continental obstruction, was notorious for high seas. Sailors trying to beat west around Cape Horn, at the tip of South America, or the Cape of Good Hope (once called, more accurately, the Cape of Storms) at the foot of Africa ran into the teeth of these winds and waves.

Sailing east, however, they became the "Roaring Forties," named for their latitude, and they sped you on your way:

The billows there lift themselves up in long ridges with deep hollows between them. They run high and fast, tossing their white caps aloft in the air, looking like the green hills of a rolling prairie capped with snow, and chasing each other in sport. Still, their march is stately and their roll majestic. The scenery among them is grand, and the Australian-bound trader, after doubling the Cape of Good Hope, finds herself followed for weeks at a time by these magnificent rolling swells, driven and lashed by the "brave west winds" furiously.

Matthew Fontaine Maury, *The Physical Geography of the Sea*

The most famous of lighthouses was once hit by the most dreaded of waves. The Pharos dominated the port and city of Alexandria in

Egypt, but on the morning of July 21, A.D. 365, it and most of the eastern Mediterranean shoreline was suddenly and violently inundated by a tsunami. The description by the Roman historian Ammianus Marcellinus, who may or may not have actually witnessed the event, might serve as the type from which the long, sad history of disaster narratives has followed:

> Shortly after dawn, while lightning and thunder crashed overhead, a massive earthquake struck. While the earth jolted and shook, the seas began to recede, the waves retreating until they disappeared altogether. The seafloor was revealed, with its myriads of strange creatures left stranded in the slime and its cliffs and valleys, once hidden by the surging brine, disclosed for the first time to the light of day. Many ships were left high and dry, and people began to drift about the remaining pools of water, collecting the stranded fish and other marine creatures. Then came a roaring: the sound of the sea returning, the roaring of its anger

Destruction of the Minot's Ledge Lighthouse, Massachusetts, 1851

at ever having been displaced at all. The sea stormed back over the shoals and shallows with a vengeance, crashing into the islands and mainland both, rolling over town and countryside, flattening innumerable buildings in its path. The elements were all in an uproar, and a terrible change came over the face of the earth. For the waters had returned when least expected, and thousands of people were drowned. Ships were overturned in the furious onslaught, and after the waters began to subside, could be seen strewn about here and there, the mariners' bodies floating face up or face down. Large vessels had been hurled onto the roofs of houses in Alexandria, while other boats had been carried nearly two miles inland, like the Laconian one I later saw near the town of Methone, gaping wide in decay, still lying where the surge had dropped it.

AMMIANUS MARCELLINUS, *Res Gestae*

The great lighthouse, the Pharos, survived, and portions of it would stand for nearly another thousand years.

THE CALLING OF THE SEA

IF YOU WOULD KNOW THE AGE OF THE EARTH," wrote Joseph Conrad, "look upon the sea in a storm. The greyness of the whole immense surface, the wind furrows upon the faces of the waves, the great masses of foam, tossed about and waving, like matted white locks, give to the sea in a gale an appearance of hoary age, lustreless, dull, without gleams, as though it had been created before light itself."

Nothing about the sea inspires the imagination like the spectacle of its storms. Seascape art is replete with visions of blackened skies and towering waves and struggling ships. Countless sea stories pivot on the dramatic crisis figured by a hurricane or typhoon. And the annals of exploration are awash with descriptions of storms that seem mythic in their apocalyptic proportions:

> The day being come, the light of sun and land was taken from us, so that there followed as it were a palpable darkness by the space of 56 days, without the sight of sun, moon, or stars, the moon only excepted, which we see in eclipse the space of a quarter of an hour or thereabouts....
>
> The winds were such as if the bowels of the earth had set all at liberty, or as if all the clouds under heaven had been called together to lay their force upon that one place. The seas, which by nature and of themselves are heavy, and of a weighty substance, were rolled up from the depths, even from the roots of the rocks, as if it had been a scroll of parchment, which by the extremity of the heat runneth together; and being aloft were carried in most strange manner and abundance as feathers or drifts of snow, by the violence of the winds, to water the exceeding tops of the high and lofty mountains. Our anchors, as false friends in such danger, gave over their holdfast, and as if it had been with horror of the thing, did shrink down and hide themselves in the miserable storm, committing the distressed ship and helpless men to the uncertain and rolling seas, which tossed them, like a ball in a racket...
>
> SIR FRANCIS DRAKE, *The World Encompassed*

To the mariner, one storm is never like another. Winds and gales, as Conrad put it—and as a former sea captain, he knew whereof he spoke— "have their own personalities":

> The olive hue of hurricane clouds presents an aspect peculiarly appalling. The inky ragged wrack, flying before a nor'-west wind, makes you dizzy with its headlong speed that depicts the rush of the invisible air. A hard sou'-wester startles you with its close horizon and its low grey sky, as if the world were a dungeon wherein there is no rest for body

or soul. And there are black squalls, white squalls, thunder squalls, and unexpected gusts that come without a single sign in the sky; and of each kind no one of them resembles another.

There is infinite variety in the gales of wind at sea, and except for the peculiar, terrible, and mysterious moaning that may be heard sometimes passing through the roar of a hurricane—except for that unforgettable sound, as if the soul of the universe had been goaded into a mournful groan—it is, after all, the human voice that stamps the mark of human consciousness upon the character of a gale.

JOSEPH CONRAD, *The Mirror of the Sea*

Human consciousness, in the age of sail, understood and appreciated the wind at sea in a way that today's anemometers fail to register. In the myriad descriptions we have of storms at sea the wind shrieks; it howls; it roars; and it moans, that "mysterious moaning" heard in the hurricane. It is tempting to say that all such verbs are poetic conceits. And yet...

There appears no reason to doubt, and I have myself experienced it in one case at sea and in another on shore, that both at the commencement and at the passage of the centres of violent Cyclones, peculiar noises are heard. At the commencement the wind sometimes rises and falls with a moaning noise, like that heard in old houses in Europe on winter nights, and this in situations both near and far from the land, and independent of the noise made by the wind in the rigging.

HENRY PIDDINGTON,
Sailor's Horn Book for the Law of Storms

Henry Piddington also knew whereof he spoke. The first person to use the word "cyclone" to describe tropical storms, he had been a captain in the India and China Seas before settling in Calcutta, where, after collecting data from numerous ships' logs, he drew up his *Sailor's Horn Book* in 1848. In that work he quoted one Captain Rundle as stating:

> We attribute it to the noise of the wind in the chimneys, or amongst the trees, or on board a ship to the rigging; yet here there can be no doubt of its being as distinctly heard at sea as the "roaring and screaming" of the wind in a tyfoon or hurricane certainly is. My present theory to account for it is this. I suppose the storm to be really formed, and to be "roaring and screaming" at, say 200 miles distance, and that the noise, if not conveyed directly by the wind, may be so reflectively from the clouds, as in the case of thunder-claps. A noise is known on some parts of the Coasts of England by the name of "the calling of the sea" as occurring in fine weather, and announcing a storm....

Suddenly a great confused murmuring is heard. There is a kind of mysterious dialogue in the air, but nothing is to be seen....There is someone beyond the horizon. Someone terrible: the wind.

—VICTOR HUGO

"I have also met with logs in which this [peculiar moaning] has been noticed," Piddington continued.

> Colonel Reid mentions that amongst the signs noticed at Barbadoes by Mr. Gittens in 1831 who appears to have been a careful observer, and well acquainted with the signs of an approaching Cyclone, was, "2ndly. The distant roar of the elements, as of the winds rushing through a hollow vault."
>
> This moaning noise has also been noticed in a Cyclone between the Cape and Australia, Lat. 41°, Long. 34°, by Capt. Leighton, of the barque *Secret*, whose chief officer was also struck by it. It is also noticed in the log

of the Dutch ship *Loopuyt*, Capt. Van Wyck, in an approaching Cyclone in the Northern Pacific, in which it is said that the wind was "increasing gradually, and producing now and then a plaintive, and the next moment a thundering noise." It has also in one instance, in the ship *John Ritson*, Captain Ritson, in the Southern Indian Ocean, been noticed at the close of a Cyclone, when the weather is described as "decidedly improving, sky breaking out clear, but wind still moaning."

The novelist Victor Hugo, who spent years in political exile on the island of Guernsey in the English Channel, also knew the sound well. When the weather was fine, it could barely be discerned—but when perceived, it was terrifying:

> Suddenly a great confused murmuring is heard. A sort of mysterious dialogue takes place in the air. Nothing unusual is seen. The wide expanse is tranquil. Yet the noises increase. The dialogue becomes more audible.
>
> There is something moving beyond the horizon. Something terrible. It is the wind.
>
> VICTOR HUGO, The Toilers of the Sea

All of which points to a moral: Should you wish to know the age of the Earth, not only look upon the face of the sea, but listen to its calling as well.

THE SEVENTH CHORD

THE GUST, THE SQUALL, THE STORM, THE GALE, THE TEMPEST, the whirlwind, and the waterspout" were to Victor Hugo the "seven chords of the wind's lyre, the seven notes of the great deep." Such dark and ominous reverberations were arranged in a mounting crescendo, with the seventh chord, the waterspout, being the most terrible. "In its presence the thunder itself is silent and seems cowed."

Few phenomena of the sea are as arresting, as mesmerizing, as frightening, as the waterspout, twisting malevolently across the face of the deep. The fiery whirlwinds of the ancients, waterspouts, according to the Roman philosopher Lucretius, howled across the sea, threatening with destruction any ship in their unpredictable path. The belief in their being demonically alive lingered even into the Renaissance. When Columbus, on his fourth voyage, was caught in a tremendous storm off the coast of Panama, and a waterspout bore down on

Waterspout at sea, 1886

his fleet, he warded the monster off by waving his sword and screaming out portions of the Gospel of St. John.

Waving a sword, or firing a broadside at the whirlwind, might seem desperate measures, but they were commonly employed in seas all over the world. Cannon fire, of course, was intended to break up the vortex rather than scare away the demon. Nevertheless, a close encounter with a waterspout was something mariners like Captain John Napier remembered for the rest of their lives. In September 1814, the 28-year-old veteran of Trafalgar was at the helm of the H.M.S. *Erne* southeast of Bermuda when an "extraordinary sort of whirlwind...was deeply impressed upon my mind." As he recalled years later in the *Edinburgh Philosophical Journal* (1821-22):

[The waterspout] continued stationary for several minutes, boiling and foaming at the base, discharging an immense column of water, with a rushing or hissing noise, into the overhanging clouds; turning itself with a quick spiral motion, constantly bending and straightening....Its approach [then became] so rapid, that we were obliged to resort to the usual expedient of a broadside, for the purpose of averting any danger that might be apprehended, when, after firing several shots, and one, in particular, having passed right through it at the distance of one-third from its base, it appeared for a minute as if cut horizontally in two parts, the divisions waving to and fro in different directions, as agitated by opposite winds, till they again joined for a time, and at last dissipated in an immense dark cloud or shower of rain.

A half century earlier, on May 18, 1773, Captain Cook had encountered six waterspouts at once. Sailing into the strait between the North and South Islands of New Zealand when a storm blew up, the always phlegmatic Cook merely put in his *Journal* this terse record:

At 4 o'Clock in the PM the sky became suddenly obscured and seemed to indicate much Wind which occasioned us to clew up all our sails, presently after Six Water Spouts were seen, four rose and spent themselves between us and the land, the fifth was at some distance without us and the

Sixth pass'd under our Stern at about fifty yards from us, the diameter of the base of this spout I judged to be about fifty or sixty feet....Some of our people said they saw a bird in the one near us which was whirled round in the same manner as the fly of a Jack while it was carried upwards...

If Cook was a dependable leader because, like Captain MacWhirr in Conrad's *Typhoon*, he had too little imagination to be swept away by it, others on board the *Resolution* found the spectacle awesome and frightening. The father-son team of Johann and Georg Forster, Germans from wherever, managed to keep their scientific poise. Georg scribbled in his journal:

On a sudden a whitish spot appeared on the sea in that quarter, and a column arose out of it, looking like a glass tube; another seemed to come down from the clouds to meet this, and they made a coalition, forming what is commonly called a water-spout. A little while after we took notice of three other columns....Their base, where the water of the sea was violently agitated, and rose in a spiral form in vapours, was a broad spot, which looked bright and yellowish when illuminated by the sun.... These columns moved forward on the surface of the sea, and the clouds not following them with equal rapidity, they assumed a bent or incurvated shape, and frequently appeared crossing each other.

His father added in his own journal that "I distinctly observed the water being hurled upwards in a Spiral: sometimes it seemed there was a hollow space in their middle, which I concluded from a darker hue towards the Axis of the column....I observed a flash of lightning , when the last broke, but heard no explosion; the same was likewise noticed by a great many more. Thus we were preserved from a very dangerous Situation...."

The expedition's artist, William Hodges, may have been the most deeply impressed of all. Hodges had learned his craft by painting scenery for the stage, and his dramatic instinct clearly surfaced in one of his best-known canvases—and one of the most famous to emerge from the age of exploration—*Waterspouts off Cape Stephens, New Zealand.*

THE MAELSTROM

Toward the end of *Ocean Scenes, or the Perils and Beauties of the Deep*, a mid-19th century miscellany of sea yarns for the "intelligent mariner," the anonymous author cheerfully described one of sailing's oldest nightmares: "When two or several currents meet each other, or cross at angles, violent circular motions of the sea are produced, which attract every thing coming within their vortex, and whirling it round in decreasing gyrations, finally ingulf it in their bosoms. These motions of the sea are called *whirlpools*...."

Whirlpools, he chattered merrily on, must mark the location of "profound abysses" that suck down the ocean like a giant drain, and among the more notorious examples were the Chalcis in Greece and Charybdis in the strait between Italy and Sicily. He concluded with the blithe statement that "the largest known whirlpool is the *Maelstrom* in the Norwegian Sea, the circumference of which exceeds 20 leagues."

That would cause any mariner to sit up and take notice, for 20 leagues equals 70 miles, making the Maelstrom a monster crouching at the northern gates of the Atlantic. If he was indeed an intelligent mariner, he had probably read Homer's description of Charybdis, which tugged everything into its vortex, including "dolphins, dogfish; somewhiles whales/If got within her when her rapine feeds." If he had also read Edgar Allan Poe's *A Descent into the Maelstrom*, published in 1841, and had cross-checked Poe's sources, he would have discovered that the writer had lifted the following account by an exuberantly imaginative 17th-century clergyman named Jonas Ramus directly from the sixth edition of the *Encyclopaedia Britannica:*

[At the southern end of Norway's Lofoten Islands the tide rushes] with a boisterous rapidity; but the roar of its impetuous ebb to the sea is scarce equalled by the loudest and most dreadful cataracts; the noise being heard several leagues off, and the vortices or pits are of such an extent and depth, that if a ship comes within its attraction, it is inevitably absorbed and carried down to the bottom, and there beat to pieces against the rocks; and when the water relaxes, the fragments thereof are thrown up again. But these intervals of tranquillity are only at the turn of the ebb and flood, and in calm weather, and last but a quarter of an hour, its violence gradually returning. When the stream is most boisterous, and its fury heightened by a storm, it is dangerous to come within a Norway mile of it. Boats, yachts, and ships have been carried away by not guarding against it before they were within its reach. It likewise happens frequently, that whales come too near the stream, and are overpowered by its violence, and then it is impossible to describe their howlings and bellowings in their fruitless struggles to disengage themselves. A bear once, attempting to swim from Lofoden to Moskoe [two local islands], was caught by

> *...the noise being heard several leagues off, and the vortices or pits are of such an extent and depth, that if a ship comes within its attraction, it is inevitably absorbed and carried down to the bottom, and there beat to pieces against the rocks; and when the water relaxes, the fragments thereof are thrown up again...*
>
> —EDGAR ALLAN POE

the stream and borne down, while he roared terribly, so as to be heard on shore. Large stocks of firs and pine trees, after being absorbed by the current, rise again broken and torn to such a degree as if bristles grew upon them. This plainly shows the bottom to consist of craggy rocks, among which they are whirled to and fro. This stream is regulated by the flux and reflux of the sea—it being constantly high and low water every six hours. In the year 1645, early in the morning of Sexagesima Sunday, it raged with such noise and impetuosity that the very stones of the houses on the coast fell to the ground.

EDGAR ALLAN POE, "A DESCENT INTO THE MAELSTROM"

Several decades later, when the ninth edition—widely esteemed as the "scholar's edition"—of the Britannica was published, it cited as authoritative this quotation from Poe's story—failing to realize that Poe had lifted it to begin with from an earlier edition of the work.

By that time, the Maelstrom had become a kind of briny black hole in the popular imagination. In Jules Verne's *Twenty-thousand Leagues under the Sea*, it was called the "navel of the ocean," the "sea's most terrifying deep"—and it sucked down Captain Nemo's *Nautilus* to a watery grave.

The Maelstrom—or Moskstraumen, as it is called in Norway—is not, of course, so terrifying, after all. Though it might be strengthened by the effect of storms, it is really only an effect of tides and eddies channeled by the undersea topography of the southern Lofoten Islands. And it is only five miles wide.

A RIVER IN THE OCEAN

THE MAIN INFLUX OF WATERS THAT FED THE COMPLEX EDDIES forming the Maelstrom came from the south; geographers would call them

the Norway Current, but it was clear those waters stemmed from a flow far grander, one that had long been washing wonders from the south and west onto European shores.

For centuries, as Alexander von Humboldt pointed out, flotsam had been washing up on the beaches of the Azores, those volcanic islands in the mid-Atlantic:

> Bamboos, artificially cut pieces of wood, trunks of an unknown species of pine from Mexico or the West Indies, and corpses of men of a peculiar race, having very broad faces, contributed to the discovery of America, as they confirmed Columbus in his belief of the existence of Asiatic countries and islands situated in the west....The mainmast of the English ship of war, the *Tilbury,* which was destroyed by fire in the Seven Years' War on the coasts of Saint Domingo, was carried...to the northern coasts of Scotland: and casks filled with palm-oil, the remains of the cargo of an English ship wrecked on a rock off Cape Lopez in Africa, were in like manner carried to Scotland, after having twice traversed the Atlantic Ocean."
>
> ALEXANDER VON HUMBOLDT, *Aspects of Nature*

By 1785, when the multitalented Benjamin Franklin became the first person to make even a rough map of this tremendous current, born in the Gulf of Mexico and passing through the Straits of Florida before drifting across the North Atlantic, it was already known by the name Gulf Stream.

The most famous description of the phenomenon came from the pen of the "Pathfinder of the Seas," the pioneering oceanographer Matthew Fontaine Maury. Although later generations have corrected and refined the conclusions expressed in his 1855 masterpiece *The Physical*

OPPOSITE: *Globe fish and coffer fish, late 19th century*

Geography of the Sea, the matchless prose of that description still reflects the majestic flow of its subject:

> There is a river in the ocean: in the severest droughts it never fails, and in the mightiest floods it never overflows; its banks and its bottom are of cold water, while its current is of warm; the Gulf of Mexico is its fountain, and its mouth is in the Arctic Seas. It is the Gulf Stream. There is in the world no other such majestic flow of waters. Its current is more rapid than the Mississippi or the Amazon, and its volume more than a thousand times greater. Its waters, as far out from the Gulf as the Carolina coasts, are of an indigo blue. They are so distinctly marked that their line of junction with the common sea-water may be traced by the eye. Often one half of the vessel may be perceived floating in Gulf Stream water, while the other half is in common water of the sea—so sharp is the line, and such the want of affinity between those waters, and such, too, the reluctance, so to speak, on the part of those of the Gulf Stream to mingle with the littoral waters of the sea.
>
> MATTHEW FONTAINE MAURY,
> *The Physical Geography of the Sea*

That demarcation was not merely one of color; it was also one of temper, as young Richard Henry Dana discovered some years earlier on the famous voyage he chronicled in *Two Years Before the Mast:*

> *Thursday, September 15th. [1836]* This morning the temperature and peculiar appearance of the water, the quantities of gulf-weed floating about, and a bank of clouds lying directly before us, showed that we were on the border of the Gulf Stream. This remarkable current, running north-east, nearly across the ocean, is almost constantly shrouded in clouds, and is the region of storms and heavy seas. Vessels often run from a clear sky and light wind, with all sail, at once into a heavy sea and cloudy sky, with double-reefed top sails. A sailor told me that on a passage from Gibraltar to Boston, his

vessel neared the Gulf Stream with a light breeze, clear sky, and studding-sails out, alow and aloft; while, before it, was a long line of heavy, black clouds, lying like a bank upon the water, and a vessel coming out of it, under double-reefed top-sails, and with royal yards sent down. As they drew near, they began to take in sail after sail, until they were reduced to the same condition; and, after twelve or fourteen hours of rolling and pitching in a heavy sea, before a smart gale, they ran out of the bank on the other side, and were in fine weather again, and under their royals and skysails.

RICHARD HENRY DANA, *Two Years Before the Mast*

The Gulf Stream was such an immense phenomenon that it not only conveyed tropical debris and warm water fishes to the far North Atlantic, it carried its own weather along as well.

GOD'S BURNING FINGER

EVERY VESSEL IS AN ARK," was one of Henry David Thoreau's oracular utterances, and though he was no seafarer, he understood a fundamental truth about the high seas: They were always perceived from the decks of a ship, which was a complete world in itself, a "fragment detached from the earth," as Joseph Conrad described it, drifting "lonely and swift like a small planet." Therefore, when something otherworldly occurred, it resonated all the more powerfully among a small crew surrounded by an immense unknown.

Describing evenings in the tropic seas, Matthew Fontaine Maury once pointed out that sometimes "30° or 40° above the horizon, a fireball arises which suddenly illumines the whole horizon, appearing to the eye the size of the fist, and fading away as suddenly as it appeared, falling into fiery nodules":

[T]hen we perceive that, in the apparent calm of nature, various forces are constantly active, in order to cause, even in the invisible air, such combinations and combustions, the appearance of which amazes the crews of ships....Again, when we go beyond the limits of the land-breeze, and come into the continuous trade-wind, we occasionally see from the low-moving, round black clouds (unless it thunders), light blue sparks collected upon the extreme points of the iron belaying-pins, &c.; then the crew appear to fear a new danger, against which courage is unavailing, and which the mind can find no power to endure. The fervent, fiery nature inspires the traveller with deep awe. They who, under the beating of the storm and terrible violence of the ocean, look danger courageously in the face, feel, in the presence of these phenomena, insignificant, feeble, anxious....

    MATTHEW FONTAINE MAURY, *The Physical Geography of the Sea*

Saint Elmo's fire is the name by which the blue, flamelike apparition is best known today, St. Elmo being a patron saint of sailors. Scientists might prefer "corona discharge," for it is apparently a halo of electrical excitement mantling such natural conductors as chimneys and mainmasts. But to sailors who understood nothing about electricity, the appearance of the flame, usually in a lightning storm, was a visitation from the beyond, and always portentous. In 1519, Magellan's ships encountered 60 days of unremitting squalls and storms in the Atlantic. When their situation seemed most desperate, the crews believed they were saved by St. Anselm, whose device was a ship, and who descended to them in the shape of the blue flame:

During these storms the body of St. Anselme appeared to us several times; amongst others, one night that it was very dark on account of the bad weather, the said saint appeared in the form of a fire lighted at the summit of the mainmast, and remained there near two hours and a half, which

comforted us greatly, for we were in tears, only expecting the hour of perish-
ing; and when that holy light was going away from us it gave out so great a
brilliancy in the eyes of each, that we were near a quarter–of–an–hour like
people blinded, and calling out for mercy. For without any doubt nobody
hoped to escape from that storm. It is to be noted that all and as many times
as that light which represents the said St. Anselme shows itself and descends
upon a vessel which is in a storm at sea, that vessel never is lost.

ANTONIO PIGAFETTA, *The First Voyage Round the World*

Herman Melville, in *Moby Dick,* vividly described the effect that an
appearance of Saint Elmo's fire has on a ship's crew. As a typhoon slams
into the *Pequod* off the coast of Japan, the crew begins lashing down the
boats. Since Starbuck and Stubb, Queequeg, Daggoo, and Tashtego are
not overly concerned with distinctions in hagiography, their name for
the apparition—"corpusants," a corruption of "corpus sancti," or "holy
body"—summons all the more strikingly the image of a visitation by
awesome and unearthly powers:

"Look aloft!" cried Starbuck. "The corpusants! the corpusants!"
All the yard-arms were tipped with a pallid fire; and touched at each
tri-pointed lightning-rod-end with three tapering white flames, each
of the three tall masts was silently burning in that sulphurous air, like
three gigantic wax tapers before an altar.
"Blast the boat! let it go!" cried Stubb at this instant, as a swashing sea
heaved under his own little craft, so that its gunwale violently jammed his
hand, as he was passing a lashing. "Blast it!"—but slipping backward on
the deck, his uplifted eyes caught the flames; and immediately shifting his
tone, he cried—"The corpusants have mercy on us all!"
To sailors, oaths are household words; they will swear in the
trance of the calm, and in the teeth of the tempest; they will imprecate
curses from the topsail-yard-arms, when most they teeter over to a

seething sea; but in all my voyagings, seldom have I heard a common oath when God's burning finger has been laid on the ship; when His "Mene, Mene, Tekel, Upharsin" has been woven into the shrouds and the cordage.

While this pallidness was burning aloft, few words were heard from the enchanted crew; who in one thick cluster stood on the forecastle, all their eyes gleaming in that pale phosphorescence, like a far away constellation of stars...

HERMAN MELVILLE, Moby Dick

This time the corposants are not beneficent—or if they are, they don't get much of a chance to work their power, as Captain Ahab, first invokes the flamelike apparition ("I leap with thee; I burn with thee; would fain be welded with thee; defyingly I worship thee!"), then extinguishes it—and the *Pequod* is doomed.

SHOALS OF STARS

STARS ARE THE MARINER'S OLDEST AND TRUEST FRIENDS. Long before the advent of nautical almanacs and sextants and chronometers, long before the medieval cross-staff and ancient astrolabe, seafarers from the Mediterranean to Polynesia were navigating by the stars using their eyes alone, watching the constellations wheel in their immense arcs in a reassuringly predictable fashion. But the upward gaze was not limited to practicing the haven-finding art; scrutiny led to contemplation, which led to rapture.

"The starry heavens, therefore, are not mere unmeaning and incomprehensible show," wrote the Lutheran pastor and stargazer Joseph Seiss in his 1882 book *The Gospel in the Stars: or, Primeval Astronomy*. Nor were they a "boundless and trackless wilderness of luminous orbs. There are paths which we can thread, sometimes dark and

Constellations of the Northern Hemisphere, 1710

rugged, and often leading into depths through which it is hard to follow them, but still not untraceable."

Tracing those paths was an activity that engaged Matthew Fontaine Maury who spent part of his professional life as superintendent of the U.S. Naval Observatory. Having been lamed in a stagecoach accident when still a young officer, he was restricted from active sea duty. But working late into the nights at the observatory, writing *The Physical Geography of the Sea,* he recalled the glorious constellations of the Southern Hemisphere, when as a midshipman he gazed at them from a ship off Valparaíso, Chile:

One who has never watched the southern sky in the stillness of the night, after the sea breeze with its turmoil is done, can have no idea of its grandeur, beauty, and loveliness.…I have stood on the deck under those beautiful skies gazing, admiring, rapt. I have seen there, above the horizon at once, and shining with a splendor unknown to these latitudes, every star of the first magnitude—save only six—that is contained in the catalogue of the 100 principal fixed stars of astronomers.…[G]lancing the eye above and around, you are dazzled with the splendors of the firmament. The moon and the planets stand out from it; they do not seem to touch the blue vault in which the stars are set. The Southern Cross is just about to culminate. Climbing up in the east are the Centaurs, Spica, Bootes, and Antares, with his lovely little companion, which only the best telescopes have power to unveil. These are all bright particular stars, differing from one another in color as they do in glory. At the same time, the western sky is glorious with its brilliants too. Orion is there, just about to march down into the sea; but Canopus and Sirius, with Castor and his twin brother, and Procyon, and Argus, and Regulus—these are high up in their course; they look down with great splendor, smiling peacefully as they precede the Southern Cross on its western way. And yonder, farther still, away to the south, float the Magellanic clouds, and the "Coal Sacks"–those mysterious, dark spots in the sky, which seem as though it had been rent, and these were holes in the "azure robe of night," looking out into the starless, empty, black abyss beyond.

MATTHEW FONTAINE MAURY, *The Physical Geography of the Sea*

Sometimes the stellar enchantment was so rapturous that it seemed to transcend the particulars of time and place. On calm, clear, moonless nights the ocean might mirror the stars so seamlessly that sky and sea lost their distinctness. The solitary wayfarer, like Henry Tomlinson one night in 1909, alone on the bridge of a tramp steamer, might then fall beneath a spell so profound that it becomes dreamlike, a suspension in a star-filled void, a wandering not over this ocean but across the great cosmic sea itself:

> There was me, and there were the stars. They were my nearest neighbours….[And I was] the only inhabitant of a congealed asteroid off the main track in space, with the sun diminished to a point through travel, and the Milky Way not reached yet; though I could see we were approaching its bay of light. An appreciable journey had been made. But by the faintness of its shine there was a timeless vacancy to be travelled still. We should make that faint glow, that congregation of suns, that archipelago of worlds; though not yet. But had we not all the night to travel in? The night would be long. We should not be disrupted any more by the old day. The final morning had passed. I had no doubt the drift of the dark lump to which I clung in space, while my hair streamed with our speed, would at length reach the bright fraternity…
>
> H. M. TOMLINSON, *The Sea and the Jungle*

STARS IN THE SEA

THE PHOSPHORESCENCE OF THE OCEAN IS ONE OF THOSE SPLENDID phenomena of nature which excite our admiration, even when we behold its recurrence every night for months together," recalled Alexander von Humboldt, writing *Aspects of Nature* in the wintry Berlin of 1808. "Wherever the ship's side rises above the waves, bluish or reddish flames seem to flash lightning-like upwards from the keel. The appearance presented in the tropical seas on a dark night is indescribably glorious, when shoals of dolphins are seen sporting around, and cutting the foaming waves in long and circling lines, gleaming with bright and sparkling light…"

No phenomenon of the sea has been more consistently and captivatingly marvelous than this scintillating, fiery luminescence. It has always made such a vivid impression that literate seafarers have often reached for their pens. Folklore might have explained the phenomenon in any number of ways, but to John Purdy, an early 19th-century British hydrographer, the display, which reminded him of the "lamps of a great city," must rise from the activity of uncounted myriads of tiny "animalcules." He was nearly, but not quite right; the culprits are usually dinoflagellates, a kind of algae, or plant:

The luminous appearance of the sea at night has often been the subject of wonder and reflection. This light, when excited by the ship's rushing through the water, assumes the form of brilliant stars, or round masses of greenish hue, frequently eighteen inches in diameter. They float by the vessel in every part of the water which her bottom has touched, as deep as the very lowest part of the keel, and form behind her a long and fiery train. At other times, when the breeze is strong, and the billows break and foam, this light appears like fields of flashing fire.

The luminous appearance of the sea at night has often been the subject of wonder and reflection. This light, when excited by the ship's rushing through the water, assumes the form of brilliant stars, or round masses of greenish hue, frequently eighteen inches in diameter.

—JOHN PURDY

Twice...I have beheld this latter sight in all its splendour; the water was highly luminous, so far as the eye could reach, and the vessel seemed to be plunging her way over billows of liquid fire. In both instances the night was dark and lowering; and the brilliance of the water formed a grand but awful contrast with the black concave above us.

JOHN PURDY, *The New Sailing Directory for the Ethiopic or Southern Atlantic Ocean*

In 1866, George Kennan, barely 20 years old but already a promising journalist, was on a ship in the North Pacific, off the coast of Russian Siberia. On an unusually warm summer's evening, the vessel seemed to float "spell-bound, in vacancy—the only earthly object in an encircling universe of stars and planets. The great luminous band of the Milky Way seemed to sweep around beneath us in a complete circle of white, misty light, and far down under our keel gleamed the three bright stars in the belt of Orion."

Then the great hollow sphere of stars suddenly vanished,

and...I saw for the first time, in all its glorious splendour, the phosphorescence of the sea. With almost incredible swiftness, a mantle of bluish-white fire had covered nearly all the dark water north of us, and its clearly defined edge wavered and trembled for an instant, like the arch of an aurora, within half a mile of the ship. Another lightning-like flash brought it all around us, and we floated, literally, in a sea of liquid radiance. Not a single square foot of dark water could be seen, in any direction, from the maintop, and all the rigging of the ship, to the royal yards, was lighted up with a faint, unearthly, blue glare. The ocean looked like a vast plain of snow, illuminated by blue fire and overhung by heavens of almost inky blackness. The Milky Way disappeared completely in the blaze of light from the sea, and stars of the first magnitude twinkled dimly, as if half hidden by fog.

Only a moment before, the dark, still water had reflected vividly a whole hemisphere of spangled constellations, and the outlines of the ship's spars were projected as dusky shadows against the Milky Way. Now, the sea was ablaze with opaline light, and the yards and sails were painted in faint tints of blue on a background of ebony. The metamorphosis was sudden and wonderful beyond description! The polar aurora seemed to have left its home in the higher regions of the atmosphere and descended in a sheet of vivid electrical fire upon the ocean. As we stood, silent with amazement, upon the quarter-deck, this sheet of blu-ish flame suddenly vanished, over at least ten square miles of water, causing, by its almost instantaneous disappearance, a sensation of total blindness, and leaving the sea, for a moment, an abyss of blackness. As the pupils of our eyes, however, gradually dilated, we saw, as before, the dark shining mirror of water around the ship, while far away on the horizon rose the faint luminous appearance which had first attracted our attention, and which was evidently due to the lighting up of the haze by areas of phosphorescent water below the horizon line.

In a moment the mate shouted excitedly: "Here it comes again!" and again the great tide of fire came sweeping up around the vessel, and we floated in a sea of radiance that extended in every direction beyond the limits of vision....

GEORGE KENNAN, Tent Life in Siberia

SHOWERS OF DIAMONDS

BRIGHT AFTERNOON ON THE HIGH SEAS, with the weather fine and the trade winds snapping, could once be relied on to provide quite a show. "There are also fish which fly," noted Antonio Pigafetta, chronicler of Magellan's 1519 voyage, "and we saw a great quantity of them together, so many that it seemed it was an island in the sea."

The anonymous compiler of the mid-19th-century miscellany *Ocean Scenes, or the Perils and Beauties of the Deep* knew the sight well:

Perhaps there is not any more characteristic evidence of our being within the tropical regions,–one, I mean, which strikes the imagination more forcibly,–than the company of those picturesque little animals, the flying-fish....No familiarity with the sight can ever render us indifferent to the graceful flight of these most interesting of all the finny, or, rather, winged tribe....I have, indeed, hardly ever observed a person so dull, or unimaginative, that his eye did not glisten as he watched a shoal, or, it may well be called, a covey of flying-fish rise from the sea, and skim along for several hundred yards. There is something in it so very peculiar, so totally dissimilar to every thing else in other parts of the world, that our wonder goes on increasing every time we see even a single one take its flight.

To Frank Bullen, a former sea captain turned writer on marine subjects, flying fish, flashing in the sun, skimmed over the surface in such numbers that the sound of their vibrating pectorals made a "musical murmur like the hum of far-off bees." At night they might even be more impressive:

There are few prettier sights to be seen at sea than is visible when, on a fairly calm night, with the smooth water highly phosphorescent, a school of Flying-fish are disturbed. Like a galaxy of meteors they may be seen streaming along very swiftly just beneath the surface, each leaving behind it a broadening track of light, until, as if at one impulse, the whole company suddenly leave the water, the points of their multitudinous exit gleaming in tiny showers of diamond spray.

FRANK BULLEN, Denizens of the Deep

Flying fish do not fly for the exultation of it; they soar to escape a host of speedy predators, including albacore, bonito, and especially dolphin (the fish, not the porpoise). In Bullen's opinion, as in that of many another mariner or saltwater angler, the dolphin is an even more marvelous creature, its iridescent sides so glowing, pulsing, and quivering with color as to really deserve his being called by his Spanish name, *el dorado,* the "gilded one":

It has long been an article of poetic faith that the dying Dolphin is more splendid in his colour changes than he ever is during life; but from this, after long experience, I must emphatically dissent. It is true that when a Dolphin suffers sudden and violent death, such as being transfixed by the granes or five-pointed fish-spear in common use on board ship, his body does exhibit a series of swiftly changing colours, fairly vivid. But they are never so brilliant as those shown by the living fish, when in the height of his activity he hurls himself in arrowy flight after his prey, or springs perpendicularly into the sunshine, the spray falling from him like a shower of diamonds, and his glorious hues flashing in the glare of the sun, with an effect beyond the power of any artist to depict or pen to describe.

When, however, the Dolphin is caught with a hook and laid on deck to die, the kaleidoscopic changes are still apparent, but oh, so faint and dulled compared with those shown by the living fish, or even with the speared creature. And some time before he dies a dull leaden shade comes over his gaudy body, and never goes away again. It is permanent and beautiful, for some reason which I do not understand. Nothing in Nature I should say can give more pleasure to a colour-loving eye than the sight of a number of Dolphin on a sunny day, when the sea is smooth enough to observe all their motions properly. Not even the amazingly beautiful tints and shadings of a flock of humming birds can vie with the marvellous splendour of this wonderful fish.

FRANK BULLEN, *Denizens of the Deep*

UNWRITTEN LIVES

IN 1872, A THREE-MASTED BRITISH NAVAL CORVETTE, THE *Challenger*, guns removed and laboratories added, weighed anchor in Portsmouth, England, and set sail for what became a four-year, globe-girdling voyage. Carrying alongside its crew a complement of scientists and naturalists,

OPPOSITE: *Sea anemones, by Ernst Haeckel, 1904*

the *Challenger* was embarked on the first cruise entirely devoted to the exploration of the deep. Supplementing the age-old fisherman's net and hempen lead line with dredges and trawls, the scientists, in seas all over the world, winched to the surface and spilled over the decks a cold, oozy mixture of starfish, sea urchins, bits of coral, strange fish with bulging eyes and distended stomachs, and myriads of other glistening creatures, first fruits of the age of marine biology.

Science had come to the deep, to the realm of tooth and maw that for so long had been consigned to monsters and marvels and Victor Hugo's pullulating horrors. Even the seafloor, for those who had the courage to imaginatively fathom the unfathomable, appeared to be just one vast, yawning maw. "When I present this great Gulf to my imagination," wrote Thomas Burnet, the 17th-century Puritan divine, "emptied of all its waters, naked and gaping at the Sun, stretching its jaws from one end of the Earth to another, it appears to me the most ghastly thing in Nature."

> 'Tis very likely there are Caves under water, and hollow passages into the bowels of the Earth, by which the Seas circulate and communicate one with another, and with Subterraneous waters; Those great Eddees and infamous Syrtes and Whirlpools that are in some Seas…that suck into them and overwhelm whatever comes within their reach, show that there is something below that sucks from them in proportion, and that drinks up the Sea as the Sea drinks up the Rivers…
>
> THOMAS BURNET, *The Sacred Theory of the Earth*

Fear and revulsion toward sea creatures ran so deep that Antonio Pigafetta, Magellan's chronicler, described sharks in such a way that untold generations of mariners might well have agreed that as a description it was complete and sufficient: "During the calm there came large fishes near the ships which they called Tiburoni (sharks), which have teeth of a terrible kind, and eat people when they find them in the sea either alive or dead."

Even those mightiest and most majestic of sea creatures, the whales, were known mostly from their need to surface frequently, and then known but imperfectly, as the fantastic whales so common in old lithographs and engravings amply testified. And the most sought-after of them, the sperm whale, "scientific or poetic, lives not complete in any literature," according to Melville. "Far above all the other hunted whales, his is an unwritten life."

If the sperm whale had not found his biographer, there was little chance that his avowed if reclusive enemy, the giant squid, who lived deep down in the maw of things, was going to be any better understood. It led such a mysterious existence that, when one occasionally surfaced or washed up on a beach, even Melville conceded that it baffled the imagination:

[We] now gazed at the most wondrous phenomenon which the secret seas have hitherto revealed to mankind. A vast pulpy mass, furlongs in length and breadth, of a glancing cream-color, lay floating on the water, innumerable long arms radiating from its centre, and curling and twisting like a nest of anacondas, as if blindly to clutch at any hapless object within reach. No perceptible face or front did it have; no conceivable token of either sensation or instinct; but undulated there on the billows, an unearthly, formless, chance-like apparition of life.

HERMAN MELVILLE, *Moby Dick*

Even as recently as 1906, there were attempts to, if not exactly write the life, then at least verify the existence of such zoological anomalies as, well, sea serpents. In the 1905 *Proceedings of the Zoological Society of London,* two naturalists, E. G. B. Meade-Waldo and Michael Nicholl, described seeing off the coast of Brazil a giant creature very like a sea serpent. The monster, which surfaced just off the yacht on which they were cruising, even had the familiar snakelike neck and frilled fin. Some might doubt that Nicholl, but 25 at the time, had sufficient experience to make such a call from a heaving deck, but Meade-Waldo was 50, and they both eventually had extremely respectable careers. Nevertheless, after that, sea serpent sightings began falling off, and the vanquished creatures have apparently retired to the only lair from which they are known to have emerged, the decorative borders of old maps.

Henry Moseley was one of the naturalists on board the *Challenger,* and his eye was not for the monsters of yore but rather was fixed on all of the tiny marvels of the sea. There were insects that lived out their entire existence far out on the open ocean, and there were bright-yellow fish or mollusks dwelling in camouflaged obscurity against the bright yellow Sargasso weed. The Sargasso Sea, in fact, was a pasture as full of life as any prairie. Their lives, and those of even tinier beings, were totally unwritten because totally unknown. Beneath the microscope, however, these diminutive little fellows with the big Latin names, dredged almost by happenstance from out of the deep, revealed themselves to be living jewels, marvels of exquisite design and entrancing, otherworldly beauty.

One thing that was not brought to the surface, however, was the primordial slime. The *Urschleim,* as the German biologist Ernst Haeckel had named it, was supposed to be the missing link between inorganic and organic existence, the literal proto-plasm, cropping into being everywhere in the depths of the sea and giving rise to all subsequent creation. "We are all sea slime," Henry David Thoreau had once mused. Tantalizingly enough, in the 1850s a deepwater trawl had brought to the surface a scoop of abyssal mud that, once safely deposited in its jar of preservative alcohol, soon revealed a dollop of globular ooze that biologists were quick to recognize as a bit of the primordial slime itself. Christened *Bathybius haeckeli* by the great Victorian scientist Thomas Henry Huxley, the slime was launched on its celebrated if inglorious career as a marvel of the sea.

Alas, its life would remain an unwritten one because, well, it didn't really exist, after all. Barely two decades later, in 1875, one of the *Challenger*'s scientists, spotting another bit of slime coating a sample jar, realized that it was only a precipitate of calcium sulfate, the result of residual seawater reacting with the preserving fluid. Huxley took the news with typical British aplomb: "*Bathybius*," he is said to have quipped, "has not fulfilled the promise of its youth."

The deepwater trawls, of course, still brought up enough bizarre creatures to crowd Victor Hugo's nightmares. As Frank Bullen—who wrote about sea creatures in such a way that, according to one commentator, " if they are not facts they ought to be"—described some of these deep-sea tyrants, they were all maw:

[*Chiasmodon niger*]...is a veritable nightmare in appearance, being entirely black in colour, with a mouth that cleaves the head asunder laterally for its whole length, so that vulgarly speaking, when its mouth is wide open it has no profile. This immense mouth is furnished with equally effective teeth, which are not only found in the jaws but on the palate also. Its front teeth are hooked and movable, so that while they may be pushed inward to admit of the entrance of prey, they effectually prevent it from coming out. This peculiarity is explained by a slight examination of the creature's feeding habits. It can and does swallow entire fish actually larger than itself —which sounds impossible, but it is not. For the belly of this atrocious glutton is like an india-rubber bladder which may be expanded amazingly. And consequently by dint of perseverance *Chiasmodon* can and does draw himself on to the body of another fish, as it were, until the visitor is snugly coiled away in that expanding bag, which being transparent, shows plainly from the outside the position of its occupant. In other respects *Chiasmodon* is rather an elegant fish, quite normally fish-like, which one would hardly expect, considering the great epths from which it has been brought. The "Challenger's" trawl brought up one in mid-Atlantic from a depth of one thousand five hundred fathoms, or nine thousand feet. Another specimen was brought up from a depth of three hundred and twelve fathoms, near Madeira. But several have been found floating upon the sea-surface, having succumbed to a very natural disaster considering their habit of gorging, namely, they have burst! And the tissues becoming inflated with gas have rapidly raised the dead mass from the immense depths in which it has lived to the revealing glare of day, to become the wonder and awe of us beings of the surface. This extraordinary creature is one of the best known and most fully described of all the abyssal fish, as it is certainly one of the most wonderful.

Melanocetus Johnsonii is really an object of terror, although only four inches in length. When closed, its lower jaw is vertical like the others, but when open it droops below a right angle—the whole front of the fish is, as it were, opened out. And it looks exactly as if the back of its head had expanded into a belly. But that useful organ, having to contain very often a fish much larger than its owner, is a loose sac attached by a cord, which floats about and apparently allows its contents to escape into the body as they are needed for its up-keep. Of course its colour is a uniform black.

Frank Bullen, Denizens of the Deep

When it came to the deepest deeps, primordial slime or not, even the genial Moseley could only offer a vision with a chilly horror all its own:

The waters of the deep sea being everywhere dark and always cold, the conditions of life in them are the same all over the world. The temperature of the deep sea is practically the same, as far as an effect on life is concerned, under the Equator and at the Poles. Hence there are absolutely no barriers to the migrations of animals in the deep sea. Time

only is required for any deep-sea animal to roam from any distant part
of the earth to another.

HENRY MOSELEY, *Notes by a Naturalist on the "Challenger"*

And time, it seems, is on the monsters' side. The rapidly evolving life
in the sunny reaches of the globe, according to Moseley, "will soon pass
away, but the deep-sea animals will very possibly remain unchanged from
their present condition long after man has died out."

ALL LEGENDARY HEAVENS

THERE ARE A GOOD MANY PEOPLE STILL LIVING who can remember when
a Cocoa-nut was a comparative rarity in some parts of England," wrote
botanist William Purdie Treloar at the close of the 19th century.

> In a few old country mansions, or on the mantel-shelves of retired sea-
> captains, and occasionally in London curiosity shops, might be seen
> strangely-figured goblets, with rims and feet of silver, and so wrought
> that here and there they were thin and almost translucent, that there was
> a gleam upon their rich, dark surfaces which gave them the appearance of
> being formed of some rare stone. These were made of the shells of the great
> cocoa-nuts, wrought in graceful or grotesque patterns by some patient
> native, or by an ingenious sailor on the long homeward voyage....Only
> the nuts themselves were articles of commerce, and they were scarce.
>
> WILLIAM PURDIE TRELOAR, *The Prince of Palms*

Botanists may never agree where the coconut palm originated; most
seem to favor the Indian Ocean, where in their uncounted millions they
have seemingly always graced the coasts of India, Ceylon, the Maldives,

and the Seychelles. They clustered thickly in the East Indies as well, where Alfred Russel Wallace admired them in the 1850s:

> The part of the village in which I resided was a grove of cocoa-nut trees, and at night, when the dead leaves were sometimes collected together and burnt, the effect was most magnificent—the tall stems, the fine crowns of foliage, and the immense fruit-clusters, being brilliantly illuminated against a dark sky, and appearing like a fairy palace supported on a hundred columns, and groined over with leafy arches. The cocoa-nut tree, when wellgrown, is certainly the prince of palms both for beauty and utility.
>
> ALFRED RUSSEL WALLACE, *The Malay Archipelago*

And, of course, they have drifted across the vast extent of the tropical Pacific, Herman Melville's "tide-beating heart of earth," for coconuts are among the greatest of ocean drifters, the ultimate castaways.

Distant coconut palms, Fiji, 1840

And that is how they became emissaries of romance: They have washed up or been carried to so many tropical islands that the rattle and sweep of those long fronds in the trades has become the whisper of paradise.

That paradise should be located in a seagirt isle is an image of immemorial antiquity. The Earthly Paradise, the Fortunate Isles, the Isles of the Blessed, the Hesperides with their golden apples are among the many variations on the fundamental idea that there must be better and happier places somewhere over the sea. Over the years these paradise isles have retreated across the globe, always staying just out of reach. The ancients might have located them in the Canaries, just off the coast of North Africa, where the peak of Tenerife, long a beacon to mariners, may have been the original Mount Atlas. Columbus claimed he found them in the Indies—the West Indies, as it turned out—because it just seemed to be axiomatically true: "In conclusion, the admiral says that the sacred theologians and learned philosophers were right in saying that the earthly paradise is at the end of the east, because it is a very temperate place, so those lands which he had now discovered are, he says, 'the end of the east.'"

There was at least one shortcoming in Columbus's paradise. The sirens, or mermaids, that he saw along the coast of Hispaniola did not live up to their billing: "I saw three sirens that came up very high out of the sea," he noted in his log for January 9, 1493. "They are not as beautiful as they are painted, since in some ways they have a face like man." He had just seen his first New World manatee.

Eventually paradise made its last stand in the South Pacific, where its deteriorated ruins still remain, more or less. The voyages of Samuel Wallis, Louis-Antoine de Bougainville, and James Cook first made Tahiti the cynosure of every wayfarer's eye, and by 1913, when the young English poet Rupert Brooke arrived there, the romance of the South Seas had become deeply rooted:

> The South Sea Islands have an invincible glamour. Any bar in 'Frisco or Sydney will give you tales of seamen who slipped ashore in Samoa or Tahiti or the Marquesas for a month's holiday, five, ten, or twenty years ago. Their wives and families await them yet. They are compound, these islands, of all legendary heavens. They are Calypso's and Prospero's isle,

and the Hesperides, and Paradise, and every timeless and untroubled spot. Such tales have been made of them by men who have been there, and gone away, and have been haunted by the smell of the bush and the lagoons, and faint thunder on the distant reef, and the colours of sky and sea and coral, and the beauty and grace of the islanders. And the queer thing is that it's all, almost tiresomely, true.

Rupert Brooke, Letters From America

Not every Pacific island seemed a paradise, however. Few coconuts originally grew along the black sand beaches of the Encantadas. That volcanic archipelago, as Herman Melville described it, was a blasted, reeking Tartarus, and its enchantments were of the malevolent kind, its tricky currents often leading to shipwreck and death:

Nor would the appellation "enchanted" seem misapplied in still another sense. For concerning the peculiar reptile inhabitant of these wilds—whose presence gives the group its second Spanish name, Galipagos—concerning the tortoises found here, most mariners have long cherished a superstition not more frightful than grotesque. They earnestly believe that all wicked sea officers, more especially commodores and captains, are at death (and in some cases before death) transformed into tortoises thenceforth dwelling upon these hot aridities, sole solitary lords of Asphaltum.

Doubtless, so quaintly dolorous a thought was originally inspired by the woebegone landscape itself; but more particularly, perhaps, by the tortoises. For, apart from their strictly physical features, there is something strangely self-condemned in the appearance of these creatures. Lasting sorrow and penal hopelessness are in no animal form so suppliantly expressed as in theirs; while the thought of their wonderful longevity does not fail to enhance the impression.

Herman Melville, Las Encantadas

No one today, of course, thinks of the Galápagos as anything other than a biological marvel, but even Charles Darwin, responsible for their change in fortune, found them initially off-putting as well:

Galápagos finches, 1839

> The day was glowing hot, and the scrambling over the rough surface and through the intricate thickets, was very fatiguing; but I was well repaid by the strange Cyclopean scene. As I was walking along I met two large tortoises, each of which must have weighed at least two hundred pounds: one was eating a piece of cactus, and as I approached, it stared at me and slowly stalked away; the other gave a deep hiss, and drew in its head. These huge reptiles, surrounded by the black lava, the leafless shrubs, and large cacti, seemed to my fancy like some antediluvian animals. The few dull-coloured birds cared no more for me than they did for the great tortoises.
>
> CHARLES DARWIN, *The Voyage of the Beagle*

Among those dull-colored birds, of course, were the finches, each collected from a separate isle and each possessing a slightly modified beak, which gave Darwin the telltale clue to natural selection, keystone of his theory of evolution.

There are islands, and then again there are islands. Robert Louis Stevenson, who lived out his short life in the South Seas, distinguished the two most important kinds:

Much of [the sea] lies vacant, much is closely sown with isles, and the isles are of two sorts. No distinction is so continually dwelt upon in

South Sea talk as that between the "low" and the "high" island, and there is none more broadly marked in nature. The Himalayas are not more different from the Sahara. On the one hand, and chiefly in groups of from eight to a dozen, volcanic islands rise above the sea; few reach an altitude of less than 4000 feet; one exceeds 13,000; their tops are often obscured in cloud, they are all clothed with various forests, all abound in food, and are all remarkable for picturesque and solemn scenery. On the other hand, we have the atoll; a thing of problematic origin and history, the reputed creature of an insect apparently unidentified; rudely annular in shape; enclosing a lagoon; rarely extending beyond a quarter of a mile at its chief width; often rising at its highest point to less than the stature of a man—man himself, the rat and the land crab, its chief inhabitants; not more variously supplied with plants; and offering to the eye, even when perfect, only a ring of glittering beach and verdant foliage, enclosing and enclosed by the blue sea.

ROBERT LOUIS STEVENSON, *In the South Seas*

Enclosing and enclosed—Old Ocean held all these far-flung islands in his deadly embrace. In the summer of 1770, Captain Cook was easing the *Endeavour* through the greatest maze of reefs on Earth, which he and his officers were calling the Labyrinth but which would soon be known as the Great Barrier Reef. They had already spent nearly seven weeks ashore in that new and strangely beautiful land repairing damage to the ship when, on August 15, having sounded and warped their careful way back into the open sea, the waves began to hurl them back against the reef wall. Joseph Banks, the wealthy 27-year-old gentleman-botanist aboard, described the encounter:

A Reef such a one as I now speak of is a thing scarcely known in Europe or indeed any where but in these seas: it is a wall of Coral rock rising almost perpendicularly out of the unfathomable ocean, always overflown at high water commonly 7 or 8 feet, and generaly bare at low water; the large waves of the vast ocean meeting with so sudden a resistance make here a most terrible surf Breaking mountain high, especially when as in our case the general trade wind blows directly upon it.

JOSEPH BANKS, *Endeavour Journal*

It was too deep to anchor, and just as the swell was about to cast the ship directly upon the knife-edge of the reef, a "small wind of air sprung up" and the ship just managed to avoid destruction and headed, ironically enough, back into the maze of reefs, preferring the dubious safety of the Labyrinth to the furious sea without. As Banks wrote in his *Journal,* "How little do men know what is for their real advantage: two days ago our utmost wishes were crownd by getting without the reef and today we were made again happy by getting within it."

THE LONELY PARADISE

EVERY ATOLL IS AN ARK, A REFUGE BUILT BY THE "multitudinous, God-omnipresent, coral insects, that out of the firmament of waters heaved the colossal orbs." And that, in Melville's finest Old Testament vein, is the story of the reef and its protecting rampart, built of its own efforts, ensuring every atoll is a world unto itself, but also a haven for the castaway.

Far out in the Indian Ocean, where the water is so deep blue it is almost black, except where the wind kicks up whitecaps on the wave crests, the Cocos, or Keeling, Islands are atolls just breaking through the surface of the sea. Very likely their first colonist was the coconut, for in the 1820s, when humans began living there, the coral was already thickly strewn with coconut palms. By the time that Joshua Slocum, in 1897, sailed his sloop, the *Spray,* into its lagoon, nearly three years into his lonely circumnavigation of the globe, he had already passed through Polynesia, yet after a five-week idyll in this isolated spot, he could declare that "if there is a paradise on this earth it is Keeling."

Nearly 3,000 miles south floated the Antarctic ice; nearly 3,500 miles west lay Madagascar; and 1,700 miles to the northwest was Ceylon, now Sri Lanka and once Serendip, whose storied princes gave us the word "serendipity," or "the faculty of making happy discoveries by chance." Most of the ocean currents, however, that surged past Cocos stemmed from Western Australia, 1,600 miles to the east, depositing on its coral beaches not only coconuts and tree trunks but also spars from wrecked ships, and once even a derelict Maori war canoe from New Zealand, which must have drifted a very long way indeed. And in 1835, they brought a ship called the *Beagle,* carrying a visitor named Charles Darwin.

> *The ocean throwing its waters over the broad reef appears an invincible, all-powerful enemy; yet we see it resisted, and even conquered, by means which at first seem most weak and inefficient*
>
> —CHARLES DARWIN

This was the only atoll Darwin ever visited, and as he wandered the barrier islands, really just heaps of shattered coral, or waded through the opaline shallows of the lagoon, shimmering with brilliantly colored marine life, he admitted that "it is excusable to grow enthusiastic over the infinite numbers of organic beings with which the sea of the tropics, so prodigal of life, teems." Mostly, however, he was swept away by the sheer bravado of the atoll, so seemingly fragile, so recently but a water-washed

OPPOSITE: *H.M.S. Beagle off Rio de Janeiro, 1832*

reef, and even during his visit but nine feet above sea level, that could not only survive the tremendous onslaught of the Indian Ocean but in its own small way triumph:

> The ocean throwing its waters over the broad reef appears an invincible, all-powerful enemy; yet we see it resisted, and even conquered, by means which at first seem most weak and inefficient. It is not that the ocean spares the rock of coral; the great fragments scattered over the reef, and heaped on the beach, whence the tall cocoa-nut springs, plainly bespeak the unrelenting power of the waves. Nor are any periods of repose granted. The long swell caused by the gentle but steady action of the trade-wind, always blowing in one direction over a wide area, causes breakers, almost equalling in force those during a gale of wind in the temperate regions, and which never cease to rage. It is impossible to behold these waves without feeling a conviction that an island, though built of the hardest rock, let it be porphyry, granite, or quartz, would ultimately yield and be demolished by such an irresistible power. Yet these low, insignificant coral-islets stand and are victorious: for here another power, as an antagonist, takes part in the contest. The organic forces separate the atoms of carbonate of lime, one by one, from the foaming breakers, and unite them into a symmetrical structure. Let the hurricane tear up its thousand huge fragments; yet what will that tell against the accumulated labour of myriads of architects at work night and day, month after month? Thus do we see the soft and gelatinous body of a polypus, through the agency of the vital laws, conquering the great mechanical power of the waves of an ocean which neither the art of man nor the inanimate works of nature could successfully resist.
>
> CHARLES DARWIN, *The Voyage of the Beagle*

But how did any of it—the coconut palms on which the slender economy depended, the crabs adapted to breaking those coconut shells, the lizards, the one species of ant, the one of earthworms, the millipedes, the birds, the flying insects—get there in the first place? The obvious and only conclusion was that they all came accidentally by sea or by air. This paradisiacal place, with its coralline beaches and waving palms, possessed the "character of a refuge for the destitute."

And that, 70 years later, is what fascinated Frederic Wood Jones: the inconceivably vast, incommensurably chance character of oceanic drift. Having himself washed up on Cocos in 1905 as a young doctor, Wood Jones learned that he was only the most recent castaway to arrive. An entire Noah's ark had preceded him. Considering the winged wayfarers alone, the birds and insects, he concluded that they were but the Elect, "appointed out of a countless host of competitors, all of whom have had equal adventures but have gone under in the struggle, through no fault of their own."

> It is impossible to conceive the numbers of the lost things perpetually flying about over the ocean, looking for some chance resting-place; it is impossible to conceive the perpetual waste going on among the flying things that have lost touch with land. These are the waifs that come aboard ships when far out at sea, and, considering the chances against an insect boarding a ship in mid-ocean, it is very astonishing how many may be picked up by any one who cares to watch the ship lights by night, and keep his eyes open by day.
>
> FREDERIC WOOD JONES, *Coral and Atolls*

Just stalking over the barrier islands led to the "discovery of many potential passenger vessels":

> The trunks of trees are naturally the most abundant of all the flotsam that might serve for the colonist, and it must be remembered that a single tree-trunk may be the only remnant of what was once a real

floating island. The very name "floating island" creates the suspicion of romance, and yet floating islands are realities. Many of the trees that fringe tropical shores (and one of the most notable features of tropical shores is the presence of dense vegetation right down to the lap of ocean waves) have complicated root systems, so that, above ground and below, the trees tangle this way and that, and form inseparable masses....

A scour of the sea-coast, or a river in flood by heavy rain, may undermine such a clump, tear it away, and set it adrift to sea, with all the earth still held in the meshes of the roots, all the trees standing—a perfect "floating island." Such things happen, and the floating island is a not uncommon phenomenon in the straits and seas of the Malay Archipelago. I know of a case, where, far out to sea, a submarine cable, on being hauled to the surface, brought up with it banana trees and portions of native houses, which had obviously gone to sea as a floating island and had encountered shipwreck.

It is easily seen that such an island might serve for the transport of a very large number of colonists. It is possible even that it carried human occupants. Such islands could not be expected to long survive the waves of the Southern Ocean, and disaster would surely overtake them when they had left the calmer landlocked seas of the Archipelago. But some portion of them, crowded with the survivors of the wreck, may float for long, and carry its living burden to new homes.

Like a prisoner on a desert island, Wood Jones then undertook an experiment. In order to determine where the currents that beset the island eventually arrived, "where they come from, and whither they go," he tried the old "message in a bottle" bit. Surely someone so suspicious of romance did not really expect this to work. All around lay thousands of miles of windswept Monsoon Sea, curling and rolling and booming with a roar of distant thunder. But he had forgotten that he was surrounded by the original sea of serendipity, and that Old Ocean always had a surprise

deep down his unfath-
omable sleeve:

Sea turtle, 1849

Many bottles went to
sea, being launched a
few at a time, during
a period of two months.
I started the experiment in
November 1905, and by June 1906,
a reply had come to hand. It was sent by Lieut. G. Piazza, the Resident of Brava, Italian Somaliland, and it told that a bottle, launched
on November 15, 1905, had been found at a place called Ras Day, at
Brava [south of Mogadishu], on May 27, 1906. My little note came back
again none the worse for its sea travel of over three thousand miles.
No other reply came in for more than a year, and then, much to my
surprise, the Resident of Brava sent me another letter telling me that
another bottle had been found, in exactly the same spot as the last, on
July 11, 1907; he again enclosed my note, and strangely enough it bore
the same date—November 15, 1905—as the first: I was glad to notice
that my kind correspondent had meanwhile ceased to be Lieutenant,
and was now Captain, Piazza.

No other messages ever came back, and considering the chances of
disaster that are likely to overtake a floating bottle—the chances of it
breaking in its landing, and the chances of its going ashore where it
would not be noticed—it is very wonderful that two ever did survive a
passage of almost the whole breadth of the Indian Ocean...

The Mournful Kingdom of Sand

THE DESERT

"And all around is the desert; a corner of the mournful kingdom of sand."
—PIERRE LOTI

NIGHT IN THE DESERT—AND MYSTERY. What by day had been so instantly recognizable, so chiseled and stony and familiar as it gazed unblinking over the centuries and across the Valley of the Nile, had with the onset of darkness been stripped of its immemorial associations, been rendered unfamiliar, insubstantial, rose-colored, almost terrifying:

And from out this kind of mummified wave a colossal human effigy emerges, rose-coloured too, a nameless, elusive rose; emerges, and stares with fixed eyes and smiles. It is so huge it seems unreal.… And behind this monster face, far away in the rear, on the top of those undefined and gently undulating sandhills, three apocalyptic signs rise up against the sky, those rose-coloured triangles, regular as the figures of geometry, but so vast in the distance that they inspire you with fear. They seem to be luminous of themselves, so vividly do they stand out in their clear rose against the deep blue of the star-spangled vault.…And all around is the desert; a corner of the mournful kingdom of sand. Nothing else is to be seen anywhere save those three awful things that stand there upright and still…

PIERRE LOTI, *The Death of Philae*

OPPOSITE: *Men and camels in the desert*

It is, of course, the Sphinx and the Pyramids. But to the French writer Pierre Loti, visiting Egypt in 1907, the familiar had been rendered unfamiliar, made alien and apocalyptic by the immemorial witchery of the desert.

Mark Twain had beheld the same sight, only in the cheerful blaze of noonday, yet that didn't make it any less unreal:

At the distance of a few miles the Pyramids rising above the palms, looked very clean-cut, very grand and imposing, and very soft and filmy, as well. They swam in a rich haze that took from them all suggestions of unfeeling stone, and made them seem only the airy nothings of a dream—structures which might blossom into tiers of vague arches, or ornate colonnades, may be, and change and change again, into all graceful forms of architecture, while we looked, and then melt deliciously away and blend with the tremulous atmosphere.

MARK TWAIN, *The Innocents Abroad*

The Pyramids looked, in fact, like all mountains do in the desert: so near you can reach out and touch them; so far that if you do so you might die trying:

The deception of distance is not infrequently accompanied by fatal consequences. The inexperienced traveler thinks the distance short, he can easily get over the ground in a few hours. But how the long leagues drag out, spin out, reach out! The day is gone and he is not there, the slight supply of water is gone and he is not there, his horse is gone and he himself is going, but he is not there. The story and its ending are familiar to those who live near the desert, for every year some mining or exploring party is lost. If there are any survivors they usually make the one report: "The distance seemed so short." But there are no short distances in the desert. Every valley-plain is an immense wilderness of space.

JOHN VAN DYKE, *The Desert*

That the desert is not what it seems was endlessly fascinating to John Van Dyke, a Rutgers art history professor with an eye for color, form, and light. Sent West to regain his health, Van Dyke soon found himself roaming the buttes and canyons and arroyos of the Sonoran and Mojave Deserts. What he saw convinced him that this was a special landscape; by day it shimmered, "the kingdom of sun-fire, where everything was tuned to the key of flame"; by night it stretched around, "the great sand-wrapped desert whose mystery no man knows, and not even the Sphinx could reveal." And it was perhaps the fundamental landscape, landscape's skeleton, lurking beneath the soil and vegetation of all leafy, well-watered lands.

The desert proper, of course, was full of skeletons. Yet even in Egypt, where the mummified remains of pharaohs and viziers slept sequestered in the honeycomb of dusty tombs flanking the Nile, those skeletons were not readily visible. They could not be spotted from the top of the Great Pyramid, where Mark Twain saw only "a mighty sea of yellow sand stretched away toward the ends of the earth, solemn, silent, shorn of vegetation, its solitude uncheered by any forms of creature life." Nevertheless, the skeletons were out there, buried in the sands, marking the caravan trails; they were skeletons of camels, those ships of the desert, reminders that every caravan was its own ark, crawling in single file from oasis to oasis, as ships of the sea sailed from island to island:

The word Oasis is Egyptian, and is synonymous with Auasis and Hyasis. Abulfeda calls the Oases *el-Wah*. In the latter time of the Caesars, malefactors were sent to the Oases, being banished to these islands in the sandy ocean, as the Spaniards and English transported their malefactors to the Falkland Islands and New Holland. The ocean affords almost a better chance of escape than the desert surrounding the Oases...

ALEXANDER VON HUMBOLDT, *Aspects of Nature*

For centuries the sight of those skeletons forcibly impressed travelers with the overwhelming mythology of the desert: Wander too far off, and you would be lost, prey to dangerous enchantments, mocking delusions, merciless sun, agonizing thirst, and inevitable death.

Bolder spirits, like Richard Francis Burton, took it all in stride. Burton, one of Victorian Britain's most notorious adventurers, pulled his own kind of desert deceit when in 1853 he clothed himself in the guise of an Arab nomad and, infidel though he was, succeeded in making the pilgrimage to Mecca. Burton was easily seduced by the romance of the desert:

Richard Francis Burton in Arab garb, 1857

It is strange how the mind can be amused by scenery that presents so few objects to occupy it…. Above, through a sky terrible in its stainless beauty, and the splendours of a pitiless blinding glare, the Samun caresses you like a lion with flaming breath. Around lie drifted sand-heaps, upon which each puff of wind leaves its trace in solid waves, flayed rocks, the very skeletons of mountains, and hard unbroken plains, over which he who rides is spurred by the idea that the bursting of a water-skin, or the pricking of a camel's hoof, would be a certain death of torture—a haggard land infested with wild beasts, and wilder men—a region whose very fountains murmur the warning words 'Drink and away!' What can be more exciting? What more sublime?

RICHARD FRANCIS BURTON,
Personal Narrative of a Pilgrimage to El-Medinah and Mecca

Charles M. Doughty, on the other hand, spent two years roaming openly and undisguised among the Bedouin of Arabia. The very type of the eccentric vagabond Englishman, Doughty also succumbed to the romance of the desert, and his deliberately archaic prose continues to bewilder and fascinate readers today. From the moment the dawn gun announces the beginning

At the distance of a few miles the Pyramids rising above the palms, looked very clean-cut, very grand and imposing, and very soft and filmy, as well.

—MARK TWAIN

of the hajj pilgrimage, there is not a page (and there are over 1,200 of them) of his masterpiece, *Travels in Arabia Deserta,* that the desert does not splinter and invade.

A less romantically inclined man, like naturalist and big-game hunter Abel Chapman, habitually squinted into sun-sheared distances, and his sharp eyes were quick to notice subtle shifts of landscape. Standing on a rock outcropping in the Sudan, Chapman discerned that the desert before him was not a featureless ocean. "After all, there are deserts and deserts," he wrote, though admitting that the difference was trifling: "it may be diagnosed as representing that between a minus quantity and a minimum."

There suggests itself a sort of weird grandeur in the very immensity of these vast voids—even a tinge of romance as horizon after horizon reveals a changeless panorama to eyes that ache with the glare of sun-blistered sand. From sunrise to sunset there may come no very palpable change in aspect, no relief or hope of relief that is not merely the mocking deceit of the mirage. That is the Sahara. But examine those deserts in closer detail and it will be found that separate landscapes, however arid, may display distinct individualities, since there are "qualities" which differentiate even the sternest sterility.

ABEL CHAPMAN, *Savage Sudan*

Yet when he put pen to paper and tried to accurately describe exactly what he saw, the desert still cheated even him in the end:

Low sand-ridges radiate afar in irregular curves like rollers in the Atlantic, their crests spangled with black volcanic debris strewn in disordered disarray….One of the nearer stone-flats being composed of the dark volcanic lava aforesaid—but embedded amidst yellow gravel—gives (under the tropical sun) the illusory effect of a stretch of purple heather! Another provides a second deceit. Its component stones are more "civilized"—or less archaic—flat discs, circular or sub-rounded, suggestive of wave-action. In the glancing sunlight, these flat grey stones resemble a sheet of rippling water! Hardly can one recognize what is full in view.

THIRST OF THE GAZELLE

IN 1914, A BRITISH MILITARY COLUMN WAS DEMARCATING THE BOUNDARY between what would become Iran and Iraq:

Our caravan…straggled over two or three miles of country, and to anyone riding somewhere near the middle the head and tail of the procession seemed always to be marching through a smooth, shallow lake;

occasionally, for some unfathomable cause, the mules and men would execute a bewildering feat of "levitation" and continue their progress in the sky. Often we saw a lake spread out on the horizon, stretching a long arm towards us to within a few hundred yards; at other times a clump of palms or a group of mounted men appeared in the distance, only to resolve themselves, as we approached nearer, into bushes of low desert scrub or a grazing flock of goats.

G. E. HUBBARD, From the Gulf to Ararat

Hubbard, of course, was describing that most famous and persistent of desert deceits, the mirage. Prosaically described today as an optical illusion, a trick of refraction and heated air, the mirage has had more poetic names in the past:

The well known phenomenon of the mirage is called in Sanskrit "the thirst of the gazelle." All objects appear to float in the air, while their forms are reflected in the lower stratum of the atmosphere. At such times the whole desert resembles a vast lake, whose surface undulates like waves. Palm trees, cattle, and camels sometimes appear inverted in the horizon. In the French expedition to Egypt, this optical illusion often nearly drove the faint and parched soldiers to distraction.

ALEXANDER VON HUMBOLDT, Aspects of Nature

The delusiveness of the mirage had inspired another name heard by Humboldt's protégé, the German Egyptologist Richard Lepsius, when he was exploring the Sudan in the 1840s:

At a very early hour in the day we saw the most beautiful mirages, both near us and at a distance, exhibiting a very deceptive resemblance to lakes and rivers, in which the mountains, blocks of stone, and everything around is reflected, as if in clear water. They form a strange contrast with the hard, arid desert, and, as it is related, must have often bitterly deceived many a poor wanderer. When we are not aware that no water can be there, it is often totally impossible to distinguish the semblance from the reality. Only a few days ago, in the neighborhood of El Mecheref, I felt perfectly certain that I saw either the Nile water which had overflowed, or a branch of the river, and I rode up, but only found Bahr Scheiten, "The water of Satan," as it is called by the Arabs.

RICHARD LEPSIUS,
Letters from Egypt, Ethiopia, and the Peninsula of Sinai

It seems, on the evidence of the first-century B.C. Greek historian Diodorus Siculus, that the "water of Satan" could instill terror in its beholders. "At certain times, and especially when there is no wind," he reported of the Libyan Desert, "shapes are seen gathering in the sky which assume the forms of animals of every kind; and some of these remain fixed, but others begin to move, sometimes retreating before a man and at other times pursuing him, and in every case, since they are of monstrous size, they strike such as have never experienced them with wondrous dismay and terror."

Even for those who understood the phenomenon, it was the seeming reality of the perception rather than the logic of the explanation that was so captivating. Richard Robert Madden, an Irish physician who toured the Near East in the 1820s, believed the mirage was not a trick of the eye but rather one of the brain: "If I were to speak of the nature of the *Mirage* from my own sensations, I should say, it was more a mental hallucination than a deception of the sight; for, although I was aware of the existence of the Mirage, I could not prevail on myself to believe that the images which were painted on my retina were only reflected, like those in a dream, from the imagination, and yet so it was":

Approach of the simoom, by David Roberts, mid-19th century

At one moment, the rippled surface of a lake was before my eyes; at another time, a thick plantation appeared on either side of me; the waving of the branches was to be seen, and this view was only changed for that of a distant glimpse of a city: the mosques and minarets were distinct, and several times I asked my Bedouins if that was not *Suez* before us; but they laughed and said it was all sand; and what appeared to me a city, a forest, or a lake, the nearer I endeavoured to approach it the farther it seemed to recede, till at last it vanished altogether, "like the baseless fabric of a vision, leaving not a wrack behind."

R. R. MADDEN, *Travels in Turkey, Egypt, Nubia, and Palestine*

John Van Dyke, in the American Southwest, was amused by the sight of horses with legs 20 feet long and cattle walking about "on the aerial ceiling in a very astonishing way." But when an entire landscape hung tremulous and colorful above the horizon, he gave his unsurpassed painterly eye free rein:

It presents certainly a very beautiful effect. The buttes rise up from the ground, first one and then another, until there is a range of them that holds the appearance of reality perhaps for hours, and then gradually fades out like a stereopticon picture—the bases going first and the tops gradually melting into the sky. When seen at sunset against a yellow sky the effect is magnificent. The buttes, even in illusion, take on a wonderful blue hue (the complementary color of yellow), and they seem to drift upon the sky as upon an open sea.

John Van Dyke, The Desert

That might not be as illusory as it seems, as Rosita Forbes, traveling in the Sahara, testified:

On clear mornings, about an hour after dawn, when the desert is very flat, a mirage of the country about a day's journey distant appears on the horizon. For a few minutes one sees a picture of what is some 50 kilometres farther on. The Arabs call it "the country turning upside down."

Rosita Forbes, The Secret of the Sahara: Kufara

If the mirage could be used as a vast map in the sky, reflecting an unseen landscape, though upside down and backward, it might not be so deceitful, after all.

Flying Sand

"The sands drove like breakers on a beach," John Van Dyke observed while riding around the Mojave and Sonoran Deserts, "washing and wearing everything up to the bases of the mountains. And the fine sand reached still higher. It whirled up the canyons and across the saddles, it eddied around the enormous taluses, it even flung itself upon the face walls of the mountain and left the smoothing marks of its fingers upon the sharp pinnacles of the peak."

The mirage aside, the most abiding, the most persistent, the most widespread and remarked-upon feature of the desert is sand—sand encroaching on cultivation's green margins, sand swirling about in violent storms, and sand piled up in tremendous, restless dunes. The humble grain of sand is the great sculptor of the desert.

Deep in the heart of the endless lands of Central Asia is a vast basin where the rivers running off the surrounding mountains all disappear into an enormous sea of sand. The grim Taklimakan Desert is one of the most desolate spots on Earth, but to Ellsworth Huntington, an American geographer exploring the area at the turn of the last century, not without its beauties:

> The backs of the larger dunes were diversified with smaller dunes, like shoals of mounting fish, and the small ones in turn were covered with ripples. All the forms, whether of dunes or ripples, were on one pattern, endlessly varied. The variety and grace of the curves in the sand, like those of drifted snow, give the sandy desert an unceasing interest and beauty. It is utterly unlike the monotonous flat deserts of gravel, clay, and salt, though even those have beauty of a certain sort. The charm increases as the dunes increase in size. The sand is truly awful in times of heat and wind, but when, as during those days at the end of September, the hours of sunshine are pleasantly warm, the nights are fresh, the air is still, the way is known, and a water supply is assured, its unique beauty is indescribable.
>
> ELLSWORTH HUNTINGTON, *The Pulse of Asia*

But beware the months of spring, as Huntington was soon informed while visiting a settlement at the edge of the desert:

A strong northwest wind had sprung up. Soon it increased to a gale, and I had to leave the roof to dust and pattering sand and two merrily rolling gourds....

That evening, as my host was entertaining me by playing on a marvelously slender and long-necked mandolin, he remarked:

"This wind is nothing. You just wait."

Two days later, we were camped in the reedy salt plain twenty miles to the east beside a white wall made of blocks of rock-salt. An evening gale came up, and blew over my tent and that of the men.

"This is nothing," said the host, who had become our guide. "Just wait till April or May. Then the wind takes the roofs off houses…"

ELLSWORTH HUNTINGTON, *The Pulse of Asia*

Huntington did not remain to find out, but his contemporary, Sven Hedin, the most famous of Central Asia's explorers, knew well that Taklimakan meant "place of flying sand" and that the winds were called the black burans, "which carry on their wings," Hedin wrote, "such vast quantities of sand and dust as to make day as black as night."

The burans begin to blow towards the end of March and continue till the close of summer....Their violence is almost inconceivable; they drive across the open, level plains with a force that is absolutely irresistible. Sheep grazing around the villages are sometimes swept bodily away...The custodian of the serai told me that ravens and other birds are often blown by unusually violent burans all the way from Kargalik to Guma, or from Guma to Kargalik, and not seldom are dashed against larger fixed objects and killed.

SVEN HEDIN, *Through Asia*

The violent sandstorms of Taklamakan were once matched by those of the Sahara, if Herodotus is any guide. The ancient Greek historian has given us the story of the Lost Army of Cambyses, the Persian overlord of Egypt who sent his legions from Thebes on the Nile to attack the Ammonians, a seven days' march away across the Libyan Desert. Apparently the army never got there—it just disappeared:

> This however is added to the story by the Ammonians themselves:—they say that as the army was going from this Oasis through the sandy desert to attack them, and had got to a point about mid-way between them and the Oasis, while they were taking their morning meal a violent South Wind blew upon them, and bearing with it heaps of the desert sand it buried them. They disappeared and were seen no more...
>
> HERODOTUS, *The Histories*

The indefatigable historian goes on to tell of the fate of the Psylloi, a Saharan people who made the mistake of waging war upon that same South Wind, with predictable results:

> Adjoining the Nasamonians is the country of the Psylloi. These have perished utterly in the following manner:—The South Wind blowing upon them dried up all their cisterns of water, and their land was waterless, lying all within the Syrtis [the ancient name for part of the Libyan-Tunisian coast]. They then having taken a resolve by common consent, marched in arms against the South Wind (I report what the Libyans say), and when they had arrived at the sandy tract, the South Wind blew and buried them in the sand. These then having utterly perished, the Nasamonians from that time forward possess their land.
>
> HERODOTUS, *The Histories*

Perhaps James Richardson unknowingly crossed the long-lost graves of the Psylloi when he crossed the Saharan sands to Ghat, the Libyan oasis

A sandstorm in the Sahara, 1821

where he served as British consul for a few months in the 1840s. One day in the nearby desert he saw a slight disturbance sweep over the ground and witnessed the aborted birth of another marvel of flying sand, the "pillar of sand," the biblical whirlwind:

> Observed to-day some curious atmospheric phenomena. A light vapour, the lightest, airiest of the airiest, swept along the surface of the ground, but as if unimpelled by any secret influence. It was also dead calm. The vapour continued to sweep before us, till at length it suddenly rose up to the sky in the form of a spiral column of air, and then disappeared....
> JAMES RICHARDSON, *Travels in the Great Desert of Sahara*

It was the Pillar of Cloud by day and the Pillar of Fire by night by which the Lord, in the book of Exodus, led the Israelites into the desert wilderness of Sinai, that "vast mountainous labyrinthine solitude of rainless valleys," as Charles Doughty memorably described it. But it was in those same valleys that Edward Palmer, a British explorer with the Palestine Exploration Fund, had an amusing encounter with the Pillar of Sand:

> A whirlwind is the most curious of all the visitations to which one is exposed; it is as violent as the most awful storm, tearing up everything in its path, but it is so partial that you may stand a yard or so off and watch its progress undisturbed. When, as once happened to me, it is your neighbor's tent which is blown about his ears while your own canvas is motionless, there is a great satisfaction to be derived from witnessing this strange atmospheric phenomenon.
>
> EDWARD HENRY PALMER, *The Desert of the Exodus*

In 1772, the Scottish explorer James Bruce, making his way north to Egypt after discovering the sources of the Blue Nile in Ethiopia, had one of the more famous encounters with these towers of flying sand. Standing transfixed on a shelf in the Nubian Desert, he watched a sublime spectacle:

> About eight we had a view of the desert to the westward as before, and saw the sands had already begun to rise in immense twisted pillars, which darkened the heavens...
>
> It was this day more magnificent than any we had as yet seen. The sun shining through the pillars, which were thicker, and contained more sand apparently than any of the preceding days, seemed to give those nearest us an appearance as if spotted with stars of gold. I do not think at any time they seemed to be nearer than two miles...

A little before twelve our wind at north ceased, and a considerable quantity of fine sand rained upon us for an hour afterwards....

JAMES BRUCE, *Travels to Discover the Source of the Nile*

His account became so famous, in fact, that it was eventually ranked with the only truly indisputable marvels, those included in children's bedside books:

"During the storms that rage in the desert, the sand is often raised in clouds, as you suppose, Lucy, and in such quantities as to fill the air and obscure the sun—but when *whirlwinds* prevail, as they sometimes do in those dreary wastes, the sand is carried up by the eddy, and assumes the form of pillars. This remarkable appearance has been described more particularly by another traveller of our own country..."

"Who was that, mamma? I wish you would tell us his description of these wonderful pillars."

"His name was Bruce; he was crossing the desert of Nubia, which you will find in the map between Egypt and Abyssinia. One day, Bruce and his companions alighted to refresh themselves under the shade of some acacia-trees, and on looking over the wide expanse of desert to the north and west of their resting-place, they were surprised and alarmed by the appearance of a number of enormous pillars of sand; many of them were so lofty that they seemed to reach the clouds. Sometimes they moved with great swiftness—sometimes stalked along majestically slow. Now they came so near that the travellers were afraid of being overwhelmed by them in a few minutes—then again they retreated to a distance, gliding almost out of sight.

"About noon the pillars advanced swiftly, the wind blowing from the north. It was vain to think of escaping by flight, they came on so rapidly that the swiftest horse could not gallop fast enough to carry his rider out of danger. Bruce was so convinced of the impossibility

of escaping that he had no desire to move—he stood quite still, looking with fear and astonishment on this magnificent spectacle. You
may suppose how relieved he must have felt when the wind presently
changing to the south-east, these giants of the desert retired before it
till they were seen no more."

"How grand!" exclaimed Harry. "It was worth while to suffer a
little from fear for the pleasure of a sight like that..."

Maria Hack, *Tales of Travellers for Winter Evenings*

THE POISON WIND

OF ALL DESERT WINDS, FEW ARE AS NOTORIOUS AS THE "POISON WIND,"
the simoom (or Samum, or simum, or any of a dozen alternative
spellings). According to John Davidson, an Englishman eventually mur-
dered on the way to Timbuktu, "the Simoum felt like the blast of a fur-
nace....It was accompanied by a line of vivid light, that looked like a train
of fire, whose murky smoke filled the whole wide expanse, and made its
horrors only the more vivid."

George Francis Lyon, who accompanied an 1818 expedition to the
Niger River, noted that "in addition to the excessive heat and dryness of
these winds, they are impregnated with sand, and the air is darkened by
it, the sky appears of a dusky yellow, and the sun is barely perceptible.
The eyes become red, swelled and inflamed; the lips and chin parched and
chapped; while severe pain in the chest is generally felt, in consequence of
the quantities of sand unavoidably inhaled."

Quite understandably, the advent of a simoom filled people with anxiety. "The fact is," reported Marco Polo, referring to Persia, "that in summer a wind often blows across the sands which encompass the plain, so
intolerably hot that it would kill everybody, were it not that when they

perceive that wind coming they plunge into water up to the neck, and so abide until the wind have ceased."

It also appears to have had another quite startling effect. As Marco Polo went on to relate, a simoom once swept over the desert near the Strait of Hormuz just when a neighboring king had sent an army of 1,600 cavalry and 5,000 infantry to subdue a rebellious vassal:

> Now, it happened one day that through the fault of their guide they were not able to reach the place appointed for their night's halt, and were obliged to bivouac in a wilderness not far from Hormos. In the morning as they were starting on their march they were caught by that wind, and every man of them was suffocated, so that not one survived to carry the tidings to their Lord. When the people of Hormos heard of this they went forth to bury the bodies lest they should breed a pestilence. But when they laid hold of them by the arms to drag them to the pits, the bodies proved to be so *baked,* as it were, by that tremendous heat, that the arms parted from the trunks, and in the end the people had to dig graves hard by each where it lay, and so cast them in.
>
> MARCO POLO, *The Travels of Marco Polo*

One might cock an eyebrow at that, but Sir Henry Yule, Marco Polo's Victorian translator, had reason to believe the tale:

> Khanikoff is very distinct as to the immediate fatality of the desert wind at Khabis, near Kerman [in Persia], but does not speak of the effect on the body after death. This Major St. John does, describing a case that occurred in June, 1871, when he was halting, during intense heat, at the post-house of Pasangan, a few miles south of Kom [also in Persia]. The bodies were brought in of two poor men, who had tried to start some hours before sunset, and were struck down by the poisonous blast

within half-a-mile of the post-house. "It was found impossible to wash them before burial....Directly the limbs were touched they separated from the trunk." About 1790, when Timur Shah of Kabul sent an army under the Sirdar-i-Sirdaran to put down a revolt in Meshed, this force on its return was struck by Simum in the Plain of Farrah, and the Sirdar perished, with a great number of his men.

SIR HENRY YULE, *The Travels of Marco Polo*

Sir Jean Chardin, a footloose 17th-century French jeweler who became Europe's preeminent expert on Persia, also testified to the simmering effects of the simoom:

The most surprising effect of the wind is not the mere fact of its caus-ing death, but its operation on the bodies of those who are killed by it. It seems as if they became decomposed without losing shape, so that you would think them to be merely asleep, when they are not merely dead, but in such a state that if you take hold of any part of the body it comes away in your hand, and the finger penetrates such a body as if it were so much dust.

SIR JEAN CHARDIN, *Travels in Persia*

There were doubters, of course, Charles Doughty, roving with the "Aarab" Beduoin, among them: "A strong simum one of these nights blew down upon us; that thin tepid air cannot fill the gasping chest nor quicken the blood, and there follows some uneasiness and head-ache. These hot winds, which the Aarab call thus, 'infected,' are common in the long summer half of the year; but no Beduin of the many I questioned had ever heard speak of any man suffocated in them."

Richard Francis Burton was inclined to agree. While on the road to Mecca, Burton examined the body of an Arnaut, an Albanian soldier in the

Ottoman army: "This Arnaut's body was swollen and decomposing rapidly, the true diagnostic of death by the poison-wind. However, as troopers drink hard, the Arabs may still be right, the Samum doing half the work, arrack the rest."

Laggard Wonders of the Night

Summing up his wartime experience of the desert, T. E. Lawrence, the famous "Lawrence of Arabia," stated in the opening paragraph of *Seven Pillars of Wisdom* that "by day the hot sun fermented us; and we were dizzied by the beating wind. At night we were stained by dew, and shamed into pettiness by the innumerable silences of the stars."

Open any celestial almanac, and alongside the Greek and Latin names of constellations are Arabic names for the stars. "Vergil's assertion as to the sailor's influence in star-naming may be true in part," wrote Richard Allen in his 1899 *Star Names,* "yet for most of this we should probably look to the Desert, where the stars would be as much required and relied upon for guidance as on the trackless ocean." Though from ancient Egypt to ancient Persia desert-bred and stargazing civilizations flourished, it was probably the wandering nomads rather than the court astronomers, Allen suspected, who did the actual naming, "their tents, nests, household articles, and ornaments; mangers and stalls; boats, biers, crosses, and thrones; wells, ponds, and rivers; fruits, grains, and nuts;—all of which they imaged in the sky."

Gertrude Bell, who alongside T. E. Lawrence helped draw the map of the modern Middle East, had traveled with the descendants of such nomads:

They had watched, as they crossed the barren watercourses, the laggard wonders of the night, when the stars seemed chained to the sky as though the dawn would never come. Imr ul Kais [medieval Islam's patron king of poets] had seen the Pleiades caught like jewels in the net of a girdle, and with the wolf that howled in the dark he had claimed fellowship...

GERTRUDE BELL, Syria: The Desert and the Sown

Those Europeans, like Bell and Lawrence, who became desert wanderers also turned their gaze to the night sky. Arthur Weigall, chief inspector of antiquities for Upper Egypt a century ago, would bed down in the desert, wrap himself in blankets, and lose himself in rapture:

If one turns to the east, one may stare at Mars flashing red somewhere over Arabia, and westwards there is Jupiter blazing above the Sahara. One looks up and up at the expanse of star-strewn blue, and one's mind journeys of itself into the place of dreams before sleep has come to conduct it thither. The dark desert drops beneath one; the bed floats in mid-air, with planets above and below. Could one but peer over the side, earth would be seen as small and vivid as the moon.

ARTHUR WEIGALL, Travels in the Upper Egyptian Deserts

All kinds of celestial phenomena were especially vivid in the desert night. The Swedish explorer Sven Hedin, while on the margins of the Gobi awaiting the return of his camel drivers, "witnessed the most brilliant display of shooting stars I have ever seen anywhere. A train of meteors of an intensely light-green color shot through the belt of Orion, and for some seconds lit up the steppe so brightly that the fire actually paled before it. Then it seemed to be darker than ever." Charles Doughty, alongside his Beduoin hosts (the "Aarab"), also watched shooting stars:

Meteors are seen to glance at every few moments in the luminous Arabian night. I asked, "What say the Aarab of these flitting stars?" *Answer:* "They go to tumble upon the heads of the heathen, O Khalil!"...I asked, "How name you this glorious girdle of the heavens?"—"*El-Mujjir;*" and they smiled at our homely name "The Milky Way." I told them, "This we see in our glasses to be a cloud of stars....But those wandering stars steadfastly shining, are like to this earth, we may see seas and lands in them." Some of the younger sort asked then, "Were there Aarab in them?—and the moon is what, Khalil?"

CHARLES DOUGHTY, *Travels in Arabia Deserta*

The moon, to John Van Dyke in the American Southwest, was encircled by radiant bands of colored light—"Rainbows by night"—which led him to conclude that the era of the fabulous was over. "How much more weird and extraordinary are the things that actually happen in this desert land." To Capt. A. H. W. Haywood, slogging alongside his caravan through the undulating sands of the Sahara in 1910, the moon so shed its light on the landscape that he found the effect to be indescribably beautiful:

The white sand of the "oueds" in which we were walking was lit up to look like a white sheet by the brilliant moonbeams; on all sides of us was this dazzling sheen spread over the surface of the ground, while in the distance one might have fancied there were the waters of a lake, so silvery crystal did the sand appear. The rocky hills on the east and west caught the glint of the moon's rays, standing out sharply defined against the deep blue of the starlit sky. The jagged peaks, which were perhaps succeeded by a rugged ridge, running thus for miles into the far-off horizon, looked for

OPPOSITE: *Temple of Karnak beneath the stars, 1875*

all the world like the towers and crenellated battlements of some ancient fortress. The grandeur of the sight filled me with a sense of awe...

That sense of awe was immeasurably heightened by a rather special celestial phenomenon:

It was about 10 p.m. on the 8th of May, the day that I left Kidal, that I first saw Halley's Comet. For many nights subsequently it was visible in the eastern sky, a beautiful, bright, luminous body with a long tail, like a streak of fire, stretching for some distance behind it. What millions of people in the world must have been watching it about this time, although I doubt if many had the opportunity of seeing it from the Sahara.

CAPTAIN A. H. W. HAYWOOD,
Through Timbuctu and Across the Great Sahara

Then there was the hypnotic, trancelike state that traveling at night might induce. Sir Francis Younghusband was a distinguished British soldier, explorer, Orientalist, and president of the Royal Geographical Society, but he also became a noted religious mystic. It is not hard to see why, when as a young officer he crossed the Gobi beneath star-drenched nights:

Upon no occasion were the wonders of the universe more impressively brought before my mind than in the long, lonely marches in the Gobi Desert...The boundless plain beneath, and the starry skies above. And skies, too, such as are not to be seen in the murky atmospheres of the less pure regions of the earth, but clear and bright as they can only be in the far, original depths of Nature. In those pure skies the stars shone out in unrivalled brilliancy, and hour after hour, through the long nights, I would watch them in their courses over the heavens, and think on what they are and what they represent, and try to realize the place which we men hold in the universe stretched out before me.

SIR FRANCIS YOUNGHUSBAND,
Heart of a Continent

For some sensitive souls, however, it was all just too overwhelming. Pierre Loti, our gloomy French novelist, recoiled in horror after beholding the myriads upon myriads of stars seen in the night sky over Thebes in Egypt:

> *Upon no occasion were the wonders of the universe more impressively brought before my mind than in the long, lonely marches in the Gobi Desert.... The boundless plain beneath, and the starry skies above. And skies, too, such as are not to be seen...*
>
> —SIR FRANCIS YOUNGHUSBAND

For the Thebans of old this beautiful vault, scintillating always with its powder of diamonds, shed no doubt, only serenity, upon their souls. But for us, *who know, alas!* it is on the contrary the field of the great fear, which, out of pity, it would have been better if we had never been able to see; the incommensurable black void, where the worlds in their frenzied whirling precipitate themselves like rain, crash into and annihilate one another, only to be renewed for fresh eternities.

PIERRE LOTI, *The Death of Philae*

For the like-minded, there was always the inevitable return of the desert dawn, when the sun, lancelike, broke over the horizon and, in Edward Fitzgerald's famous words:

...scattered into flight
The Stars before him from the Field of Night...

In the Palace of Demons

THERE WERE OTHER, WEIRDER ENCHANTMENTS IN THE DESERT NIGHT. "Out of the black darkness is heard the distant boom of a heavy bell," wrote George Nathaniel Curzon, recalling his travels in Persia. "Mournfully, and with perfect regularity of iteration, it sounds, gradually swelling nearer and louder, and perhaps mingling with the tones of smaller bells":

> But nearer and louder as the sound becomes, not another sound, and not a visible object, appear to accompany it. Suddenly, and without the slightest warning, there looms out of the darkness, like the apparition of a phantom ship, the form of the captain of the caravan. His spongy tread sounds softly on the smooth sand, and, like a great string of linked ghouls, the silent procession stalks by and is swallowed up in the night.
> GEORGE NATHANIEL CURZON, *Persia and the Persian Question*

He had been hearing, of course, the camel bells of a passing caravan. To the future viceroy of India, it was the "weirdest and most impressive" moment of his journey.

Col. Thomas Holdich, army officer, geographer, and another future president of the Royal Geographical Society, successfully navigated the phantasmagoric, labyrinthine terrain that was Baluchistan by night:

> Night travelling under clear skies in a desert has attractions of its own which go far to balance its inconveniences. The pure, fresh, invigorating air—air that may be eaten, as the natives say—produces sensations akin to those of intoxication, a light-hearted gladness which is never born of a thicker atmosphere. The mere physical sensation of pleasure in living is a delight in itself. Then there is the purple starlit sky, alight with

A caravan in the desert, 1893

familiar constellations that come back like old friends at the appointed time; and the soft talk of the desert wind, which breaks rippling over the tops of the sand waves with a sound like the sound of a far-away sea. The glint of the guiding fire ahead, flashing into sight or dropping back to darkness, is an object of intense interest, especially when it has disappeared for any length of time. It seems so close, whatever the distance may really be; and only the weird look of figures around it, as they grow from little black sand sprites into full-grown human shadows, measures the intervening space.

Col. T. H. Holdich, *The Indian Borderland*

Those guiding fires were at least as old as Marco Polo, who described similar beacons in the deserts of Lop Nor, deep in the desiccated heart of Central Asia, one of the most desolate spots on Earth—and apparently one of the spookiest:

> [T]here is a marvellous thing related of this Desert, which is that when travellers are on the move by night, and one of them chances to lag behind or to fall asleep or the like, when he tries to gain his company again he will hear spirits talking, and will suppose them to be his comrades. Sometimes the spirits will call him by name; and thus shall a traveller oft-times be led astray, so that he never finds his party. And in this way many have perished. Sometimes the stray travellers will hear as it were the tramp and hum of a great cavalcade of people away from the real line of road, and taking this to be their own company they will follow the sound; and when day breaks they find that a cheat has been put on them and that they are in an ill plight. Even in the day time one hears those spirits talking. And sometimes you shall hear the sound of a variety of musical instruments, and still more commonly the sound of drums. Hence in making this journey 'tis customary for travellers to keep close together. All the animals too have bells at their necks, so that they cannot easily get astray. And at sleeping-time a signal is put up to show the direction of the next march.
>
> MARCO POLO, *The Travels of Marco Polo*

Superstitious nonsense, according to James Richardson, the British consul in Ghat in southwestern Libya. Traversing the nearby desert one day, he had an opportunity to help banish such tales from desert lore. Not far away a fantastically sculpted hill loomed out of the sands. It was called Kesar Jenoun, the "Palace of Demons," and his caravan men would have nothing whatsoever to do with it. So, as "an Englishman and a Christian," Richardson set out—alone—to prove to them the childishness of their fears:

I got within the mysterious precincts of the Great Mountain Rock, in the course of three-quarters of an hour. I had, however, still more fear of the living than the dead, and said to myself mechanically aloud, "Man has more to fear from the living than the dead;" and I looked around anxiously this way, and that way, and every way, if perchance there might lurk, as the demon of the mountain, some stray bandit. Reassuring myself, my thoughts turned on science. I wished to astonish the boobies of the British Museum by geological specimens from the far-famed palace of mortal and immortal spirits, built in the heart of The Great Desert. I picked up various pieces of stone which lay scattered at its rocky base....This done, as connoisseur of geology, I stood stock still and gaped open-mouthed like an idiot, at the huge pyramidal ribs of The Rock. Then I bethought me I would ascend some of these off shoots of the mountain, and take a quiet seat of observation from off one of the battlemental turrets which capped its many-towered heights, over all the subjected desert and lesser hills and rocks below. But I soon changed my mind; not recognizing any decided advantage in scrambling up—God knows where—over heaps upon heaps of crumbling falling rock. I now turned my back to the Demons' Cavern, without having had the honour or pleasure of making a single acquaintance amongst these demi-immortals, much to my regret, and my face was towards the encampment. At least I thought so...

I saw at once that the king of day was fast going down to sup on the other side of The Palace, or perhaps with the Demons, and I must hasten back to my supper. I started on my return as carelessly as I came, with this foolish difference, that, although not remarking a single part of my way hither, I fancied I would take a shorter cut back to supper, beginning to feel hungry, having eaten nothing since morning....

In ten minutes I made sure of my encampment, and ran right up to some mounds of sand topped with bushes, where I expected to find Said with the supper already cooked, and the nagah lying snugly by, eating her dates and barley. But that was not the encampment. The sun was now gone, and following hard upon his heels were lurid fleecy clouds of red, the last attendants of his daily march through the desert heavens. I now looked a little farther, and said to myself, "There they are!" I went to "There they are," and found no encampment. I continued still farther, and said, "Ah, there they are!" and went to "Ah, there they are!" and found no encampment. I now made a turn to the south, and saw them quietly encamped under "various mounds," and went to "various mounds," but the encampment sunk under the earth, for they "were not." All was right, and "never mind," I should soon see their fires, and was extremely glad to notice all the light of day quenched in the paling light of a rising crescent, some five or six days old. I thus continued cheerfully my search another quarter of an hour, when all at once, as if struck by an electric shock, it flashed

Every moment a camel loomed in sight, which was no camel. There was also a hideous sameness! The reason, indeed, I was lost. For there were no distinguishing marks, the mounds followed shrubs, the shrubs mounds, then a little plain, then sand, then again the mounds and shrubs...

—JAMES RICHARDSON

across my mind, "Peradventure, I might be lost for the night!" and be obliged to make my bed in Open Desert.

The fear and thought of being lost in The Desert now mastered every other consideration, and I started unappalled to the Black Rock, without ever thinking of the myriads of spirits which at the time were keeping their midnight revels within its mysterious caverns. Got near The Rock, but I saw no place which I had seen before. The mountain had now at night assumed other shapes, other forms, other colours. Probably the demons were dancing all over it, or fluttering round it like clouds of bats and crows, preventing me from seeing its real shape and proportions...

All was vain. Fatigue was overpowering me, and my senses began to reel like a drunken man. Now was the time to see the visions and mysteries of this dread abode, and unconsciously to utter sounds of unknown tongues. Now, indeed, I fancied I heard people call me; now I saw lights; now I saw a camel with a person mounted in search of me, to whom I called. And, what is strange, these sights and sounds were all about the natural and not the supernatural...

They were phantom sights and sounds, however, and thoroughly terrified, Richardson scooped out a bed—or a grave—in a sandy mound. But all night he continued seeing phantoms. To his amazement, however, he survived until dawn, when with renewed vigor and "unshrinking mind" he sallied forth on his quest for camp. It was a little premature:

Every tuft of grass, every bush, every little mound of earth, shaped itself into a camel, a man, a sheep, a something living and moving....Although the day was pretty well developed I was staggered at the deceptions and phantasms of The Desert. Every moment a camel loomed in sight, which was no camel. There was also a hideous sameness! The reason, indeed, I was lost. For there were no distinguishing marks, the mounds followed shrubs, the shrubs mounds, then a little plain, then sand, then again the mounds and shrubs, plain and sand, and always the same—an eternal sameness....

Another camel appeared. Yes, it was a small black bush, on the top of a little hillock, shaping itself into a camel. Now a marvel—life I was sure I saw. Two beautiful antelopes, light as air, bounded by me with amazing agility, and were lost in a moment amongst the shrubs and mounds of the desert plain....

By the greatest stroke of good fortune, he managed to stumble onto the campsite of his caravan men. There, chastened, he allowed himself to be soundly berated for so tempting the demons.

So it came to pass, that I nearly lost my life for the sake of confirming them more strongly than ever in their superstitions. I, who was to have taught them the folly of their fears by practical and demonstrable defiance of the Genii confirmed and sealed the power of the Genii over this Desert.

JAMES RICHARDSON, *Travels in the Great Desert of Sahara*

DESTROYER AND PRESERVER

CLIMBING ONE OF THE LOST MOUNTAINS, AS HE CALLED THEM, deep in the Sonoran Desert between Arizona and Mexico, John Van Dyke noticed the sharp-toed print of a mule deer's hoof. "But it looks a little odd," he relates. "The impression is so clear cut that I stoop to examine it. It is with no little astonishment that I find it sunk in stone instead of earth—petrified in rock and overrun with silica. How many thousands of years ago was that impression stamped upon the stone? By what strange chance has it escaped destruction?"

That the desert is its own archive, preserving the memory, the impression, of whatever occurs in it, was not the least of its marvels. If Van Dyke came off his mountain and rode away toward the California border, he would have traversed an area once called "The Valley of the Ancient Lake," the former floor of a vast inland sea, the impression of which was still visible:

Both dunes and beach are plainly visible winding across the desert for many miles. The southwestern shore, stretching under a spur of the Coast Range, shows the same formation in its beach-line. The old bays and lagoons that led inland from the sea, the river-beds that brought down the surface waters from the mountains, the inlets and natural harbors are all in place. Some of them are drifted half full of sand, but they have not lost their identity. And out in the sea-bed still stand masses of cellular rock, honeycombed and water-worn (and now for many years wind-worn), showing the places where once rose the reefs of the ancient sea.

JOHN VAN DYKE, *The Desert*

The fennec, or Saharan fox, stalking jerboa, 1863

A half century before and half a world away, James Richardson had noticed something similar in the Sahara:

> The action of water remains a long time visible in The Great Desert, perhaps twelve, twenty, nay, fifty years, during which several periods, even in the driest regions of The Sahara, there is sure to be a heavy drenching rain....The action of rain on the earthy bosom of The Desert is very much like the action of the sea on its shores, which has led to the remark, that The Sahara looks as if it had been "washed over" by the ocean.
>
> JAMES RICHARDSON, *Travels in the Great Desert of Sahara*

Tracks in the desert need not have been laid down in stone. The Egyptologist Arthur Weigall, roaming about the rugged hills between the Nile and the Red Sea, saw tracks everywhere he rested:

Around me, on the face of the desert, there lies a jumbled collection of things beautiful: brown flints, white pebbles of limestone, yellow fragments of sandstone, orange colored ochre, transparent pieces of gypsum, carnelian and alabaster chips, glittering quartz. Across the clear patches of sand there are all manner of recent footprints, and the incidental study of these is one of the richest delights of a desert journey. Here may one see the four-pronged footprints of a wagtail, and there the larger marks of a crow. An eagle's and a vulture's footmarks are often to be observed, and the identification of those of birds such as the desert partridge or of the creamy-coloured courser is a happy exercise for one's ingenuity. Here the light, wiggly line of a lizard's rapid tour abroad attracts the attention... and there footprints of the jerboa are seen leading in short jumps towards its hole. Jackals or foxes leave their dainty pad-marks in all directions, and one may sometimes come across the heavy prints of a hyaena, while it is not unusual to meet with those of a gazelle.

ARTHUR WEIGALL, *Travels in the Upper Egyptian Deserts*

Weigall's professional life revolved around monuments of another order of magnitude altogether, for the desert preserved in its sands the broken record of human civilization like no other environment on Earth.

Nowhere was that record more ancient and apparent than along the desert shores bordering the valley of the Nile. Near the river's delta, Mark Twain could marvel at the most celebrated survivor of "five thousand slow revolving years," the Sphinx, how it gazed out "over the ocean of Time—over lines of century-waves which, further and further receding, closed nearer and nearer together, and blended at last into one unbroken tide, away toward the horizon of remote antiquity..." Five hundred miles upriver from this oldest of Egyptian statues stood one of the youngest of ancient Egyptian temples. The huge columns of Kom Ombo, rising dramatically from the river, were erected as late as the first century B.C.—but were almost swallowed in desert:

The rising sun disclosed the ruins of Kom Ombo, which we had seen in the distance the night before like an island rising out of the waters.... There are two great temples side by side; everything is duplex. In this they are unique. Nothing of the kind exists elsewhere in the world. One temple is dedicated to Amen, the representative of God as personified in the sun; the other is dedicated to Sebek, the evil deity, represented by the crocodile. Thus the good people of ancient Ombos endeavoured to make the best of both worlds.

JOHN WARD, *Pyramids and Progress*

Until 1893, when it was cleared and restored, the sand had so filled the majestic courts and chapels that visitors to Kom Ombo had a first-hand look at the painted ceilings over which the sun and the stars sailed in boats. Even the hieroglyphic inscription stating that the temple was "founded as a work to endure for ever" had been buried for centuries.

Still, it was worth the journey to see, and one of those who made the trip was President Ulysses S. Grant, just after he took leave of office:

The first stop on the return trip was at Kom Ombo, on the east bank of the river, twenty-six miles below Assuaan. At this point, the desert comes to the river. The old town and its surrounding walls were buried in the sand, which also covered so large a part of its vast and well preserved temple, that its grandeur was then unknown, and scarcely suspected even by Egyptologists. The rear of the temple was completely buried. In the front part the sand had accumulated up to a level with the capitals of the great columns of its hypostyle hall...

There is a certain fascination in a half buried ruin. It is probable that the General and Mrs. Grant received quite as much pleasure in viewing the great pylon, the beautiful floral and palm-capitals of the columns of the great hall, the finely decorated ceilings, and the interesting astronomical figures then in view, supplying the rest with their imaginations, as they would have received from seeing the whole temple.

ELBERT ELI FARMAN, *Along the Nile with General Grant*

If there was a certain fascination for half-buried ruins, there might be much more for half-buried cities. All over the deserts of the Old World the remains of vanished civilizations were swallowed up in sand. Austen Henry Layard, the excavator of Nineveh in modern Iraq, found in the deserts around Baghdad villages deserted and canals abandoned. "In this region the habitations of men are turned almost in a day to mere heaps of earth.... The grave of the wandering Arab is rarely far beneath the surface of the soil, and the wild beasts of the Desert soon scrape away the scanty earth. Human skulls and remains, scarcely yet bleached by the sun, were scattered over the ruins, mingled with bricks, pottery, broken glass, and other relics of ancient population." Col. Thomas Holdich, surveying the border region between Afghanistan and Iran, was astonished at what he saw:

> As we progressed we encountered strange sights, the sights of the cit-
> ies of the dead spreading out like gigantic cemeteries for miles on either
> side the river, gaunt relics of palaces and mosques and houses, upright
> and bleached, scattered over acres of débris, masses of broken pottery,
> mounds of mud ruins.
>
> T. H. HOLDICH, *The Indian Borderland*

In the vast desert in the dead heart of Asia, Sven Hedin discovered forests of upright wooden rafters sticking out of the sand that were all that remained of the legendary city of Taklimakan:

OPPOSITE: *The temple of Gyrshe in Egypt, by David Roberts, mid-19th century*

This city, of whose existence no European had hitherto any inkling, was one of the most unexpected discoveries that I made throughout the whole of my travels in Asia. Who could have imagined that in the interior of the dread Desert of Gobi, and precisely in that part of it which in dreariness and desolation exceeds all other deserts on the face of the earth, actual cities slumbered under the sand, cities wind-driven for thousands of years, the ruined survivals of a once flourishing civilization? And yet there stood I amid the wreck and devastation of an ancient people, within whose dwellings none had ever entered save the sandstorm in its days of maddest revelry; there stood I like the prince in the enchanted wood, having awakened to new life the city which had slumbered for a thousand years, or at any rate rescued the memory of its existence from oblivion.

SVEN HEDIN, *Through Asia*

In this irresistible creeping march, the desert was destroyer as well as preserver.

When not buried in sand, the monumental ruins of vanished civilizations—the soaring columns, the triumphal arches, the fallen temples, the upright pillars upholding nothing—still withstood the centuries of sun and sand and wind. Yet there were those who thought that even such grand sites as Palmyra in Syria were dwarfed by their setting, the desert reducing the noble ruins to insignificance. So there developed a fascination not for half-buried cities, but for hidden ones, and there was no hidden city like Petra.

In the early 19th century the intrepid Swiss adventurer, Johann Ludwig Burckhardt, emerged from the desert with tales of having visited a fabulous abandoned city hidden in a rocky enclave in northern Arabia (now part of Jordan). Soon thereafter every desert traveler worth his or her salt had to visit Petra, the stronghold of the Nabataean civilization before the shifting tides of history ebbed and left it behind.

The approach, however, was a bit treacherous and the local tribes fiercely discouraged intruders. Yet those who did get there never forgot the sight. In 1835, the peripatetic lawyer John Lloyd Stephens was the first American to see it:

> The only access is by clambering over this wall of stone, practicable only in one place, or by an entrance the most extraordinary that Nature, in her wildest freaks, has ever framed. The loftiest portals ever raised by the hands of man, the proudest monuments of architectural skill and daring, sink into insignificance by the comparison. It is, perhaps, the most wonderful object in the world, except the ruins of the city to which it forms the entrance...
>
> In a few words, this ancient and extraordinary city is situated within a natural amphitheatre of two or three miles in circumference, encompassed on all sides by rugged mountains five or six hundred feet in height. The whole of this area is now a waste of ruins, dwelling-houses, palaces, temples, and triumphal arches, aprostrate together in undistinguishable confusion. The sides of the mountains are cut smooth, in a perpendicular direction, and filled with long and continued ranges of dwelling-houses, temples, and tombs, excavated with vast labor out of the solid rock; and while their summits present Nature in her wildest and most savage form, their bases are adorned with all the beauty of architecture and art, with columns, and porticoes, and pediments, and ranges of corridors, enduring as the mountains out of which they are hewn, and fresh as if the work of a generation scarcely yet gone by...
>
> JOHN LLOYD STEPHENS,
> *Incidents of Travel in Egypt, Arabia Petraea, and the Holy Land*

In the heart of a lost mountain, located deep in a desert, it was not a hoofprint but a city that was found petrified in stone.

Desert Monsters

"It is a very old trick of the poets and retailers of the marvellous to people The Desert with dragons, and serpents, and monsters of every kind," noted James Richardson, whose own travels—or travails—were in the Sahara. "It would have been very nice to fight one's way through The Desert in the midst of every kind of beast and monster which the gloomy imagination of men may have conjured up from the beginning of the annals of adventure"—but, he concluded, they were not necessary. "Sufficient are the evils of The Desert to the wayfarer who sojourns therein."

By his day, most desert monsters had been reduced considerably in size, if not in reputation. Snakes, despite the many legends entwined about them, were rarely seen. Perhaps that was because, as Herodotus told it, the hordes of winged serpents that each year rose out of Arabia were stopped at the mountain passes by ibises, sacred birds to the Egyptians. No birds, however, could stop that biblical scourge, the locust, from still rising out of the deserts in immense numbers, and the diminutive scorpion also retained his outsize reputation. Charles Doughty knew both from his travels in the wastes of Arabia:

> We saw "pillars" of locusts again, the desolation of the land that is desolate, reeling high above the soil in the evening wind, from the westward and drive towards el-Ally and Kheybar: the deep clouds of flickering insects passed without dimming the waning sunlight…
>
> Scorpions lurk under the cool stones; I have found them in my tent, upon my clothing, but never had any hurt. I have seen many grown persons and children bitten, but the sting is not perilous; some wise man is called to "read" over them. The wounded part throbs with numbness and aching till the third day; there is not much swelling.
>
> CHARLES DOUGHTY, *Travels in Arabia Deserta*

Other desert creatures once deified by the Egyptians, from falcons to crocodiles, could still be seen along the Nile. Johann Burckhardt encountered "the bird Zakzak, frequently seen in Upper Egypt, which is said to creep into the crocodile's mouth, and to feed upon the digested food which that animal throws up from its stomach," but he was particularly taken with the scarab beetles:

> On the sandy shore, on the west side of the Nile, are numberless beetles (Scarabaei), of great variety in size and shape; I often found the sandy road on that side completely covered with the traces of their feet. The Nubians, who call them Kafers, or Infidels, dread them from a belief that they are venomous, and that they poison whatever kind of food they touch. Their color is generally black, and the largest I have seen were of the size of a half-crown piece. The worship paid to this animal by the ancient Egyptians may probably have had its origin in Nubia; it might well be adopted as a symbol of passive resignation to the decrees of Providence; for it is impossible, from the sandy mounds which they inhabit, that these beetles can ever taste water, and the food they partake of must be very scanty; they are however always seen busily and unweariedly toiling their way over the sands.
>
> JOHANN BURCKHARDT, *Travels in Nubia*

Scorpions lurk under the cool stones; I have found them in my tent, upon my clothing, but never had any hurt. I have seen many grown persons and children bitten…

—CHARLES DOUGHTY

Those beetles worked no harder than did the proverbial ant, whose buried cities Charles Doughty found so fascinating. "Many are the cities under this desert sand, of seed-gathering ants; I have measured some watling-street of theirs, eighty-five paces; to speed once this length and come again, loaded as camels, is these small busybodies' summers day journey." Those admirable fellows, however, appear to be the exception, for ants and other insects seemed to be the real monsters of the desert, as Edward Palmer discovered in the rugged, dry, empty wilderness of Sinai:

Egyptian cobra, 1849

No sooner had the shades of night fallen than we were visited by such a plague of insects as it has never been my lot to witness before or since. Mosquitoes, moths and gnats literally swarmed in upon us, extinguishing the candles, filling our ink bottles, settling in large bunches even on the pens with which we wrote, and ultimately driving us out into the dark night-air, to be again charged at by gigantic beetles, and stung by flying ants.

E. H. PALMER, *The Desert of the Exodus*

In 1873, while making his epic crossing of Australia's Great Sandy Desert, Col. Peter Warburton had enough to worry about—his water was going and his imported camels were faltering—without having to face the insects:

A small black ant seems to have been the avowed enemy of this expedition. The ground literally swarmed with them, and a stamp of the foot brought them up in thousands. When the wearied men threw themselves down under the shade of a bush, to snatch the half-hour's slumber their exhausted frames required, the merciless little insects attacked them, and not only effectually routed sleep, but even rendered a recumbent position impossible. The scanty clothing possessed by the travellers was no protection; so feeble a bulwark was speedily under-run by the enemy, and their successful invasion announced by sharp painful nips from their powerful mandibles. Often, when the vertical sun poured down in full fierceness on their heads, and the poor shade afforded even by a bush would have been an inestimable blessing, the travellers were driven away from the shelter by their relentless persecutors, and in despair flung themselves down on the burning sand, where it was too hot even for an ant. By day or by night the little insects gave them no respite...

The number of flies in Australia, and the rapidity with which they breed, are quite horrible. Nothing in the shape of meat can be left exposed for a moment, otherwise a swarm of flies descend and seem to emit living maggots on the flesh. They assail the ears, nostrils, and eyes of the traveller, who is unable to stir without a veil...A little scratch, that under other circumstances would pass unnoticed, here became a troublesome, ulcerous sore. Some idea of the condition of this camel's back may be imagined when the reader hears that the maggots were *scooped out with a pint pot.*

PETER EGERTON WARBURTON,
Journey across the Western Interior of Australia

Flies so bedeviled Charles Doughty that he was forced to seek the shelter of the cliffs—where he found his own heroic bird willing to battle the winged monsters of Arabia:

Where I sat, there came tripping a little fly-catcher bird, slender and slate-coloured and somewhat as our common wagtail, which coursing nimbly upon the tormenting flies, snatched her prey without ever missing: I spread upon her my kerchief, and took and caressed the little friendly bird without hurt, and let her go from my hand: but for all this she only removed a little and did not fly from me.

While the Glow Holds

"NO DOUBT IT IS AN ACQUIRED TASTE THAT LEADS ONE TO ADMIRE greasewood and cactus," John Van Dyke admitted. Sometimes, however, even he was hard-pressed to admire a desert plant:

> The crucifixion thorn is a bush or tree somewhat like the palo verde, except that it has no leaf. It is a thorn and little else. Each small twig runs out and ends in a sharp spike of which the branch is but the supporting shaft. It bears in August a small yellow flower but this grows out of the side of the spike. In fact the whole shrub seems created for no other purpose than the glorification of the thorn as a thorn.
>
> JOHN VAN DYKE, *The Desert*

Desert finch and desert lark, late 19th century

To which Van Dyke's contemporary, Mary Hunter Austin, might have shrugged: "The manner of the country makes the usage of life there," she wrote, "and the land will not be lived in except in its own fashion."

By the time she began writing the essays collected in her classic *The Land of Little Rain,* Mary Austin's marriage was failing and her daughter had been born retarded. But she found solace in the desert, in those regions where the Mojave reached out and kissed the feet of the California mountains:

East away from the Sierras, south from Panamint and Amargosa, east and south many an uncounted mile, is the Country of Lost Borders.

Ute, Paiute, Mojave, and Shoshone inhabit its frontiers, and as far into the heart of it as a man dare go. Not the law, but the land sets the limit. Desert is the name it wears upon the maps, but the Indian's is the better word. Desert is a loose term to indicate land that supports no man; whether the land can be bitted and broken to that purpose is not proven. Void of life it never is, however dry the air and villainous the soil.

Mary Hunter Austin, *The Land of Little Rain*

She saw the desert through different eyes—Shoshone eyes, perhaps— and as a result her book would help change the way that future generations would come to see it, too. It was still the desert, with all its bewitching enchantments, but the desert transfigured:

None other than this long brown land lays such a hold on the affections. The rainbow hills, the tender bluish mists, the luminous radiance of the spring, have the lotus charm. They trick the sense of time, so that once inhabiting there you always mean to go away without quite realizing that you have not done it…

Out West, the west of the mesas and the unpatented hills, there is more sky than any place in the world. It does not sit flatly on the rim

Saberwing hummingbirds, late 19th century

of earth, but begins somewhere out in the space in which the earth is poised, hollows more, and is full of clean winey winds....In summer the sky travails with thunderings and the flare of sheet lightnings to win a few blistering big drops, and once in a lifetime the chance of a torrent. But you have not known what force resides in the mindless things until you have known a desert wind. One expects it at the turn of the two seasons, wet and dry, with electrified tense nerves. Along the edge of the mesa where it drops off to the valley, dust devils begin to rise white and steady, fanning out at the top like the genii out of the Fisherman's bottle. One supposes the Indians might have learned the use of smoke signals from these dust pillars as they learn most things direct from the tutelage of the earth...

Now and then a palm's breadth of the trail gathers itself together and scurries off with a little rustle under the brush, to resolve itself into sand again. This is pure witchcraft. If you succeed in catching it in transit, it loses its power and becomes a flat, horned, toad-like creature, horrid looking and harmless...

Go as far as you dare in the heart of a lonely land, you cannot go so far that life and death are not before you. Painted lizards slip in and out of rock crevices, and pant on the white hot sands. Birds, hummingbirds even, nest in the cactus scrub; woodpeckers befriend the demoniac yuccas; out of the stark, treeless waste rings the music of the night-singing mockingbird. If it be summer and the sun well down, there will be a burrowing owl to call....Late afternoons [they] may be seen blinking at the doors of their hummocks with perhaps four or five elfish nestlings atow, and by twilight begin a soft *whoo-oo-ing,* rounder, sweeter, more incessant in mating time. It is not possible to disassociate the call of the burrowing owl from the late slant light of the mesa. If the fine vibrations which are the golden-violet glow of spring twilights were to tremble into sound, it would be just that mellow double note breaking along the blossom-tops. While the glow holds one sees the thistle-down flights and pouncings after prey, and on into the dark hears their soft *pus-ssb!* clearing out of the trail ahead.

MARY HUNTER AUSTIN, *The Land of Little Rain*

When John Van Dyke bade his long good night to the desert, he felt a touch of that same indefinable dread to which so many desert travelers have succumbed:

A dusk is gathering on the desert's face, and over the eastern horizon the purple shadow of the world is reaching up to the sky. The light is fading out. Plain and mesa are blurring into unknown distances, and mountain-ranges are looming dimly into unknown heights. Warm drifts of lilac-blue are drawn like mists across the valleys; the yellow sands have shifted into a pallid gray. The glory of the wilderness has gone down with the sun. Mystery—that haunting sense of the unknown—is all that remains.

Before she closed her eyes, Mary Austin just wrapped that mystery around her:

For all the toll the desert takes of a man it gives compensations, deep breaths, deep sleep, and the communion of the stars. It is hard to escape the sense of mastery as the stars move in the wide clear heavens to risings and settings unobscured. They look large and near and palpitant; as if they moved on some stately service...Wheeling to their stations in the sky, they make the poor world-fret of no account. Of no account you who lie out there watching, nor the lean coyote that stands off in the scrub from you and howls...

ONE BOUNDLESS PASTURE
THE GRASSLANDS

"I had a most delightfull view of…immence herds of Buffaloe, Elk,
deer, & Antelopes feeding in one common and boundless pasture."
—MERIWETHER LEWIS

ERIWETHER LEWIS WAS NOT OVERLY CONCERNED WITH spelling. Scribbling journal entries by a campfire's flickering light was not conducive to grammatical niceties, nor could his pen adequately represent what his eyes had just beheld:

September 17, 1804

…this senery already rich pleasing and beatiful was still farther hightened by immence herds of Buffaloe deer Elk and Antelopes which we saw in every direction feeding on the hills and plains. I do not think I exagerate when I estimate the number of Buffaloe which could be compre[hend]ed at one view to amount to 3000.

April 22, 1805

I asscended to the top of the cutt bluff this morning from whence I had a most delightfull view of the country, the whole of which except the vally formed by the Missouri is void of timber or underbrush, exposing

OPPOSITE: *Buffalo on the prairie, early 20th century*

to the first glance of the spectator immence herds of Buffaloe, Elk, deer, & Antelopes feeding in one common and boundless pasture.

Thursday, April 25, 1805
the whol face of the country was covered with herds of Buffaloe, Elk & Antelopes; deer are also abundant, but keep themselves more concealed in the woodland. the buffaloe Elk and Antelope are so gentle that we pass near them while feeding, without apearing to excite any alarm among them; and when we attract their attention, they frequently approach us more nearly to discover what we are, and in some instances pursue us a considerable distance apparently with that view.

MERIWETHER LEWIS, *The Journals of Lewis and Clark*

Such entries crop up everywhere in the journals, interspersed with observations on weather or Indian customs or the "tremendious" grizzly bear. For Lewis and Clark were fortunate enough to have beheld one of the great marvels of the wild grasslands: the spectacle, extending to the limits of vision, of thousands of animals roaming openly over the plains.

It could still be seen in 1846, when a 22-year-old Harvard graduate named Francis Parkman, chasing a summer idyll on the wild prairie, found one evening that he had strayed too far from his companions and needed to find his way back:

But in the mean time my ride had been by no means a solitary one. The whole face of the country was dotted far and wide with countless hundreds of buffalo. They trooped along in files and columns, bulls, cows and calves, on the green faces of the declivities in front. They scrambled away over the hills to the right and left; and far off, the pale blue swells in the extreme distance were dotted with innumerable specks.

Sometimes I surprised shaggy old bulls grazing alone, or sleeping behind the ridges I ascended. They would leap up at my approach, stare stupidly at me through their tangled manes, and then gallop heavily away. The antelope were very numerous; and as they are always bold when in the neighborhood of buffalo, they would approach quite near to look at me, gazing intently with their great round eyes, then suddenly leap aside, and stretch lightly away over the prairie, as swiftly as a race-horse. Squalid, ruffian-like wolves sneaked through the hollows and sandy ravines. Several times I passed through villages of prairie-dogs, who sat, each at the mouth of his burrow, holding his paws before him in a supplicating attitude, and yelping away most vehemently, energetically whisking his little tail with every squeaking cry he uttered. Prairie-dogs are not fastidious in their choice of companions; various long, checkered snakes were sunning themselves in the midst of the village, and demure little gray owls, with a large white ring around each eye, were perched side by side with the rightful inhabitants. The prairie teemed with life. Again and again I looked toward the crowded hill-sides, and was sure I saw horsemen; and riding near, with a mixture of hope and dread, for Indians were abroad, I found them transformed into a group of buffalo. There was nothing in human shape amid all this vast congregation of brute forms.

When I turned down the buffalo path, the prairie seemed changed; only a wolf or two glided past at intervals, like conscious felons, never looking to the right or left. Being now free from anxiety, I was at leisure to observe minutely the objects around me; and here, for the first time, I noticed insects wholly different from any of the varieties found farther to the eastward. Gaudy butterflies fluttered about my horse's head; strangely formed beetles, glittering with metallic lustre, were crawling upon plants that I had never seen before; multitudes of lizards, too, were darting like lightning over the sand.

I had run to a great distance from the river. It cost me a long ride on the buffalo path, before I saw, from the ridge of a sand-hill, the pale

Zebras on the savanna, late 19th century

surface of the Platte glistening in the midst of its desert valleys, and the faint outline of the hills beyond waving along the sky.

FRANCIS PARKMAN, *The Oregon Trail*

A few years later and an ocean away, David Livingstone was following the course of the Zambezi River in Africa. As one of the first Europeans to extensively explore the bushy savannas of what are now Zambia and Zimbabwe, he found himself frequently stopping to gaze in admiration, if not amazement:

When we came to the top of the outer range of the hills we had a glorious view. At a short distance below we saw the Kafue wending away over the forest-clad plain to the confluence, and on the other side of the Zambezi, beyond that, lay a long range of dark hills. A line of fleecy clouds appeared lying along the course of the river at their base. The plain below us had more game on it than anywhere I had seen in Africa. Hundreds of buffaloes and zebras grazed on the open spaces, and there stood lordly elephants feeding majestically, nothing moving apparently but the proboscis. When we descended we found all the animals remarkably tame. The elephants stood beneath the trees, fanning themselves with their large ears, as if they did not see us at two hundred yards' distance. The number of animals was quite astonishing, and made me think that here I could realize an image of the time when megatheria fed undisturbed in the primeval forests.

DAVID LIVINGSTONE,
Missionary Travels and Researches in Southern Africa

It was Livingstone's fellow Scot, a 25-year-old explorer named Joseph Thomson, who in 1883, a thousand miles to the north, crested a rise near the foot of Mount Kilimanjaro to behold what would soon become one of the world's most famous wildlife spectacles: the East African savanna in all its pristine glory:

Leaving the forest country round the base of Kibonoto, and traversing a rich and varied scene, we suddenly emerged, at a height of 6000 feet, on a great treeless plain covered with a close and succulent coating of grass quite undistinguishable from the pasture of more temperate climates. In the immediate foreground, the country spread out before us in gently waving plains diversified by low, rounded ridges, small humpy hills or volcanic cones...

Such is the country: but see its inhabitants! There, towards the base of Kilimanjaro, are three great herds of buffalo slowly and leisurely moving up from the lower grazing-grounds to the shelter of the forest for their daily snooze and rumination in its gloomy depths. Farther out on the plains enormous numbers of the harmless but fierce-looking wildebeest continue their grazing, some erratic members of the herd gambolling and galloping about, with waving tail and strange uncouth movements. Mixed with these are to be seen companies of that loveliest of all large game, the zebra, conspicuous in their beautiful striped skin,—here marching with stately step, with heads down bent, there enjoying themselves by kicking their heels in mid-air or running open–mouthed in mimic fight, anon standing as if transfixed, with heads erect and projecting ears, watching the caravan pass. But these are not all. Look! Down in that grassy bottom there are several specimens of the great, unwieldy rhinoceros, with horns stuck on their noses in a most offensive and pugnacious manner. Over that ridge a troop of ostriches are scudding away out of reach of danger, defying pursuit, and too wary for the stalker. See how numerous are the herds of hartebeest; and notice the graceful pallah springing into mid-air with great bounds, as if in pure enjoyment of existence. There also, among the tall reeds near the marsh, you perceive the dignified waterbuck, in twos and threes, leisurely cropping the dewy grass. The wart-hog, disturbed at his morning's feast, clears off in a bee-line with tail erect, and with a steady military trot truly comical. These do not exhaust the list, for there are many other species of game. Turn in whatever direction you please, they are to be seen in astonishing numbers, and so rarely hunted, that unconcernedly they stand and stare at us…

JOSEPH THOMSON, *Through Masai Land*

When that description was published, the great game herds had largely disappeared from the North American prairie. In Africa they would linger into our own day, though in ever diminishing numbers. Yet there were observers even at that time who were finding other things in the world of grass and sky than the fading splendor of the wild and once boundless pasture.

The Flying Summer

WHEN VICTOR HUGO, THE FRENCH NOVELIST EXILED TO THE ISLE of Guernsey in the English Channel, turned his all-encompassing gaze onto the grass at his feet, he beheld there a microcosm of all of those lush meadows that made much of Europe ideal pasture and dairy country. He saw, and could identify, at least two dozen kinds of grasses, ranging from the *Phalaris* of the Canary Islands to the sow thistle of Siberia. Peering closer, he then studied its wonderful bazaar of bizarre inhabitants:

> Now, imagine a thousand insects running through and flying above this, some disgusting, others charming. Under the grass the longi-cornes (insects with long antennae), longinases (insects with long proboscides), weevils, ants occupied milking the grubs, their cows; the driveling grasshopper, the small beetle, ladybugs...in the air, the dragon-fly, the wasp, the golden rose-beetle, the bumble-bee, the lace-winged fly, ruby-tailed flies, the noisy volucellae, and you will have some idea of this sight...offered at noon of a June day on the ridge of Jerbourg or Fermain Bay to a dreamy entomologist and to a poet who is also some-thing of a naturalist.
>
> VICTOR HUGO, *The Toilers of the Sea*

Hugo would have found such a man in W. H. Hudson. Dreamer, poet, naturalist—Hudson had just that combination of acute eye, pro-found sensibility, and fluid pen that, molded by an idyllic childhood on the Argentine Pampas of the 1840s, made for a man who saw grassland marvels everywhere.

The Pampas, an apparently illimitable sea of grass, was so fecund with insect life that it spilled, so to speak, over its borders. Charles Darwin, standing on the *Beagle* off the coast of that great Pampas stream, the River

Plate, saw "vast numbers of butterflies, in bands or flocks of countless myriads, extended as far as the eye could range. Even by aid of a glass it was not possible to see a space free from butterflies. The seamen cried out 'it was snowing butterflies.'"

That was just the kind of thing that Hudson would notice. Butterflies might be one thing, but who, for instance, had ever heard of "dragon fly storms"? Dragonflies, large and small, sober green and brilliant scarlet, were abundant on the Pampas, and mostly each clung to its own kind. On occasion, though, they mixed together in huge flights composed of countless thousands of individuals—all flying before the strong southwest wind, the pampero:

> It is in summer and autumn that the large dragon-flies appear; not with the wind, but—and this is the most curious part of the matter—in advance of it...flying before the wind at a speed of seventy or eighty miles an hour. On some occasions they appear almost simultaneously with the wind, going by like a flash, and instantly disappearing from sight. You have scarcely time to see them before the wind strikes you. As a rule, however, they make their appearance from five to fifteen minutes before the wind strikes; and when they are in great numbers the air, to a height of ten or twelve feet above the surface of the ground, is all at once seen to be full of them, rushing past with extraordinary velocity in a north-easterly direction...and of the countless millions flying like thistledown before the great pampero wind, not one solitary traveller ever returns.
>
> W. H. HUDSON, *The Naturalist in La Plata*

Hudson concluded that the insects were seized with "a sudden panic," and told of a horse race near the town of El Carmen in Patagonia that was struck by a violent pampero, preceded by a huge dragonfly storm. The insects "settled on the people in such quantities that men and horses were quickly covered with clinging masses of them. My informant said—and this agrees with my own observation—that he was greatly impressed by the appearance of terror shown by the insects; they clung to him as if for dear life, so that he had the greatest difficulty in ridding himself of them."

Dragonfly, circa 1800

When he was not watching for dragonflies, Hudson might be observing spiders gathering in equally immense numbers. Once he found gossamer web lying in such quantities as to hide the grass and thistles:

> The white zone was about twenty yards wide, and outside it only a few scattered webs were visible on the grass; its exact length I did not ascertain, but followed it for about two miles without finding the end. The spiders were so numerous that they continually baulked one another in their efforts to rise in the air. As soon as one threw out its lines they would become entangled with those of another spider, lanced out at the same moment; both spiders would immediately seem to know the cause of the trouble, for as soon as their lines fouled they would rush angrily towards each other, each trying to drive the other from the elevation. Notwithstanding these difficulties, numbers were continually floating off on the breeze which blew from the south.

They were gathering for migration, he concluded, heading north, like the birds do in the Southern Hemisphere.

> When great numbers of spiders rise up simultaneously over a large area, then, sometimes, the movement forces itself on our attention; for at such times the whole sky may be filled with visible masses of

floating web. All the great movements of gossamers I have observed have occurred in the autumn, or, at any rate, several weeks after the summer solstice; and, like the migrations of birds at the same season of the year, have been in a northerly direction....On the continent of Europe it also seems probable that a great autumnal movement of these spiders takes place; although, I must confess, I have no grounds for this statement, except that the floating gossamer is called in Germany "Der fliegender Sommer"—the flying or departing summer.

> *You have scarcely time to see them before the wind strikes you. As a rule, however, they make their appearance from five to fifteen minutes before the wind strikes; and when they are in great numbers the air, to a height of ten or twelve feet...is all at once seen to be full of them rushing past with extraordinary velocity in a northeasterly direction.*
>
> —W. H. HUDSON

A man of Hudson's sensibility could not help but find something remarkable in the grasshopper, most proverbial of all the fleeting summer creatures. One hot day while driving sheep he came to a stony sierra looming several hundred feet over the plain. He rode up to it and began climbing:

Coming to a place where ferns and flowering herbage grew thick, I began to hear all about me sounds of a character utterly unlike any natural sound I was acquainted with—innumerable low clear voices tinkling or pealing like minute sweet-toned, resonant bells—for the sounds were purely metallic and perfectly bell-like. I was completely ringed round with the mysterious music, and as I walked it rose and sank rhythmically, keeping time to my steps. I stood still, and immediately the sounds ceased. I took a step forwards, and again the fairy-bells were set ringing, as if at each step my foot touched a central meeting point of a thousand radiating threads, each thread attached to a peal of little bells hanging concealed among the herbage....Eventually we discovered that the sound was made by grasshoppers; but they were seen only to be lost, for I could not capture one, so excessively shy and cunning had the perpetual ringing of their own little tocsins made them. And presently I had to return to my muttons; and afterwards there was no opportunity of revisiting the spot to observe so singular a habit again and collect specimens. It was a very slender grasshopper, about an inch and a half long, of a uniform, tawny, protective colour...

Hudson concluded, since other grasshoppers are silent when alarmed, that this strange race or colony, living in isolation, unknown and unseen by the roving eyes of naturalists, had acquired a gregarious habit, which served to warn and protect the community at large.

A continent away, the novelist Willa Cather recalled from her own Nebraska childhood the glorious transfiguration of the autumn prairies, when the red-gold grass was like the "bush that burned with fire and was not consumed":

The rabbits were unusually spry that afternoon. They kept starting up all about us, and dashing off down the draw as if they were playing a game of some kind. But the little buzzing things that lived in the grass were all dead—all but one. While we were lying there against the warm bank, a little insect of the palest, frailest green hopped painfully out of the buffalo grass and tried to leap into a bunch of bluestem. He missed it, fell back, and sat with his head sunk between his long legs, his antennae quivering, as if he were waiting for something to come and finish him. Tony made a warm nest for him in her hands; talked to him gaily and indulgently in Bohemian. Presently he began to sing for us—a thin, rusty little chirp. She held him close to her ear and laughed, but a moment afterward I saw there were tears in her eyes.

When the bank on the other side of the draw began to throw a narrow shelf of shadow, we knew we ought to be starting homeward; the chill came on quickly when the sun got low, and Ántonia's dress was thin. What were we to do with the frail little creature we had lured back to life by false pretenses? I offered my pockets, but Tony shook her head and carefully put the green insect in her hair, tying her big handkerchief down loosely over her curls.

WILLA CATHER, My Ántonia

The day, like the year, always winds down into the diurnal autumn that is dusk—a time when W. H. Hudson could usually be found stirring abroad:

Riding on the pampas one dark evening an hour after sunset, and passing from high ground overgrown with giant thistles to a low plain covered with long grass, bordering a stream of water, I found it all ablaze with myriads of fireflies. I noticed that all the insects gave out an exceptionally large, brilliant light, which shone almost steadily. The long grass was thickly studded with them, while they literally swarmed in the air, all moving up the valley with a singularly slow and languid flight. When I galloped down into this river of phosphorescent fire, my horse plunged and snorted with alarm. I succeeded at length in quieting him, and then rode slowly through, compelled to keep my mouth and eyes closed, so thickly did the insects rain on to my face. The air was laden with the sickening phosphorous smell they emit, but when I had once got free of the broad fiery zone, stretching away on either hand for miles along the moist valley, I stood still and gazed back for some time on a scene the most wonderful and enchanting I have ever witnessed.

W. H. HUDSON, The Naturalist in La Plata

Deathwatch and Flutter and Hiss

IN THE LLANOS, THE VAST GRASSLAND CLOAKING HUGE TRACTS OF Venezuela and Colombia, the dry season is a time of searing heat and drought. Cattle and horses were once seen roaming about in an endless torment of thirst, persecuted by insects each day, by vampire bats each night. Though they might snuff the air expectantly when the first distant thunder rumbled, heralding the approach of the rainy season, the animals would find no release from their tortures. Once rain began to soak into the cracked clay, titanic forces began to stir:

> At times, according to the account of the natives, the humid clay on the banks of the morasses, is seen to rise slowly in broad flakes. Accompanied by a violent noise, as on the eruption of a small mud-volcano, the upheaved earth is hurled high into the air. Those who are familiar with the phenomenon fly from it; for a colossal water-snake or a mailed and scaly crocodile, awakened from its trance by the first fall of rain, is about to burst from his tomb...
>
> ALEXANDER VON HUMBOLDT, *Views of Nature*

And with the streams overflowing their banks and turning what was once dry and sere into a "vast inland sea," those monsters went on the prowl. Horses and cattle might retreat to the ever shrinking land still projecting like islands above the spreading waters, but the monsters were sure to follow. "Many foals are drowned," continued Humboldt's grisly account, "many are seized by crocodiles, crushed by their serrated tails, and devoured. Horses and oxen may not unfrequently be seen which have escaped from the fury of this bloodthirsty and gigantic lizard, bearing on their legs the marks of its pointed teeth." Even then the horror was not ended, for onto the flooded plains swam innumerable electric eels, "who

can at pleasure discharge from every part of their slimy, yellow-speckled bodies a deadening shock":

> This species of gymnotus is about five or six feet in length. It is powerful enough to kill the largest animals when it discharges its nervous organs at one shock in a favourable direction. It was once found necessary to change the line of road from Uritucu across the Steppe, owing to the number of horses which, in fording a certain rivulet, annually fell a sacrifice to these gymnoti, which had accumulated there in great numbers.

The seasonal extremes of the llanos notwithstanding, the world's grasslands hold their fair share of scaly monsters, most of them, because of the dry environment, being snakes. The unreasoning, and often unreasonable, human aversion to snakes inevitably accompanied all those explorers who first ventured onto the pristine prairies and savannas. There was, of course, just cause for some concern. The cobras of India and Africa led a long list of venomous serpents that made the adder of the Eurasian steppe look tame. In Australia one was hard-pressed to find a snake that wasn't deadly. And in North America, those hunters and trappers and members of Lewis and Clark's Corps of Discovery who first penetrated the wild grasslands found their nemesis in the rattlesnake. Josiah Gregg, traversing the Santa Fe Trail in the 1830s, had no lost love for rattlesnakes:

> Rattlesnakes are proverbially abundant upon all these prairies, and as there is seldom to be found either stick or stone with which to kill them, one hears almost a constant popping of rifles or pistols among the vanguard, to clear the route of these disagreeable occupants, lest they should bite our animals. As we were toiling up through

OPPOSITE: *African cobra and gazelles, 1885*

the sandy hillocks which border the southern banks of the Arkansas, the day being exceedingly warm, we came upon a perfect den of these reptiles. I will not say "thousands," though this perhaps were nearer the truth—but hundreds at least were coiled or crawling in every direction. They were no sooner discovered than we were upon them with guns and pistols, determined to let none of them escape.

JOSIAH GREGG, Commerce of the Prairies

On the other hand, W. H. Hudson, as might be expected, never met a snake he couldn't admire. The great naturalist of the Argentine grasslands had many unusual—almost magical—encounters with strange creatures, including that which occurred one summer while riding alone across the dry brown Pampas. Galloping over a low plain covered with unusally green grass, he noticed a vast number of snakes had congregated there, all of a single species, and all lying like ribbons on the turf:

> Pausing at length, before quitting this green plain, to give my horse a minute's rest, I got off and approached a large snake; but when I was quite twelve yards from it, it lifted its head, and, turning deliberately round, came rather swiftly at me. I retreated, and it followed, until, springing on to my horse, I left it, greatly surprised at its action, and beginning to think that it must be venomous. As I rode on the feeling of surprise increased, conquering haste; and in the end, seeing more snakes, I dismounted and approached the largest, when exactly the same thing occurred again, the snake rousing itself and coming angrily at me when I was still at an absurd distance from it. Again and again I repeated the experiment, with the same result. And at length I stunned one with a blow of my whip to examine its mouth, but found no poison-fangs in it.
>
> I then resumed my journey, expecting to meet with more snakes of the same kind at my destination; but there were none, and very soon business called me to a distant place, and I never met with this species afterwards.

But when I rode away from that green spot, and was once more on the higher, desolate, wind-swept plain surrounding it—a rustling sea of giant thistles, still erect, although dead, and red as rust, and filling the hot blue sky with silvery down—it was with a very strange feeling.…There seemed to be something mysterious, extra-natural, in that low level plain, so green and fresh and snaky, where my horse's hoofs had made no sound— a place where no man dwelt, and no cattle pastured, and no wild bird folded its wing. And the serpents there were not like others—the mechanical coiled-up thing we know, a mere bone-and-muscle man-trap, set by the elements, to spring and strike when trodden on: But these had a high intelligence, a lofty spirit, and were filled with a noble rage and astonishment that any other kind of creature, even a man, should venture there to disturb their sacred peace. It was a fancy, born of that sense of mystery which the unknown and the unusual in nature wakes in us—an obsolescent feeling that still links us to the savage. But the simple fact was wonderful enough…

Rattlesnakes are proverbially abundant upon all these prairies.…one hears almost a constant popping of rifles or pistols among the vanguard, to clear the route of these disagreeable occupants, lest they should bite our animals.

—Josiah Gregg

W. H. Hudson, *The Naturalist in La Plata*

That sense of mystery, that regard for serpents of high intelligence, even that fancy, may have been born in Hudson's childhood, when his family began refurbishing a dilapidated old dwelling house on the magical Pampas:

[A]t all seasons a nest or colony of snakes existed in the thick old foundations of the house, and under the flooring. In winter they hibernated there, tangled together in a cluster no doubt; and in summer nights when they were at home, coiled at their ease or gliding ghost-like about their subterranean apartments, I would lie awake and listen to them by the hour. For although it may be news to some closet ophiologists, serpents are not all so mute as we think them. At all events this kind, the *Philodryas aestivus*—a beautiful and harmless colubrine snake, two and a half to three feet long, marked all over with inky black on a vivid green ground—not only emitted a sound when lying undisturbed in his den, but several individuals would hold a conversation together which seemed endless, for I generally fell asleep before it finished. A hissing conversation it is true, but not unmodulated or without considerable variety in it; a long sibilation would be followed by distinctly-heard ticking sounds, as of a husky-ticking clock, and after ten or twenty or thirty ticks another hiss, like a long expiring sigh, sometimes with a tremble in it as of a dry leaf swiftly vibrating in the wind. No sooner would one cease than another would begin; and so it would go on, demand and response, strophe and antistrope; and at intervals several voices would unite in a kind of low mysterious chorus, death-watch and flutter and hiss; while I, lying awake in my bed, listened and trembled. It was dark in the room, and to my excited imagination the serpents were no longer under the floor, but out, gliding hither and thither over it, with uplifted heads in a kind of mystic dance; and I often shivered to think what my bare feet might touch if I were to thrust a leg out and let it hang down over the bedside.

W. H. Hudson, *Far Away and Long Ago*

The Grandest of All Earthly Music

A CENTURY AGO, THE "TOWNSHIPS" OF THE VIZCACHA, THE SOUTH American equivalent of the prairie dog, were found everywhere on the pampas, and W. H. Hudson, recalling boyhood pleasures beneath those far-flung skies, remembered the tremendous din the animals made at night when suddenly startled by a loud noise:

> When we had visitors from town, especially persons new to the country who did not know the vizcacha, they would be taken out after supper, a little distance from the house, when the plain was all dark and profoundly silent, and after standing still for a few minutes to give them time to feel the silence, a gun would be discharged, and after two or three seconds the report would be followed by an extraordinary hullabaloo, a wild outcry of hundreds and thousands of voices, from all over the plain for miles round, voices that seemed to come from hundreds of different species of animals, so varied they were, from the deepest booming sounds to the high shrieks and squeals of shrill-voiced birds. Our visitors used to be filled with astonishment.
>
> <div align="right">W. H. HUDSON, <i>Far Away and Long Ago</i></div>

Hudson himself never ceased being astonished by another strange, almost terrifying voice in the night. The "big venomous toad-like creature called *escuerzo*" (*Ceratophrys ornata*) emitted, he recalled, an unearthly roar that could, at times, turn symphonic:

> I never knew any spot where these creatures were more abundant than in that winter lake of ours, and at night in the flooded time we used to lie awake listening to their concerts. The *Ceratophrys* croaks when angry, and as it is the most truculent of all batrachians it works itself into a rage if you go near it. Its first efforts at chanting or singing sounds like the deep, harsh, anger-croak prolonged, but as the time goes on they gradually acquire, night by night, a less raucous and a louder, more sustained and far-reaching sound. There was always very great variety in the tones; and while some continued deep and harsh—the harshest sound in nature—others were clearer and not unmusical; and in a large number there were

always a few in the scattered choir that out-soared all others in high, long-drawn notes, almost organ-like in quality.

With their big skies and far horizons, their trillions of insects, rodents, night-singing birds, grunting predators, and all that hidden but rustling life, the world's grasslands have always poured forth a night music that has made a deep impression upon listeners. David Livingstone, camping one night in 1853 in a vast sea of reeds off a tributary of Africa's Zambezi River, listened, above the whine of mosquitoes, to one such concert. "We were close to the reeds and could listen to the strange sounds that are often heard there," he wrote in his Missionary Travels. "Curious birds... jerked and wriggled among the reedy masses, and we heard human-like voices and unearthly sounds with splash, guggle, jupp, as if rare fun were going on in their uncouth haunts."

A half century later, the famous hunter Frederick Selous recalled a memorable night he once passed near the Zambezi. Though by 1908, when he wrote, tourists were hoping to visit Victoria Falls:

> ...no man will ever again sit by a camp fire near one of the little rivers the railway will cross, eating prime pieces of fat elephant's heart, roasted on a forked stick, nor watch the great white rhinoceroses coming to drink just before dark, nor lie and listen to herd after herd of elephants drinking and bathing in the river near their camp. On one particular night in 1873 which I shall never forget, the splashing and trumpeting of troop after troop of hot and thirsty elephants was kept up from soon after dark till long past midnight.
>
> FREDERICK SELOUS, *African Nature Notes and Reminiscences*

Selous was a young elephant hunter at the time, but he eventually concluded, as did many old Africa hands, that the "grandest of all earthly

African elephant, late 19th century

music" was heard in the deep, reverberating roar of the lion. His friend Sir Alfred Pease who hunted lions by horseback in Kenya's tsetse-free Athi Plains, concurred. "There is no sound which issues from the throat of any creature to compare with that of the lion's voice," Pease declared. "Heard near at hand, in the dark or in daylight, his roar is a truly terrible and earth-shaking sound":

Any one may hear the noise a lion can make, at feeding time, in the lion house at the Zoo, yet somehow, though the air vibrates and the sound comes thundering out of the depths of their insides, it gives little sensation compared with that of standing in the bush on a still night, and not only hearing, but feeling it close at hand. I have led my horse in the dusk when light failed too much to ride among the trees, and heard but the deep grunt of a lion, perhaps a quarter of a mile away, and felt it so full of meaning that my blood has run cold and I have cocked my rifle and tugged at my horse to hurry him home. The roar proper consists of an ascending scale of half a dozen awfully deep and loud moaning, reverberating roars, ending either with a sigh that makes the air quiver, or low rumbling growls which shake the earth. Until you are familiar with them the mere deep staccato chest grunts of a lion, when you suddenly disturb one or come up with one, are very disconcerting.

SIR ALFRED PEASE, *The Book of the Lion*

Even Selous could be rattled by the lion's roar issuing out of the darkness. Camping one inky night near a water hole, his fire dying into embers, he heard the roar of approaching lions:

They roared three times in the river-bed just below us, and the volume of sound they emitted when all roaring in unison was nerve-shaking. My Kafirs sat motionless and silent, holding their hands over their mouths. There were no trees of any size near us, only small bushes, so they could not make a run for it to any place of safety. They confessed to me the next morning that when they heard the lions roaring so near them "their hearts died," meaning that they were terrified; and although I myself was not then of a very nervous disposition, and moreover believed that when lions roared loudly they were not hungry, and would therefore be unlikely to attack a human being, I was very glad when they at last left the water and we heard them go roaring back to where they had probably been feeding on the carcase of a buffalo or some other animal before they came to drink.... When moving about at night, lions sometimes give vent to a low purring growl—very different in sound to a roar—which may be a call-note to others of their party, and if driven off by shots from a horse or an ox they have killed in the night, they will growl loudly. In approaching a camp with the intention of killing oxen, horses, donkeys, or human beings, lions are absolutely silent, as I believe they always are when approaching any kind of wild game.

FREDERICK SELOUS, *African Nature Notes and Reminiscences*

Yet to Selous, who spent thousands of nights on the open veld, the lion, despite being the grandest musician, was not the virtuoso in the nocturnal symphony. That honor went to another:

Spotted hyaenas are very noisy animals, and their eerie, mournful howling is the commonest sound to break the silence of an African night.

Lion and lioness, 1849

The ordinary howl of the spotted hyaena commences with a long-drawn-out, mournful moan, rising in cadence till it ends in a shriek, altogether one of the weirdest sounds in nature....[W]hen a lot of hyaenas have gathered round the carcase of a large animal, such as an elephant or a rhinoceros, and are feasting on it undisturbed, the noises they make are most interesting to listen to. They laugh, they shriek, they howl, and in addition they make all kinds of gurgling, grunting, cackling noises, impossible to describe accurately.

PRAIRIE FEVER

BY THE SPRING OF 1541, FRANCISCO VÁSQUEZ DE CORONADO, with his gilded armor and plumed helmet, had spent months in a fruitless quest to find the legendary gold-rich Seven Cities of Cibola. Having dragged his weary legions all over what is now New Mexico, he soon emerged onto an immense plain of grass, nothing but grass, grass and sky and natives who lived in tents like Arabs and the strangest cattle they had ever seen—cattle with beards like goats, wool like sheep, humps like camels, haunches like lions, and tails like scorpions. They were still chasing tall tales of fabulous treasure somewhere over the horizon, only the horizon seemed ever to recede before them, and the grass simply swallowed them up:

For these things were remarkable and something not seen in other parts. I dare to write of them because I am writing at a time when many men are still living who saw them and who will vouch for my account. Who could believe that 1,000 horses and 500 of our cows and more than 5,000 rams and ewes and more than 1,500 friendly Indians and servants, in traveling over those plains, would leave no more trace where they had passed than if nothing had been there—nothing—so that it was necessary to make piles of bones and cow dung now and then, so that the rear guard could follow the army. The grass never failed to become erect after it had been trodden down, and, although it was short, it was as fresh and straight as before...

PEDRO DE CASTAÑEDA, "THE CORONADO EXPEDITION, 1540–1542"

Foragers and hunters quickly became lost, "wandering about the country as if they were crazy, in one direction or another, not knowing how to get back where they started from." Every night the army fired guns, blew trumpets, beat drums, and built great fires to draw the stragglers in. Out there in the grass, men lost their sense of direction. "The only thing to do," the foot soldier and chronicler Casteñeda continued, was "to stay near the game quietly until sunset, so as to see where it goes down, and even then they have to be men who are practiced to it."

[T]hese things were remarkable and something not seen in other parts....The grass never failed to become erect after it had been trodden down, and...it was as fresh and straight as before...

—PEDRO DE CASTAÑEDA

Coronado eventually struggled back to Mexico, beaten and disillusioned, leaving behind him those strange cattle—the bison—and that world of endless grass and sky.

His men would not be the last Europeans affected with what came to be called prairie fever. Later settlers on the High Plains of Texas and Kansas, where Coronado had wandered, were sometimes driven mad by the hideous monotony of the landscape, by the endless horizon and empty sky.

It could be, of course a matter of temperament. When the poet Walt Whitman crossed the plains he exultingly described it as "an exhilaration!"

Comparing those long levels with mountains and other scenic marvels, he concluded, "I am not so sure but the prairies and plains, while less stunning at first sight, last longer, fill the esthetic sense fuller, precede all the rest, and make North America's characteristic landscape."

But others saw the same scene differently. Robert Louis Stevenson, crossing Nebraska by rail in the 1870s, admitted that "there was a certain exhilaration in this spacious vacancy, this greatness of the air, this discovery of the whole arch of heaven, this straight, unbroken, prison-line of the horizon." But he also concluded that it wasn't the land but the settler "at whom we have a right to marvel." Stevenson, like Coronado's soldiers, recoiled at the overwhelming changelessness of it, the tediousness of the landscape:

> Our consciousness, by which we live, is itself but the creature of variety. Upon what food does it subsist in such a land? What livelihood can repay a human creature for a life spent in this huge sameness? ... A sky full of stars is the most varied spectacle that he can hope for. He may walk five miles and see nothing; ten, and it is as though he had not moved; twenty, and still he is in the midst of the same great level, and has approached no nearer to the one object within view, the flat horizon which keeps pace with his advance. We are full at home of the question of agreeable wall-papers, and wise people are of opinion that the temper may be quieted by sedative surroundings. But what is to be said of the Nebraskan settler? His is a wall-paper with a vengeance—one quarter of the universe laid bare in all its gauntness.
>
> ROBERT LOUIS STEVENSON, *Across the Plains with Other Memories and Essays*

Willard Johnson saw it slightly differently. As a U.S. Geological Survey topographer, he knew, from having squinted at it across plane tables, that the horizon did not always recede; it very often encroached:

Coronado's March, *by Frederic Remington, 1898*

The horizon is, in fact, not distant, as seen from the ground. It is not so distant as that at sea, for normally it is viewed from an elevation much lower than the deck of a ship, and there is no lift of a wave at intervals to extend it. The ranchman gets a widened view from his windmill tower on oiling days, but his accustomed point of observation is the back of a horse. With his motion in the saddle, antelope, feeding along the sky- line, will have the deceptive appearance of moving vertically in unison, so responsive is that boundary of vision to vertical change in the position of the eye. The ranchman's wife views the world from the doorway, and hers is a still narrower horizon. And the small boy, as he soon learns, can step off the radius to his. He finds, moreover, that to do so is no great adventure. He lives in a pent-up Utica, but he has the measure of it. He discovers that he is tethered in effect to his windmill tower; that to put that familiar object hull down, and finally out of sight, is to go adrift. Beyond would be the open sea. Indeed, he has his foot at the edge of it when, on looking back, tiptoeing, he can but just discern the rim of the windmill wheel turning dark and solitary against the sky.

WILLARD JOHNSON, "CLOUD SCENERY OF THE HIGH PLAINS"

Willa Cather knew how the grasslands appeared in the eyes of a child. She had grown up in Nebraska, and it was the prairie, as seen by a small boy, that she delineated in her novel *My Ántonia*. Young Jim Burden's first encounter with that world occurred at night from the bed of the wagon carrying him to his grandparents:

> There seemed to be nothing to see; no fences, no creeks or trees, no hills or fields. If there was a road, I could not make it out in the faint starlight. There was nothing but land: not a country at all, but the material out of which countries are made. No, there was nothing but land—slightly undulating, I knew, because often our wheels ground against the brake as we went down into a hollow and lurched up again on the other side. I had the feeling that the world was left behind, that we had got over the edge of it, and were outside man's jurisdiction. I had never before looked up at the sky when there was not a familiar mountain ridge against it. But this was the complete dome of heaven, all there was of it.
>
> WILLA CATHER, *My Ántonia*

The blankness, the aridity, the desolation, the huge emptiness of grass and sky that drove so many to despair were lost on the child. What Jim saw come morning was not the endless monotony on the surface, but the rustle of life beneath it:

> Everywhere, as far as the eye could reach, there was nothing but rough, shaggy, red grass, most of it as tall as I.
>
> As I looked about me I felt that the grass was the country, as the water is the sea. The red of the grass made all the great prairie the colour of wine-stains, or of certain seaweeds when they are first washed up. And there was so much motion in it; the whole country seemed, some-how, to be running...

I can remember exactly how the country looked to me as I walked beside my grandmother along the faint wagon-tracks on that early September morning. Perhaps the glide of long railway travel was still with me, for more than anything else I felt motion in the landscape; in the fresh, easy-blowing morning wind, and in the earth itself, as if the shaggy grass were a sort of loose hide, and underneath it herds of wild buffalo were galloping, galloping...

ONE WIDE SEPULCHRE

AMONG THE MANY MARVELS ENCOUNTERED BY CORONADO'S BEWILDERED expedition, straying across the otherwise featureless prairie in 1541, were immense piles of bones:

> Another thing was a heap of cow bones [bison bones], a crossbow shot long, or a very little less, almost twice a man's height in places, and some 18 feet or more wide, which was found on the edge of a salt lake in the southern part, and this in a region where there are no people who could have made it. The only explanation of this which could be suggested was that the waves which the north winds must make in the lake had piled up the bones of the cattle which had died in the lake, when the old and weak ones who went into the water were unable to get out. The noticeable thing is the number of cattle that would be necessary to make such a pile of bones.
>
> PEDRO DE CASTEÑEDA, "THE CORONADO EXPEDITION, 1540-1542"

Three centuries later, when Francis Parkman sat down to admire prairie wildflowers, he reached for the first seat available: a buffalo skull. There were still plenty of them about. "Huge skulls and whitening bones of buffalo were scattered every where," Parkman recalled of

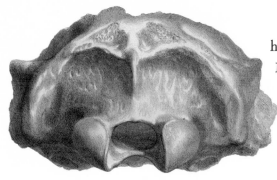

Megatherium fossil, Argentina, circa 1839

his ride along the foot of the Rocky Mountains to Fort Laramie. Drought, fire, wolves, and the depredations of red and white hunters had all contributed their pound of bone. Generally it was shrugged off and taken for granted.

Not by Charles Darwin, however, who was as staggered as was Coronado's historian by the sheer numbers of animals that must have perished on the plains. While fossil hunting in the Argentine Pampas in the 1830s, Darwin began to wonder why "vast numbers of animals of all kinds" were found embedded together in the fossil deposits:

The period between the years 1827 and 1830 is called the "gran seco" or the great drought. During this time, so little rain fell, that the vegetation, even to the thistles, failed; the brooks were dried up, and the whole country assumed the appearance of a dusty high-road....Very great numbers of birds, wild animals, cattle, and horses, perished from the want of food and water. A man told me, that the deer used to come into his courtyard to the well, which he had been obliged to dig to supply his own family with water; and that the partridges had hardly strength to fly away when pursued. The lowest estimation of the loss of cattle in the province of Buenos Ayres alone, was taken at one million head. A proprietor at San Pedro had previously to these years 20,000 cattle; at the end not one remained...

I was informed by an eyewitness, that the cattle in herds of thousands rushed into the Parana, and being exhausted by hunger they were unable to crawl up the muddy banks, and thus were drowned. The arm which runs by San Pedro was so full of putrid carcasses, that the master of a vessel told me, that the smell rendered it quite impossible to pass that way. Without doubt several hundred thousand animals thus perished in the river. Their bodies when putrid floated down the stream, and many in all probability were deposited in the estuary of the Plata. All the small rivers became highly saline, and this caused the death of vast numbers in particular spots; for when an animal drinks of such water it does not recover. I noticed, but probably it was the effect of a gradual increase, rather than of any one period, that the smaller streams in the Pampas were paved with a breccia of bones.

CHARLES DARWIN, The Voyage of the Beagle

Once the rains returned, Darwin reasoned, the subsequent floods would bury that breccia in mud, and over time some future geologist might surmise that the animals had all died by flood rather than by drought. That led Darwin to an inescapable conclusion: The fossils found in estuaries were but the exposed edges of an unbelievably vast breccia of bones underlying all of those wildflowers and all that waving grass:

> The number of bones embedded in the grand estuary deposit of the Pampas must be very great; I myself heard of, and saw many groups. The names of such places as "the stream of the animal," "the hill of the giant," tell the same story. At other times I heard of the marvellous property of certain rivers, which had the power of changing small bones into large; or as some maintained, the bones themselves grew. As far as I am aware, not one of these animals, as was formerly supposed, perished in the marshes, or muddy river-beds of the present land, but their bones have been exposed by the streams intersecting the deposit in which their remains were formerly buried. We may therefore conclude that the whole area of the Pampas is one wide sepulchre for these extinct quadrupeds.

GRASSLAND STORMS

THE NORTHERN PLAINS OF AFGHANISTAN SLOPE DOWN OFF THE Hindu Kush before leveling out toward the great Kara Kum Desert and the mighty Oxus River, once fabled for its golden sands. In the midst of those plains, near the old caravan city of Balkh, there is a stretch of territory once called the Chol, or "desert," the "description of which," according to Col. Thomas Holdich, who in the late 19th century helped survey the Afghan border, "seemed to oscillate between that of a prairie or a waste. The fact is that it is both prairie and waste at different seasons of the year"—largely because it was subject to the *shamshir,* the "scimitar" wind that knifed down those slopes, making of the Chol an illustration of how short and violent the life of a grassland might be:

It is prairie in the greenness of spring and early summer, when these breezy hills lie knee-deep in grass and flowers—flowers of all descriptions, but consisting chiefly of scarlet tulips and gorgeous purple thistles. These are replaced later by poppies as scarlet as the tulips; and yet more thistles. But this is just by way of full dress for Nature's levee once a year. There is little water; and what little there is, is found at far intervals in the one or two river beds which intersect the Chol. When the spring rains cease, all this gaiety ceases too. The flowers wither and the stalks dry up and stiffen. Then comes the wind, and it just scrapes all the dry stalks from the surface of the downs. It blows them off, and then rolls them up into huge bundles which collect in the folds and gullies of the hills, a tangled mass of dry nothingness; which is, however, thick enough to conceal the shaggy-hided wild boar....When the snows descend, and the floods finally come again, out goes all this mass of debris, sailing after the manner of detached haystacks, into the open plains that lie south of the Oxus. None of it ever reaches the Oxus, for

The Eurasian steppe, late 19th century

none of the local streams ever reach that river. So the debris gets piled into the Akcha swamps, and there gives cover to countless pheasants... and finally becomes submerged....[I]t is in this way that the coal beds of the Oxus plains must have been formed, there being no appearance of forest since Eocene periods.

SIR THOMAS HOLDICH, *The Indian Borderland*

Grasslands are often swept by fierce winds. It was once thought that the Argentine Pampas were virtually treeless because the winds so continually scoured them, though the most notorious and violent of Pampas wind, the pampero, always struck without warning—usually carrying a storm on its wings:

It was in sultry summer weather, and towards evening all of us boys and girls went out for a ramble on the plain, and were about a quarter of a mile from home when a blackness appeared in the south-west, and began to cover the sky in that quarter so rapidly that, taking alarm, we started homewards as fast as we could run. But the stupendous slaty-black darkness, mixed with yellow clouds of dust, gained on us, and before we got to the gate the terrified screams of wild birds reached our ears, and glancing back we saw multitudes of gulls and plover flying madly before the storm, trying to keep ahead of it. Then a swarm of big dragon-flies came like a cloud over us, and was gone in an instant, and just as we reached the gate the first big drops splashed down in the form of liquid mud. We had hardly got indoors before the tempest broke in its full fury, a blackness as of night, a blended uproar of thunder and wind, blinding flashes of lightning, and torrents of rain. Then as the first thick darkness began to pass away, we saw that the air was white with falling hailstones of an extraordinary size and appearance. They were big as fowls' eggs, but not egg-shaped: they were flat, and about half-an-inch thick, and being white, looked like little blocks or bricklets made of compressed snow. The hail continued falling until the earth was white with them, and in spite of their great size they were driven by the furious wind into drifts two or three feet deep against the walls of the buildings.

It was evening and growing dark when the storm ended, but the light next morning revealed the damage we had suffered. Pumpkins, gourds, and water-melons were cut to pieces, and most of the vegetables, including the Indian corn, were destroyed. The fruit trees, too, had suffered greatly. Forty or fifty sheep had been killed outright, and hundreds more were so much hurt that for days they went limping about or appeared stupefied from blows on the head. Three of our heifers were dead, and one horse—an old loved riding-horse with a history, old Zango—the whole house was in grief at his death.

W. H. Hudson, *Far Away and Long Ago*

The North American prairie also bred huge, towering thunderstorms quite as violent as their Argentine cousins. Coronado's wayward legions were struck by one in 1541, a storm with hail "as large as bowls and even larger, and as thick as raindrops" that carpeted the ground with ice in some places a foot deep, ripping up the tents and shattering the crockery. The horses were pummeled so hard that they stampeded, all except those held by soldiers wearing steel helmets, dented by the hail. Some of Lewis and Clark's men were caught in a similar storm. "The rain fell like one voley of water falling from the heavens," Clark reported, "the hail & wind being so large and violent" that men were "much brused, and some nearly killed, one knocked down three times, and others without hats or any thing on their heads bloody & complained verry much. I refreshed them with a little grog."

Pasture thistle, 1886

Then there was lightning. Josiah Gregg, a merchant and jack-of-all-trades along the old Santa Fe Trail, had clearly experienced the worst of both hail and lightning:

Storms of hail-stones larger than hen's eggs are not uncommon, frequently accompanied by the most tremendous hurricanes. The violence of the wind is sometimes so great that, as I have heard, two road-wagons were once capsized by one of these terrible thunder-gusts; the rain, at the same time, floating the plain to the depth of several inches. In short, I doubt if there is any known region out of the tropics, that can "head" the great prairies in "getting up" thunder-storms, combining so many of the elements of the awful and sublime. I was deeply impressed with a scene I witnessed in the summer of 1832, about two days' journey beyond the Colorado, which I may be excused for alluding to in this connection. We were encamped at noon, when a murky cloud issued from behind the mountains, and, after hovering over us for a few minutes, gave vent to one of those tremendous peals of thunder which seem peculiar to those regions, making the elements tremble, and leaving us so stunned and confounded that some seconds elapsed before each man was able to convince himself that he had not been struck by lightning. A sulphureous stench filled the atmosphere; but the thunderbolt had skipped over the wagons and lighted upon the *caballada* [herd of horses], which was grazing hard by; some of which were afterward seen stretched upon the plain. It was not a little singular to find an ox lying lifeless from the stroke, while his mate stood uninjured by his side, and under the same yoke.

JOSIAH GREGG, Commerce of the Prairies

Sometimes it was more show than storm, the thunderheads piling up to an immense height, only to be headed elsewhere. The topographer Willard Johnson, who saw nothing but despair in the monotonous high plains landscape in which he worked during the 1890s, instead became captivated by such "cloud scenery":

Then begin the heavy marshallings and for some days these continue. Ranches disappear in premature night under mere accumulation of shadow, and again are sought out in the glare of recessed furnaces of illumination and seemingly consumed. The plain is thundered over continuously, and penetrated at innumerable points by vertical lightning. Fires thus are sometimes originated, and areas as great as a New England state become blackened over with a film of grass charcoal, which the winds whirl into columns as much as a mile in height and trail along both plain and sky. In this display there is grandeur in the magnitude of details and the deeply glowing colors…Soon, however, arise the winds, and slow evolution gives place to tumult. The solitary inhabitant, wherever the occasion may have found him, drops all pretense of occupation, and with hat gripped in both hands, leaning back against the rush of air, surrenders himself to awed contemplation of the spectacle.

WILLARD JOHNSON, "CLOUD SCENERY OF THE HIGH PLAINS"

THE ALL-DEVOURING CONFLAGRATION

AT THE END OF THE 18TH CENTURY, SETTLERS PUSHING WEST FOUND THAT a vast tongue of tallgrass prairie, encompassing most of Illinois and part of Indiana, had invaded and interpenetrated the prevailing oak and hickory forest. That prairie, it was widely believed, had been maintained for ages by fire—seasonal fire set by the Indians for hunting purposes. By the time William Faux, an English-born farmer, arrived in Illinois, something about those fires had clearly gotten out of hand:

The season called the Indian Summer, and which here commences in October by a dark, thick, hazy atmosphere, is caused by millions of acres, for thousands of miles round, being in a wide-spreading, flaming, blazing, smoking fire, rising up through wood and prairie, hill and dale, to the tops of low shrubs and high trees, which are kindled by a coarse, thick, long prairie grass and dying leaves, at every point of the compass, and far beyond the foot of civilization, darkening the air, heavens, and earth, over the whole extent of the northern part to the Southern Continent, from the Atlantic to the Pacific; and, in the neighbourhoods contiguous to the all-devouring conflagration, filling the whole horizon with yellow, palpable, tangible smoke, ashes, and vapour, which affect the eyes of man and beast, and obscure the sun, moon, and stars for many days; or until the winter rains descend to quench the fire, and purge the thick, ropy air, which is seen, tasted, handled, and felt.

WILLIAM FAUX, *Memorable Days in America*

And that is all one sentence. Hyberbole aside, there was something decidedly mesmerizing about prairie fires. In the 1790s, Mungo Park, the Scottish explorer who discovered the course of the Niger River in Africa, had marveled at the fires racing over the West African grasslands:

The burning of the grass in Manding exhibits a scene of terrific grandeur. In the middle of the night I could see the plains and mountains, as far as my eye could reach, variegated with lines of fire; and the light reflected on the sky made the heavens appear in a blaze. In the daytime pillars of smoke were seen in every direction; while the birds of prey were observed

Buffalo escape a prairie fire, 1887

hovering round the conflagration, and pouncing down upon the snakes, lizards, and other reptiles which attempted to escape from the flames.

MUNGO PARK, *Travels in the Interior Districts of Africa*

Thirty years later, in 1832, George Catlin, the artist and student of the American Indian, was hunting one day on the Kansas prairie when he cast his painterly eye on a very similar spectacle:

The prairies burning form some of the most beautiful scenes that are witnessed in the country, and also some of the most sublime. Every acre of these vast prairies (being covered for hundreds and hundreds of miles with a crop of grass, which dies and dries in the fall) burns over during the fall or early in the spring, leaving the ground a black and doleful color.

There are many modes by which the fire is communicated to them, both by white men and by Indians—par accident, and yet many more where it is done for the purpose of getting a fresh crop of grass, and for the grazing of their horses, and also for easier traveling during the next summer, when there will be no old grass to lie upon the prairies, entangling the feet of man and horse, as they are passing over them.

Over the elevated lands and prairie bluffs, where the grass is thin and short, the fire slowly creeps with a feeble flame, which one can easily step over; where the wild animals often rest in their lairs until the flames almost burn their noses, when they will reluctantly rise and leap over it, and trot off amongst the cinders, where the fire has past and left the ground as black as jet. These scenes at night become indescribably beautiful, when their flames are seen at many miles distance, creeping over the sides and tops of the bluffs, appearing to be sparkling and brilliant chains of liquid fire (the hills being lost to the view), hanging suspended in graceful festoons from the skies.

GEORGE CATLIN, *Letters and Notes*

Yet there was a difference between what would come to be called a "controlled burn," and a roaring inferno, as Catlin pointed out:

> But there is yet another character of burning prairies that requires another Letter, and a different pen to describe—the war, or hell of fires! where the grass is seven or eight feet high, as is often the case for many miles together, on the Missouri bottoms; and the flames are driven forward by the hurricanes, which often sweep over the vast prairies of this denuded country. The fire in these, before such a wind, travels as fast as a horse at full speed, but that the high grass is filled with wild pea-vines and other impediments, which render it necessary for the rider to guide his horse in the zig-zag paths of the deers and the buffaloes, retarding his progress, until he is overtaken by the dense column of smoke that is swept before the fire—alarming the horse, which is wafted in the wind, falls about him, kindling up in a moment a thousand new fires, which are instantly wrapped in the swelling flood of smoke that is moving on like a black thunder-cloud, rolling on the earth, with its lightning's glare, and its thunder rumbling as it goes.

Such a conflagration consumed the small things—the grasshoppers, spiders, snakes, lizards, bees, wasps, ticks, ground-nesting birds, rodents, and all the intertwined flowers—but also left behind the charred carcasses of deer, wolves, and buffalo. "The plains are burned in every direction," observed the trapper Alexander Henry in North Dakota, "and blind buffalo are seen every moment wandering about. The poor beasts have all the hair singed off; even the skin in many places is shriveled up and terribly burned, and their eyes are swollen and closed fast. It was really pitiful to see them staggering about, sometimes running afoul of a large stone, at other times tumbling downhill and falling into creeks not yet frozen over. In one spot we found a whole herd lying dead." The Canadian geologist Henry Hind, exploring the Red River of the North, admired such doughty survivors. "Blind buffalo are frequently found accompanying herds," he wrote in his *Narrative,* "and sometimes they are met with alone. Their eyes have been destroyed by prairie fires; but their increased alertness enable them to guard against danger, and makes it more difficult to approach them in quiet weather than those possessing sight."

The terrific violence of a fire roaring through tall grass was vividly impressed on Joseph Thomson while he was exploring the East African savannas in the 1880s. He and his caravan had just set up camp for the night in a grove of trees by a spring when they sprang to their feet:

> The tall dry grass had been set on fire some distance to the south of us, probably by the Wa-seri. As the wind was blowing to the north with unusual violence, the flames came down on us with terrific speed and the most appalling noise. Before we were fairly aware what was up, the camp was completely surrounded and the whole heavens were overcast with the lurid glow. The scenes and sounds that followed were past description. Monkeys screamed and birds cried in abject terror. Several hundred men rushed about and shouted in uncontrollable excitement, tearing down branches to thrash out the flames or labouring away in the very midst of the relentless element, looking amid their fiery surroundings the very incarnation of evil spirits; some ran to save the donkeys outside and to prevent a stampede, and soon the donkeys, panic-stricken, added to the chaos and confusion by rushing pell-mell into camp with their great ears uplifted, knocking down men or whatever came in their way.
>
> JOSEPH THOMSON, *Through Masai Land*

It had been a close call. Some loads were destroyed and several men had been badly burned. "Nothing could have saved us from immense damage and loss of life if we had been camped in the open," Thomson admitted. They were saved because they had arrived at a place where they could step from the open world of the grasslands into the refuge of the forest.

Arborious Wonders

THE FOREST

"The mind sees that dark region as an impenetrable density of green and secret leaves; which, literally, when you go there, is what you will find. You enter the leaves, and vanish..."

—H.M. Tomlinson

EUROPEANS HAVE A LONG HISTORY OF MARVELING AT TREES. Their civilization was nurtured in the forest. A forest tamed and felled, turned to field and pasture, copse and hedgerow, town and city, but still at root the forest. Though deeply buried, that root remained alive, and the forest kept blooming in the fallow places of the European imagination.

So anyone who read the anonymously written "Walks in a Brazilian Forest," published in the September 9, 1848, edition of *Chamber's Edinburgh Journal,* already harbored a buried image of what the primeval woodlands of Africa, Asia, and the Americas might look like:

> It is indeed allowed that the whole kingdom of nature presents no spectacle more grand, and at the same time more pleasing and curious, than the Brazilian Forest....There is a subdued and indefinite murmur pervading these majestic groves, like the hum of human life heard afar off: the tiny horn of the insects, the strange voices of birds, and the distant cries

OPPOSITE: *A tropical forest in Ceylon, late 19th century*

Spix and Martius in the Amazon, mid-19th century

of the monkeys, make the solemn scene vocal with nature's hymn. But disregarding these, the traveller turns to the contemplation of the stupendous vegetation crowding around him, which coats the soil, creeps up the trees, flings its airy garlands aloft; which forms the foreground, the background, and the very sky of this sylvan picture...

In the deeper recesses of the forest are trees of colossal proportions. Dr Von Martius gives the particulars of a locust-tree which fifteen Indians with outstretched arms could only just embrace. Several others were upwards of eighty *feet* in circumference at the bottom, and sixty feet where the boles became cylindrical. By counting the concentric rings of such parts as were accessible, he arrived at the conclusion that they were of *the age of Homer,* and 332 years old in the days of Pythagoras: one estimate, indeed, *reduced* their antiquity to 2052 years, while another carried it up to 4104! The effect produced upon the imagination by the sight of these vegetable patriarchs can scarcely be described...

Carl Friedrich von Martius was a Prussian botanist who, accompanied by his colleague Johann von Spix, had explored Brazil in 1817-19. The first non-Portuguese scientists allowed into the remote Amazon, they carried this tangled European legacy with them. On the one hand, they were Romantic enthusiasts for nature; "there is more to be learned in forests than in books," they quoted a Brazilian guide telling them. Yet they were also heirs to a folk memory of the gloomy Teutonic woods of their forebears. While the scientists were in Brazil, the brothers Grimm were publishing their collections of folk and fairy tales—Hansel and Gretel, Little Red Riding Hood, and all those woodcutters, witches, and wolves—most of them set in an all-pervading forest as menacing as it was enchanting.

THE SACRED OAK

BEHIND IT ALL STOOD THE LONG SHADOW OF THE DARK AND mysterious Hercynian Forest, which once blanketed most of Europe east of the Rhine. To Julius Caesar, it was so extensive that no one had ever reached its utmost edge. Unicorns were supposed to live there, and Pliny the Elder asserted that birds whose feathers blazed at night were found there, too. So were gargantuan oaks, as old as the world, their protruding roots, like the gates to some giant's city, large enough to raise mountains.

The brothers Grimm grew up in the remnants of the Hercynian Forest, in the wooded hills of Hesse, not far from the spot where once towered Thor's Oak, sacred to the god of thunder and revered by many of the ancient German tribes. To Sir James Frazer, the Scottish anthropologist who at the turn of the last century was harvesting the anthropological fruit of his era, Thor's Oak was but one instance of an oak cult widespread in the forests of prehistoric Europe:

It is a plausible theory that the reverence which the ancient peoples of Europe paid to the oak, and the connexion which they traced between the tree and their sky-god, were derived from the much greater frequency with which the oak appears to be struck by lightning than any other tree of our European forests....However we may explain it, whether by the easier passage of electricity through Oakwood than through any other timber, or in some other way, the fact itself may well have attracted the notice of our rude forefathers, who dwelt in the vast forests which then covered a large part of Europe; and they might naturally account for it in their simple religious way by supposing that the great sky-god, whom they worshipped and whose awful voice they heard in the roll of thunder, loved the oak above all the trees of the wood and often descended into it from the murky cloud in a flash of lightning, leaving a token of his presence or of his passage in the riven and blackened trunk and the blasted foliage. Such trees would thenceforth be encircled by a nimbus of glory as the visible seats of the thundering sky-god. Certain it is that, like some savages, both Greeks and Romans identified their great god of the sky and of the oak with the lightning flash which struck the ground; and they regularly enclosed such a stricken spot and treated it thereafter as sacred. It is not rash to suppose that the ancestors of the Celts and Germans in the forests of Central Europe paid a like respect for like reasons to a blasted oak.

Sir James Frazer, *The Golden Bough*

Thor's Oak, and those Hercynian ones as old as time, were thus among the earliest of forest marvels. Even when that sacred tree was felled in A.D. 723 by Saint Boniface, Apostle to the Germans—a supernatural wind blew it over at the first stroke of the ax, while a young fir sprang up in its roots, origin, it is said, of the Christmas Tree—even when it came crashing down, the widespread reverence for oak trees did not die with it. As the 18th-century poet and landscape gardener William Shenstone put it, "a large, branching, aged oak, is perhaps the most venerable of all inanimate objects." And a century later, Washington Irving observed of the English landed gentry that many traveled considerable distances to see gnarled and aged oaks, for "it seems that trees, like horses, have their established points of excellence; and that there are some in England which enjoy very extensive celebrity among tree-fanciers from being perfect in their kind."

Whether or not Frazer's prehistoric oak cult ever really existed, the oak has retained its primacy in the European imagination over the beech, the ash, the birch, the maple, the pine, or any other tree. When those Europeans began to venture around the world, it was the image of the oak's sturdy, rugged trunk and branching pattern that was projected on some quite wonderful trees found elsewhere. And when scientists and explorers, like Spix and Martius, fanned out across the globe they discovered new woods to enchant and terrify them. The painstaking classification of the profusion of botanical exotica that resulted—it took three-quarters of a century for Martius's masterpiece, the *Flora Brasiliensis,* to be completed, all 40 parts of it—might have been an expiation for the ancient sin of felling their own groves, and their wanderings throughout the world's leafy recesses a quest to recover that lost forest primeval.

Arborious Wonders

THE HAUNTED WOODS OF EUROPEAN LORE HAD NOT ENTIRELY RECEDED by the early 19th century. They still clung to the Balkans, where a later generation would locate its vampire and werewolf stories. Those woods, and their horrors, were real enough when in 1835 young Alexander Kinglake, fresh from Eton and Cambridge, turned up in Serbia to begin a tour of "the East." Facing a two-week journey by horseback in order to reach Constantinople, he hired Gypsy-like Suridgees as hostlers and guides and got under way. It was like riding into a tale by Grimm:

We had ridden on for some two or three hours; the stir and bustle of our commencing journey had ceased, the liveliness of our little troop had worn off with the declining day, and the night closed in as we entered the great Servian forest. Through this our road was to last for more than a hundred miles. Endless, and endless now on either side, the tall oaks closed in their ranks and stood gloomily lowering over us, as grim as an army of giants with a thousand years' pay in arrear. One strived with listening ear to catch some tidings of that forest world within—some stirring of beasts, some night-bird's scream, but all was quite hushed, except the voice of the cicadas that peopled every bough, and filled the depths of the forest through and through, with one same hum everlasting—more stifling than very silence.

At first our way was in darkness, but after a while the moon got up, and touched the glittering arms and tawny faces of our men with light so pale and mystic, that the watchful Tatar felt bound to look out for demons, and take proper means for keeping them off: forthwith he determined that the duty of frightening away our ghostly enemies (like every other troublesome work) should fall upon the poor Suridgees, who accordingly lifted up their voices, and burst upon the dreadful stillness of the forest with shrieks and dismal howls. These precautions were kept up incessantly, and were followed by the most complete success, for not one demon came near us...

There are few countries less infested by "lions" than the provinces on this part of your route. You are not called upon to "drop a tear" over the tomb of "the once brilliant" anybody, or to pay your "tribute of respect"

European oak, 1898

to anything dead or alive. There are no Servian or Bulgarian litterateurs with whom it would be positively disgraceful not to form an acquaintance; you have no staring, no praising to get through; the only public building of any interest that lies on the road is of modern date, but is said to be a good specimen of Oriental architecture; it is of a pyramidical shape, and is made up of thirty thousand skulls, contributed by the rebellious Servians in the early part (I believe) of this century: I am not at all sure of my date, but I fancy it was in the year 1806 that the first skull was laid. I am ashamed to say that in the darkness of the early morning we unknowingly went by the neighbourhood of this triumph of art, and so basely got off from admiring "the simple grandeur of the architect's conception," and "the exquisite beauty of the fretwork."

> *...the only public building of any interest that lies on the road is of modern date, but is said to be a good specimen of Oriental architecture; it is of a pyramidical shape, and is made up of thirty thousand skulls, contributed by the rebellious Servians in the early part (I believe) of this century...*
>
> —A. W. KINGSLAKE

There being no "lions," we ought at least to have met with a few perils, but the only robbers we saw anything of had been long since dead and gone. The poor fellows had been impaled upon high poles, and so propped up by the transverse spokes beneath them, that their skeletons, clothed with some white, wax-like remains of flesh, still sat up lolling in the sunshine, and listlessly stared without eyes.

A. W. KINGSLAKE, *Eothen*

By and large, however, the old gods had retreated to the scattered groves and lightning-blasted, wind-shattered trees that were the sentinels of Europe's fields and pastures. To England's John Evelyn, the

17th-century diarist and author of *Sylva: A Treatise on Forest Trees,* such prodigies still bore their nimbus of glory. "As the fall of a very aged oak, giving a crack like thunder, has often been heard at many miles distance," he wrote, "constrained though I often am to fell them with reluctancy, I do not at any time remember to have heard the groans of those nymphs (grieving to be dispossessed of their ancient habitations) without some emotion and pity." Combing biblical and classical literature and travelers' accounts, Evelyn compiled an astonishing list of marvelous trees, all characterized by tremendous height, vast spread of leaves, or "massy bodies" requiring the "years of divers Methuselahs, before they determine their days." There was a hollow oak that served as a prison, and a hollow chestnut that contained "within the bowels of it a pretty wainscotted room inlighten'd with windows." There were trees in the Congo large enough to fashion canoes able to hold 200 men, and a tree in China "whose amplitude is so stupendously vast, as fourscore persons can hardly embrace." Nor was Evelyn the first admirer of such "arborious wonders," citing as he did the curious case of a Roman consul: "And certainly, a goodly tree was a powerful attractive, when that a prudent consul, Passienus Crispus, fell in love with a prodigious beech of a wonderful age and stature, which he us'd to sleep under, and would sometimes refresh it with pouring wine at the roots."

While artists tramped all over Europe to depict such celebrated marvels as the great chestnut growing on the slopes of Mount Etna or the great yew in the churchyard at Fortingall, Scotland, more exacting admirers, like Alexander von Humboldt, were setting forth with measuring rod in hand. Humboldt thought the grandest oak in Europe was one near Saintes in France, which—30 feet in diameter—he concluded was 1,800 to 2,000 years old. Though modern botanists might be skeptical, Humboldt and his generation readily believed that such "colossal living forms" could be incredibly ancient. The great dragon tree of Orotava, a famous sight on the island of Tenerife, was—Humboldt measured it—48 feet in circumference, and "in the year

1402, which was the period of Béthencourt's first expedition, it was as large and hollow as in the present day." In 1749, the French botanist Michel Adanson had measured some of the magnificent baobabs he found in Senegal, trees so large in girth that their hollow interiors were used not only for rooms but for workshops and crypts as well, estimating they might attain 6,000 years of age—to which Humboldt commented, that "would make them coeval to the builders of the Pyramids, or even with Menes, and would place them in an epoch when the Southern Cross was still visible in Northern Germany."

The measuring rod became one of the explorer's most treasured tools. In 1826, when Scottish botanist David Douglas encountered the magnificent Sugar Pine in the forests of Oregon, he scribbled madly in his journal:

> "New and strange things seldom fail to make strong impressions, and are therefore frequently over-rated; so that, lest I should never see my friends in England to inform them verbally of this most beautiful and immensely grand tree, I shall here state the dimensions of the largest I could find among several that had been blown down by the wind. At 3 feet from the ground its circumference is 57 feet 9 inches; at 134 feet, 17 feet 5 inches; the extreme length 245 feet..."

Even John Muir, rhapsodist of California's natural wonders, took a measuring rod in hand. The largest tree he found—over 35 feet in diameter—was nearly 5,000 years old (he claimed), "which showed that this tree was in its prime, swaying in the Sierra winds, when Christ walked the earth."

Vegetable Roofs

EUROPEANS MIGHT HAVE SUBLIMATED THEIR DEEP-ROOTED impulse toward tree worship, using the sober language of measurement to express it, but other people around the world still expressed it openly. Paul Du Chaillu, one of the early explorers of the African rain forests, reported seeing a colossal tree in Gabon:

When we stopped for breakfast next day, I noticed a little way from us an extraordinary tree, quite the largest in height and circumference I ever saw in Africa. It was a real monarch of even this great forest. It rose in one straight and majestic trunk entirely branchless, till the top reached far above all the surrounding trees. There at the top the branches were spread out somewhat like an umbrella, but could not give much shade, being so high. I found that this tree was highly venerated by the people, who call it the *oloumi*. Its kind are not common even here, where its home is said to be. Its bark is said to have certain healing properties, and is also in request from a belief that if a man going off on a trading expedition washes himself first all over in a decoction of its juices in water, he will be lucky and shrewd in making bargains. For this reason great strips were torn off this tree to the height of at least twenty feet.

PAUL DU CHAILLU, *Explorations and Adventures in Equatorial Africa*

Humboldt, too, encountered a leafy phenomenon in Venezuela:

On quitting the village of Turmero, we discover, at a league distant, an object, which appears at the horizon like a round hillock, or tumulus, covered with vegetation. It is neither a hill, nor a group of trees close to each other, but one single tree, the famous zamang del Guayre, known throughout the province for the enormous extent of its branches, which form a hemispheric head five hundred and seventy-six feet in circumference. The zamang is a fine species of mimosa, and its tortuous branches are divided by bifurcation. Its delicate and tender foliage was agreeably relieved on the azure of the sky. We stopped a long time under this vegetable roof....The inhabitants of these villages, but particularly the Indians, hold in veneration the zamang del Guayre, which the first conquerors found almost in the same state in which it now remains.

ALEXANDER VON HUMBOLDT, *Personal Narrative of a Journey to the Equinoctial Regions of the New Continent*

Of all the trees venerated around the world, however, surely none surpass the sacred figs of India in the sheer number of their worshippers. The bo tree, or pipal (*Ficus religiosa*), is the sacred tree of Buddhism, the one beneath which Siddartha Gautama, in the sixth century B.C., achieved enlightenment. Wherever Prince Waldemar of Prussia, grandson of Frederick the Great, saw a bo tree in mid-1840s Ceylon, he was sure to find a nearby shrine, decked with blossom of hibiscus or frangipani. Visiting the famous temple complex at Anaradjapura, he inquired whether the young stems growing some distance away from an old Bo Tree bore any relation to it. Yes, he was told, "the young venerable lords are the offspring of the old venerable lord."

The bo tree could be found growing wild in the forest, but the banyan (*Ficus indica*) was a forest in itself. Sacred to the Hindu deity Vishnu, the many-stemmed banyan was a justifiable marvel, as Georg Hartwig, a mid-19th-century scientific popularizer, enthused:

> No baobab rears its monstrous trunk on the banks of the Ganges; no dragon-tree of patriarchal age here reminds the wanderer of centuries long past; but the beautiful and stately *Banyan* (*Ficus indica*) gives him but little reason to regret their absence. Each tree is in itself a grove, and some of them are of an astonishing size, as they are continually increasing, and, contrary to most other animal and vegetable productions, seem to be exempted from decay; for every branch from the main body throws out its own roots, at first in small tender fibers, several yards from the ground, which continually grow thicker, until, by a gradual descent, they reach its surface, where, striking in, they increase to a

large trunk and become a parent-tree, throwing out new branches from the top. These in time suspend their roots, and, receiving nourishment from the earth, swell into trunks and send forth other branches, thus continuing in a state of progression so long as the first parent of them all supplies her sustenance. The Hindoos are peculiarly fond of this tree; they consider its long duration, its outstretching arms and overshadowing beneficence, as emblems of the Deity; they plant it near their temples; and in those villages where there is no structure for public worship they place an image under a banyan, and there perform a morning and evening sacrifice.

Many of these beautiful trees have acquired an historic celebrity; and the famous "Cubbeer-burr," on the banks of the Nerbuddah, thus called

Banyan tree, circa 1860

by the Hindoos in memory of a favorite saint, is supposed to be the same as that described by Nearchus, the admiral of Alexander the Great, as being able to shelter an army under its farspreading shade. High floods have at various times swept away a considerable part of this extraordinary tree, but what still remains is near 2,000 feet in circumference, measured round the principal stems; the overhanging branches not yet struck down cover a much larger space; and under it grow a number of custard-apple and other fruit trees. The large trunks of this single colossus amount to a greater number than the days of the year, and the smaller ones exceed 3,000, each constantly sending forth branches and hanging roots, to form other trunks and become the parents of a future progeny. In the march of an army it has been known to shelter 7,000 men. Such is the banyan —more wonderful, and infinitely more beautiful and majestic, than all the temples and palaces which the pride of the Moguls has ever reared!

GEORG HARTWIG, *The Polar and Tropical Worlds*

Not to be outdone, Baron de Santa-Anna Nery, a Brazilian booster and corresponding member of the Royal Geographical Society, could best that tree with one the ancients would surely have deified:

In 1863, Gustave Walles, in studying the flora of the upper rio Branco, stated the existence of a gigantic tree whose proportions surpassed those of the famous Baobab of Senegambia, and the no less wonderful Wellingtonias of the Sierra Nevada and California. This tree of the rio Branco is the veritable giant of the tropical flora, and constitutes a small forest in itself. It is over 153 feet in height from the roots to the first branches, and is a mass of verdure. Its circumference at the ends of the branches is 840 feet, and it shades more than 5,500 square yards of soil, so that more than 12,000 men could encamp under it....

By the side of this tree of the rio Branco, what are the most marvellous pines of the North, with which the streets of Paris are paved? What are the old oaks that once sheltered the Druids? The celebrated chestnut tree of Etna itself, by the side of this leafy colossus, is but a vulgar pygmy, for although it is growing in a volcano, warmed by subterranean lava, it has never been able to attain, during the 4000 years that it has seen the Sicilian sun, more than 160 feet in circumference.

BARON DE SANTA-ANNA NERY, *The Land of the Amazons*

That chestnut grew in the Old World, but the tree on the Rio Branco waved in the New World, where everything was gigantic.

A Land "Buried in Foliage"

AMERICA WAS STILL A LAND OF WONDER. THE ANCIENT SPELL still hung unbroken over the wild, vast world of mystery beyond the sea—a land of romance, adventure, and gold."

That was Francis Parkman describing the New World as it was in the 17th century, when pioneers were in a North American forest that, with its oaks and beeches, maples and birch, its deer and wolves and bears, bore great similarities to that of Europe. That forest was doomed, of course, yet before it was tamed and felled it was an extensive, largely broad-leaved temperate woodland stretching from the shores of the Atlantic to the banks of the Mississippi—"a whole country," Parkman put it, "lay buried in foliage."

That was literally the image summoned up by James Fenimore Cooper in the opening pages of *The Pathfinder,* one of his Leatherstocking Tales, in which a former sailor and his niece take in a sweeping view from the hills of New York State:

Truly, the scene was of a nature, deeply to impress the imagination of the beholder. Towards the west, in which direction the faces of the party were turned, and in which alone could much be seen, the eye ranged over an ocean of leaves, glorious and rich in the varied but lively verdure of a generous vegetation, and shaded by the luxuriant tints that belong to the forty-second degree of latitude. The elm, with its graceful and weeping top, the rich varieties of the maple, most of the noble oaks of the American forest, with the broad leafed linden, known in the parlance of the country as the bass-wood, mingled their uppermost branches, forming one broad and seemingly interminable carpet of foliage, that stretched away towards the setting sun, until it bounded the horizon, by blending with the clouds, as the waves and sky meet at the base of the vault of heaven. Here and there, by some accident of the tempests, or by a caprice of nature, a trifling opening among these giant members of the forest, permitted an inferior tree to struggle upward toward the light, and to lift its modest head nearly to a level with the surrounding surface of verdure. Of this class were the birch, a tree of some account, in regions less favored, the quivering aspen, various generous nut-woods, and divers others, that resembled the ignoble and vulgar, thrown by circumstances, into the presence of the stately and great. Here and there, too, the tall, straight trunk of the pine, pierced the vast field, rising high above it, like some grand monument reared by art on the plain of leaves.

It was the vastness of the view, the nearly unbroken surface of verdure, that contained the principle of grandeur. The beauty was to be traced in the delicate tints, relieved by gradations of light and shade, while the solemn repose, induced a feeling allied to awe.

"Uncle," said the wondering, but pleased girl, addressing her male companion, whose arm she rather touched...to steady her own light but firm footing—"this is like a view of the ocean you so much love!"

"So much for ignorance, and a girl's fancy, Magnet"—a term of affection, the sailor often used in allusion to his niece's personal attractions; "no one but a child would think of likening this handful of leaves, to a look at the real Atlantic. You might stop all these tree-tops to Neptune's jacket, and they would make no more than a nosegay in his bosom."

"More fanciful than true, I think, uncle. Look, thither; it must be miles on miles, and yet we see nothing but leaves! What more could one behold, if looking at the ocean?"

"More!" returned the uncle, giving an impatient gesture with the elbow the other touched, for his arms were crossed, and the hands were thrust into the bosom of a vest of red cloth, a fashion of the times,—"More, Magnet; say, rather, what less? Where are your combing-seas, your blue-water, your rollers, your breakers, your whales, or your water-spouts and your endless motion, in this bit of a forest, child?"

"And where are your tree-tops, your solemn silence, your fragrant leaves and your beautiful green, uncle, on the ocean?"

"Tut, Magnet; if you understood the thing, you would know that green water is a sailor's bane. He scarcely relishes a green horn, less."

"But green trees are a different thing.—Hist! that sound is the air breathing among the leaves!"

"You should hear a nor-wester breathe, girl, if you fancy wind aloft. Now where are your gales, and hurricanes, and trades, and levanters and such like incidents in this bit of forest? and what fishes have you swimming beneath yonder tame surface?"

"That there have been tempests here, these signs around us plainly show; and beasts, if not fishes, are beneath those leaves."

James Fenimore Cooper, The Pathfinder

"Ayerie Regiments"

Not all beasts were beneath those leaves, however, and the tempests were often of the feathered kind. If ever there were a forest marvel, then those early settlers in the woods of North America beheld it in the passenger pigeons.

When the first Europeans arrived on those wooded shores, they were stupefied by the enormous flocks of pigeons they watched migrating with the seasons or seeking out the beechnuts, acorns, and chestnuts on which they subsided. Cotton Mather, the Puritan divine who witnessed the Salem witchcraft trials and penned *Wonders of the Invisible World,* was so amazed by the birds that he believed they sprang from "some undiscovered Satellite, accompanying the Earth at a near distance."

For most observers the marvel didn't extend quite that far. What they witnessed was quite marvel enough: The birds were like "Ayerie regiments" as they passed overhead; they darkened the sun for hours at a stretch; their wing beats were so deafening one could not hear oneself

A vast flock of passenger pigeons, circa 1875

shout. Settling in a forest, they broke stout limbs with the sheer weight of their numbers. They covered the trees, said the Baron Louis de Lahontan, "more than with Leaves." And the noise of their cooing was something else again. According to John Mactaggart, an early 19th-century traveler in Canada, "they breed together in the woods by millions, and the singular noise they make in their crowded nursery, or matrimonial haunt, surpasses any sound I have ever heard—it is a loud and confused buzz of love."

> *The multitudes of wild pigeons in our woods are astonishing. Indeed, after having viewed them so often, and under so many circumstances, I even now feel inclined to pause, and assure myself that what I am going to relate is fact...*
>
> —JOHN JAMES AUDUBON

The pigeons seemed especially numerous in the extensive forested regions drained by the Ohio River. Alexander Wilson, the Scottish-born naturalist who was one of the first great American ornithologists, was mesmerized by the numbers of pigeons he saw in Kentucky. As they crossed the sky, their "glittering undulations" resembled the "winding of a vast and majestic river." One such flock, he estimated, contained over two billion birds:

From right to left as far as the eye could reach, the breadth of this vast procession extended, seeming everywhere equally crowded....It was then half past one. I sat for more than an hour, but instead of diminution of this prodigious procession, it seemed rather to increase both in numbers and rapidity....About four o'clock in the afternoon I crossed the Kentucky river, at the town of Frankfort, at which time the living torrent above my head seemed as numerous and as extensive as ever. Long after this I observed them, in large bodies that continued to pass for six or eight minutes, and these again were followed by other detached bodies, all moving in the same south-east direction, till after six in the evening.

ALEXANDER WILSON, American Ornithology

It was Wilson's great successor, John James Audubon, who, as an awestruck young man newly arrived in the Kentucky wilderness, also gazed wonderingly at the living streams passing overhead. Years later he described his experiences in *Ornithological Biographies:*

"The multitudes of Wild Pigeons in our woods are astonishing. Indeed, after having viewed them so often, and under so many circumstances, I even now feel inclined to pause, and assure myself that what I am going to relate is fact. Yet I have seen it all, and that too in the company of persons who, like myself, were struck with amazement.

In the autumn of 1813, I left my house at Henderson, on the banks of the Ohio, on my way to Louisville. In passing over the Barrens a few miles beyond Hardensburgh, I observed the pigeons flying from north-east to south-west, in greater numbers than I thought I had ever seen them before, and feeling an inclination to count the flocks that might pass within the reach of my eye in one hour, I dismounted, seated myself on an eminence, and began to mark with my pencil, making a dot for every flock that passed. In a short time finding the task which I had undertaken impracticable, as the birds poured in in countless multitudes, I rose, and counting the dots then put down, found that 163 had been made in twenty-one minutes. I traveled on, and still met more the farther I proceeded. The air was literally filled with pigeons; the light of noonday was obscured as by an eclipse, the dung fell in spots, not unlike melting flakes of snow, and the continued buzz of wings had a tendency to lull my senses to repose.

Whilst waiting for dinner at Young's inn at the confluence of Salt river with the Ohio, I saw, at my leisure, immense legions still going by,

with a front reaching far beyond the Ohio on the west, and the beech-wood forests directly on the east of me. Not a single bird alighted; for not a nut or acorn was that year to be seen in the neighborhood....I cannot describe to you the extreme beauty of their aerial evolutions , when a Hawk chanced to press upon the rear of a flock. At once, like a torrent, and with a noise like thunder, they rushed into a compact mass, pressing upon each other towards the center. In these almost solid masses, they darted forward in undulating and angular lines, descended and swept close over the earth with inconceivable velocity, mounted perpendicularly so as to resemble a vast column, and, when high, were seen wheeling and twisting within their continued lines, which then resembled the coils of a gigantic serpent.

Before sunset I reached Louisville, distant from Hardensburgh fifty-five miles. The pigeons were still passing in undiminished numbers and continued to do so for three days in succession...

Investigating a roosting place in Kentucky, Audubon found that it was like picking his way across a battlefield:

It was, as is always the case, in a portion of the forest where the trees were of great magnitude, and where there was little underwood. I rode through it upwards of forty miles, and, crossing it in different parts, found its average breadth to be rather more than three miles...The dung lay several inches deep, covering the whole extent of the roosting-place. Many trees two feet in diameter, I observed, were broken off at no great distance from the ground, and the branches of many of the largest and tallest had given way as if the forest had been swept by a tornado. Everything proved to me that the number of birds resorting to this part of the forest must be immense beyond conception...

OPPOSITE: *Passenger pigeons, by Audubon, circa 1830*

Yet they are all gone now. Annihilated by overhunting and the destruction of those wide tracts of mature hardwood forest they so depended upon, the passenger pigeons plummeted to extinction. The last known individual having died in the Cincinnati Zoo in 1914, we are left with only a few stuffed specimens and the historical accounts, which are so numerous and so similar that, as the ornithologist Arthur Cleveland Bent put it, "we are compelled to believe what seems to pass belief."

LIGHT IN THE WILDERNESS

HENRY DAVID THOREAU BELIEVED, THOUGH HE WAS DARKLY prophetic, when on May 9, 1852, he wrote in his journal: "Saw pigeons in the woods, with their inquisitive necks and long tails, but few representatives of the great flocks that once broke down our forests."

Forests were much on Thoreau's mind. He was soon to depart on the second of three journeys he undertook to Maine, where, having lived at Walden Pond within two miles of his mother, he went to seek the forest primeval. The swamps and somber woods of Maine were outriders of the most far-flung plant empire on Earth, the kingdom of spruce and fir that stretched from Newfoundland around the globe to Norway. Locked in the grip of ice and snow in winter, plagued by clouds of insects in summer, the North Woods were a formidable environment—though, according to Thoreau, not a howling wilderness. "A howling wilderness does not howl. It is the imagination of the traveler that does the howling." With his own imagination primed and ready throughout his Maine journeys, even the smallest thing might occasion an epiphany. Camping one night on the shores of Moosehead Lake, Thoreau was "just in the frame of mind to see something wonderful":

It was a dense and damp spruce and fir wood in which we lay, and, except for our fire, perfectly dark; and when I awoke in the night, I either heard an owl from deeper in the forest behind us, or a loon from a distance over the lake. Getting up some time after midnight to collect the scattered brands together, while my companions were sound asleep, I observed, partly in the fire, which had ceased to blaze, a perfectly regular elliptical ring of light, about five inches in its shortest diameter, six or seven in its longer, and from one eighth to one quarter of an inch wide. It was fully as bright as the fire, but not reddish or scarlet like a coal, but a white and slumbering light, like the glowworm's. I could tell it from the fire only by its whiteness. I saw at once that it must be phosphorescent wood, which I had so often heard of, but never chanced to see. Putting my finger on it, with a little hesitation, I found that it was a piece of dead moose-wood (*Acer striatum*) which the Indian had cut off in a slanting direction the evening before. Using my knife, I discovered that the light proceeded from that portion of the sap-wood immediately under the bark, and thus presented a regular ring at the end, which, indeed, appeared raised above the level of the wood, and when I pared off the bark and cut into the sap, it was all aglow along the log. I was surprised to find the wood quite hard and apparently sound, though probably decay had commenced in the sap, and I cut out some little triangular chips, and placing them in the hollow of my hand, carried them into the camp, waked my companion, and showed them to him. They lit up the inside of my hand, revealing the lines and wrinkles, and appearing exactly like coals of fire raised to a white heat, and I saw at once how, probably, the Indian jugglers had imposed on their people and on travellers, pretending to hold coals of fire in their mouths.

I also noticed that part of a decayed stump within four or five feet of the fire, an inch wide and six inches long, soft and shaking wood, shone with equal brightness.

I neglected to ascertain whether our fire had anything to do with this, but the previous day's rain and long-continued wet weather undoubtedly had.

I was exceedingly interested by this phenomenon, and already felt paid for my journey. It could hardly have thrilled me more if it had taken the form of letters, or of the human face. If I had met with this ring of light while groping in this forest alone, away from any fire, I should have been still more surprised. I little thought that there was such a light shining in the darkness of the wilderness for me...

HENRY DAVID THOREAU, *The Maine Woods*

Thoreau had read where Peter Kalm, the Swedish-Finnish botanist who had roamed the woods about 1750, had described in *Travels in North America* the sound trees made when they fell in the forest: "We heard several great trees fall of themselves in the night, though it was so calm that not a leaf stirred. They made a dreadful cracking noise." A century later, Thoreau, deep in the Maine woods with his Indian guide, heard something similar, but more distant:

[I]t was a fine, clear night above. There were very few sounds to break the stillness of the forest. Several times we heard the hooting of a great horned-owl, as at home, and told Joe that he would call out the moose for him, for he made a sound considerably like the horn,—but Joe answered, that the moose had heard that sound a thousand times, and knew better; and oftener still we were startled by the plunge of a musquash. Once, when Joe had called again, and we were listening for moose, we heard, come faintly echoing, or creeping from far, through the moss-clad aisles, a dull, dry, rushing sound, with a solid core to it, yet as if half smothered under the grasp of the luxuriant and fungus-like forest, like the shutting of a door in some distant entry of the damp and shaggy

Balsam fir, early 19th century

wilderness. If we had not been there, no mortal had heard it. When we asked Joe in a whisper what it was, he answered,—"Tree fall." There is something singularly grand and impressive in the sound of a tree falling in a perfectly calm night like this, as if the agencies which overthrow it did not need to be excited, but worked with a subtle, deliberate, and conscious force, like a boa-constrictor, and more effectively then than even in a windy day. If there is any such difference, perhaps it is because trees with the dews of the night on them are heavier than by day...

Trees falling—at roughly the same time, the 1850s, but 3,000 miles to the south, a former hosier's apprentice from Leicestershire was sleeping one night on a riverboat deep in the Brazilian wilderness when he was awakened by a tremendous noise:

One morning I was awoke before sunrise by an unusual sound resembling the roar of artillery. I was lying alone on the top of the cabin; it was very dark, and all my companions were asleep, so I lay listening. The sounds came from a considerable distance, and the crash which had aroused me was succeeded by others much less formidable. The first explanation which occurred to me was that it was an earthquake; for, although the night was breathlessly calm, the broad river was much agitated and the vessel rolled heavily. Soon after, another loud explosion took place, apparently much nearer than the former one; then followed others. The thundering peal rolled backwards and forwards, now seeming close at hand, now far off; the sudden crashes being often succeeded by a pause, or a long-continued dull rumbling. At the second explosion, Vicente, who lay snoring by the helm, awoke and told me it was a "terra cahida"; but I could scarcely believe him. The day dawned after the uproar had lasted about an hour, and we then saw the work of destruction going forward on the other side of the river, about three miles off. Large masses of forest, including trees of colossal size, probably 200 feet in height, were rocking to and fro, and falling head-long one after the other into the water. After each avalanche the wave which it caused returned on the crumbly bank with tremendous force, and caused the fall of other masses by undermining them. The line of coast over which the landslip extended was a mile or two in length; the end of it, however, was hid from our view by an intervening island. It was a grand sight; each downfall created a cloud of spray; the concussion in one place causing other masses to give way a long distance from it, and thus the crashes continued, swaying to and fro, with little prospect of a termination. When we glided out of sight, two hours after sunrise, the destruction was still going on.

The onetime hosier's apprentice was Henry Walter Bates, and the river, of course, was the Amazon.

THE STUPENDOUS AMAZON

THERE IS A MOMENT IN W. H. HUDSON'S *Green Mansions* WHEN "Mr. Abel," who has exiled himself in the depths of unexplored Venezuela, takes Rima the "bird girl" to the top of a mountain and shows her the world surrounding her bit of enchanted forest:

There yet remained to be described all that unimaginable space east of the Andes; the rivers—what rivers!—the green plains that are like the sea—the illimitable waste of water where there is no land—and the forest region. The very thought of the Amazonian forest made my spirits drop. If I could have snatched her up and placed her on the dome of Chimborazo she would have looked on an area of ten thousand square miles of earth, so vast is the horizon at that elevation. And possibly her imagination would have been able to clothe it all with an unbroken forest. Yet how small a portion this would be of the stupendous whole—of a forest region equal in extent to the whole of Europe! All loveliness, all grace, all majesty are there...

Such testaments had been streaming forth since at least 1504, when Amerigo Vespucci, after whom the continent was named, declared that "if there is a paradise in this world, without doubt it cannot be far from here." The Amazon, broadly speaking, was the land of marvels: marvelous trees, marvelous forests, and a river system that equaled those of the Ganges, the Nile, and the Euphrates put together. El Dorado, city of the "golden one," was said to be there, though it remained inconveniently elusive, buried now here, now there in the great green sea of leaves. In 1594, Sir Walter Raleigh went looking for it via the Orinoco River; he missed it, too, but did report seeing, "a farre off," a "mountain of Christall," shining with diamonds and other precious stones. Glimpsed once, it has never been seen since.

The Amazon was also a terrifying place. A year after its departure, the starving survivors of Gonzalo Pizarro's 1541 expedition to the "Land of Cinnamon" limped back to civilization clothed in leaves and furs. Pizarro's lieutenant, Francisco de Orellana, became the first European to navigate the entire length of the Amazon River, largely because he was forced to do so, harried by native canoemen unleashing flights of arrows at him. Well into the 19th century explorers were hearing reports of tribes of dwarfs, tribes of giants, tribes with backward-facing feet, tribes with Cyclopean eyes, tribes with tails, tribes of women warriors (who gave the river its name), and other curiosities that might have filled a medieval book of marvels.

It was all simply irresistible to Henry M. Tomlinson, the short, city-bred, pipe-smoking Everyman who left a secure Fleet Street job to go not just there, but *there*: into the deepest heart of the green abyss, a place described on the map with but two words: "Forest" and "Unexplored":

When I take the map of South America now, and hold it with the estuary of the Amazon as its base, my thoughts are like those might be of a lost ant, crawling in and over the furrows and ridges of an exposed root as he regards all he may of the trunk rising into the whole upper cosmos of a spreading oak. The Amazon then looks to me, properly symbolical, as a monstrous tree, and its tributaries, paranas, furos, and igarapes, as the great boughs, little boughs, and twigs of its ascending and spreading ramifications, so minutely dissecting the continent with its numberless watercourses that the mind sees that dark region as an impenetrable density of green and secret leaves; which, literally, when you go there, is what you will find. You enter the leaves, and vanish...

H. M. TOMLINSON, *The Sea and the Jungle*

Among the books Tomlinson read in preparation for his 1909 journey were two classics then on every naturalist's shelf, *The Naturalist on the River Amazons*, by Henry Walter Bates, and *Travels on the Amazon and Rio Negro*, by Alfred Russel Wallace.

It was the words "Promising indeed to lovers of the marvellous is that land"—one of the opening sentences of W. H. Edwards's *A Voyage up the River Amazon* (1847)—that inspired Bates, the former hosier's apprentice, and his friend Wallace, a former surveyor's apprentice, to embark together on their grand adventure. Both men were keen entomologists, though when in the field neither one limited his collecting to insects alone. Bates remained in Brazil for eleven years, 1848-59, collecting over 14,000 specimens, most of them new to science. Wallace was there four years before he left for his famous odyssey in the East Indies. Both were wry observers as well as ardent naturalists, and their writings influenced the way a whole generation of Victorian readers would imagine a primeval forest:

Exploring the Amazon, 1820

At about two miles from the city [Magoary] we entered the virgin forest, which the increased height of the trees and the deeper shade had some time told us we were approaching. Its striking characteristics were, the great number and variety of forest-trees, their trunks rising frequently for sixty or eighty feet without a branch, and perfectly straight; the huge creepers, which climb about them, sometimes stretching obliquely from their summits like the stays of a mast, sometimes winding around their trunks like immense serpents waiting for their prey. Here, two or three together, twisting spirally round each other, form a complete living cable, as if to bind securely these monarchs of the forest; there, they form tangled festoons, and, covered themselves with smaller creepers and parasitic plants, hide the parent stem from sight.

Among the trees the various kinds that have buttresses projecting around their base are the most striking and peculiar. Some of these buttresses are much longer than they are high; springing from a distance of eight or ten feet from the base, and reaching only four or five feet high on the trunk, while others rise to the height of twenty or thirty feet, and can even be distinguished as ribs on the stem to forty or fifty. They are complete wooden walls, from six inches to a foot thick, sometimes branching into two or three, and extending straight out to such a distance as to afford room for a comfortable hut in the angle between them. Large square pieces are often cut out of them to make paddles, and for other uses, the wood being generally very light and soft.

Other trees, again, appear as if they were formed by a number of slender stems growing together. They are deeply furrowed and ribbed for their whole height, and in places these furrows reach quite through them, like windows in a narrow tower, yet they run up as high as the loftiest trees of the forest, with a straight stem of uniform diameter. Another most curious form is presented by those which have many of their roots high above the surface of the ground, appearing to stand on many legs, and often forming archways large enough for a man to walk beneath.

ALFRED RUSSEL WALLACE, *Travels on the Amazon and Rio Negro*

We often read, in books of travels, of the silence and gloom of the Brazilian forests. They are realities, and the impression deepens on a longer acquaintance. The few sounds of birds are of that pensive or mysterious character which intensifies the feeling of solitude rather than imparts a sense of life and cheerfulness. Sometimes, in the midst of the stillness, a sudden yell or scream will startle one; this comes from some defenceless fruit-eating animal, which is pounced upon by a tiger-cat or stealthy boa-constrictor. Morning and evening the howling monkeys make a most fearful and harrowing noise, under which it is difficult to keep up one's buoyancy of spirit. The feeling of inhospitable wildness which the forest is calculated to inspire is increased tenfold under this fearful uproar. Often, even in the still hours of midday, a sudden crash will be heard resounding afar through the wilderness, as some great bough or entire tree falls to the ground. There are, besides, many sounds which it is impossible to account for. I found the natives generally as much at a loss in this respect as myself. Sometimes a sound is heard like the clang of an iron bar against a hard, hollow tree, or a piercing cry rends the air; these are not repeated, and the succeeding silence tends to heighten the unpleasant impression which they make on the mind.

HENRY WALTER BATES, *The Naturalist on the River Amazons*

Henry Tomlinson was more imaginatively susceptible than his two more phlegmatic idols. By the time he arrived *there,* that spot far up the Madeira River that seemed utterly back of even the Brazilian beyond, he was in a place where he imagined the ancient gods must have their ultimate sanctuary:

This central forest was really the vault of the long-forgotten; dank, mouldering, dark, abandoned to the accumulations of eld and decay. The tall pillars rose, upholding night, and they might have been bastions of weathered limestone and basalt, for they were as grim as ancient and ruinous masonry. There was no undergrowth. The ground was hidden in a ruin of perished stuff, uprooted trees, parchments of leaves, broken boughs, and mummied husks, the iron globes of nuts, and pods. There was no day, but some breaks in the roof were points of remote starlight. The crowded columns mounted straight and far, almost branchless, fading into indistinction. Out of that overhead obscurity hung a wreckage of distorted cables, binding the trees, and often reaching the ground. The trees were seldom of great girth, though occasionally there was a dominant basaltic pillar, its roots meandering over the floor like streams of old lava. The smooth ridges of such a fantastic complexity of roots were sometimes breast high. The walls ran up the trunk, projecting from it as flat buttresses, for great heights. We would crawl round such an occupying structure, diminished groundlings, as one would move about the base of a foreboding, plutonic building whose limits and meaning were ominous and baffling. There were other great trees with compound boles, built literally of bundles of round stems, intricate gothic pillars, some of the props having fused in places. Every tree was the support of a parasitic community, lianas swathing it and binding it. One vine moulded itself to its host, a flat and wide compress, as though it were plastic. We might have been witnessing what had been a riot of manifold and insurgent life. It had been turned to stone when in the extreme pose of striving violence. It was all dead now.

But what if these combatants had only paused as we appeared? It was a thought which came to me. The pause might be but an appearance for our deception. Indeed, they were all fighting as we passed through, those still and fantastic shapes, a war ruthless but slow, in which the battle day was ages long. They seemed but still. We were deceived. If time had been accelerated, if the movements in that war of phantoms had been speeded, we should have seen what really was there, the greater trees running upwards to starve the weak of light and food, and heard the continuous collapse of the failures, and have seen the lianas writhing and constricting, manifestly like serpents, throttling and eating their hosts. We did see the dead everywhere, shells with the worms at them. Yet it was not easy to be sure that we saw anything at all, for these were not trees, but shapes in a region below the day, a world sunk abysmally from the land of living things, to which light but thinly percolated down to two travellers moving over its floor, trying to get out to their own place.

H. M. TOMLINSON, *The Sea and the Jungle*

With most of the animals lost in a billowing ocean of leaves, even the naturalists were afforded only a rare glimpse or two of certain creatures— but those were unforgettable moments:

OPPOSITE: *Ferns and tree ferns, by Ernst Haeckel, 1904*

As I was walking quietly along I saw a large jet-black animal come out of the forest about twenty yards before me, which took me so much by surprise that I did not at first imagine what it was. As it moved slowly on, and its whole body and long curving tail came into full view in the middle of the road, I saw that it was a fine black jaguar. I involuntarily raised my gun to my shoulder, but remembering that both barrels were loaded with small shot, and that to fire would exasperate without killing him, I stood silently gazing. In the middle of the road he turned his head, and for an instant paused and gazed at me, but having, I suppose, other business of his own to attend to, walked steadily on, and disappeared in the thicket. As he advanced, I heard the scampering of small animals, and the whizzing flight of ground birds, clearing the path for their dreaded enemy.

This encounter pleased me much. I was too much surprised, and occupied too much with admiration, to feel fear. I had at length had a full view, in his native wilds, of the rarest variety of the most powerful and dangerous animal inhabiting the American continent. I was, however, by no means desirous of a second meeting, and, as it was near sunset, thought it most prudent to turn back towards the village.

ALFRED RUSSEL WALLACE, *Travels on the Amazon and Rio Negro*

Henry Bates had many noteworthy encounters with birds. Urubu vultures would march into his kitchen and "lift the lids of the saucepans with their beaks to rob them of their contents." A flock of toucans once scolded him point-blank for wounding one of its members. And far up the Amazon Valley, where Indians built thatched huts on the banks of secluded streams, he heard the bird about which it was said, when it began to sing, all other birds paused:

I frequently heard in the neighbourhood of these huts, the "realejo," or organ bird (Cyphorhinus cantans), the most remarkable songster, by far, of the Amazonian forests. When its singular notes strike the ear for the first time, the impression can not be resisted that they are produced by a human voice. Some musical boy must be gathering fruits in the thicket, and is singing a few notes to cheer himself. The tunes become more fluty and plaintive; they are now those of a flageolot, and notwithstanding the utter impossibility of the thing, one is for a moment convinced that some one is playing that instrument. No bird is to be seen, however closely the surrounding trees and bushes may be scanned, and yet the voice seems to come from the thicket closest to one's ear. The ending of the song is rather disappointing. It begins with a few very slow and mellow notes, following each other like the commencement of an air; one listens expecting to hear a complete strain, but an abrupt pause occurs, and then the song breaks down, finishing with a number of clicking unmusical sounds like a piping barrel organ out of wind and tune. I never heard the bird on the Lower Amazon, and very rarely heard it even at Ega; it is the only songster which makes an impression on the natives, who sometimes rest their paddles whilst travelling in their small canoes, along the shady by-streams, as if struck by the mysterious sounds.

HENRY WALTER BATES, *The Naturalist on the River Amazons*

Sound, it seems, could be more haunting than sight in this extraordinarily imposing environment. Charles Darwin had remarked upon the contrast between the shrill of uncounted trillions of insects, heard from ships standing off the Brazilian coast, and the cathedral-like silence of the forest interior. Life, of course, was found in the treetops; or, as the Reverend Charles Kingsley put it, after his first rapturous experience of a tropical forest, "You are in the empty nave of the cathedral, and the service is being celebrated aloft in the blazing roof."

Yet there were few things as unsettling as the twilight roar of the jungle at sundown. Something tremendous must be awakening. Henry Bates heard it far up at the lonely falls of the Cupari River:

In this remote and solitary spot I can say that I heard for the first and almost the only time the uproar of life at sunset, which Humboldt describes as having witnessed towards the sources of the Orinoco, but which is unknown on the banks of the larger rivers. The noises of animals began just as the sun sank behind the trees after a sweltering afternoon, leaving the sky above of the intensest shade of blue. Two flocks of howling monkeys, one close to our canoe, the other about a furlong distant, filled the echoing forests with their dismal roaring. Troops of parrots, including the hyacinthine macaw we were in search of, began then to pass over; the different styles of cawing and screaming of the various species making a terrible discord. Added to these noises were the songs of strange Cicadas, one large kind perched high on the trees around our little haven setting up a most piercing chirp; it began with the usual harsh jarring tone of its tribe, but this gradually and rapidly became shriller, until it ended in a long and loud note resembling the steam-whistle of a locomotive engine. Half-a-dozen of these wonderful performers made a considerable item in the evening concert. I had heard the same species before at Para, but it was there very uncommon: we obtained here one of them for my collection by a lucky blow with a stone. The uproar of beasts, birds, and insects lasted but a short time: the sky quickly lost its intense hue, and the night set in. Then began the tree-frogs—quack-quack, drum-drum, hoo-hoo; these, accompanied by a melancholy night-jar, kept up their monotonous cries until very late.

Cicada, 1849

HENRY BATES, The Naturalist on the River Amazons

Of course, to Henry Tomlinson, way up *there,* the sound was almost apocalyptic:

Then, almost imperceptibly, the frogs begin their nightlong din. The crickets and cicadas join. Between the varying pitch of their voices come other nocturnes in monotones from creatures unknown to complete the gamut. There are notes so profound, but constant, that they are a mere impression of obscurity to the hearing, as when one peers listening into an abysm in which no bottom is seen, and others are stridulations so attenuated that they shrill beyond reach....

The noise comes nearer and louder until it is palpitating around us. It might be the life of the forest, immobile and silent all day, now released and beating upwards in deafening paroxysms...

LORDS OF THE JUNGLE

LIONS AND TIGERS AND BEARS—OUTSIDE OF OZ, THERE WAS ONLY one land, India, where all three might be found in close conjunction. Lions, however, were already fading from the scene by the 1890s, when Rudyard Kipling penned *The Jungle Book,* which he peopled with all those anthropomorphized denizens of the fictional Seeonee Hills: Akela the Wolf, Bagheera the panther, Baloo the Bear, Hathi the Elephant, Kaa the Python, Rikki-Tikki-Tavi the Mongoose, Shere Khan the Tiger, alongside the host of monkeys and peacocks and cobras making up the supporting cast.

This was the original jungle—the English word derives from Hindi *jangal*—and in its infinite variety of forms it stretched from practically the foot of the Himalaya to embrace what on maps of Kipling's day included India, Ceylon, Burma, Malaya, Thailand, French Indochina, and the near isles of the Dutch East Indies. Sal and teak trees, banyans and rattan palms, and wonderful, if infragrant, three-foot-broad rafflesia flowers ranked among its botanical marvels. Stalking in and among them was the tiger, widely considered lord of these forests.

Despite enough tiger lore to fill the shelves of entire libraries, and despite their being so numerous in parts of India at the beginning of the 19th century that all a region's villages might be deserted, it was very hard, unless you were involved in an organized hunt, to actually see a tiger in the jungle. If you did, however, it was the kind of heart-stopping moment likely to remain vivid the rest of your—possibly shortened—life. Capt. James Forsyth, who spent ten years roaming central India during Queen Victoria's reign, described one such encounter:

> About the centre of the cover I came upon the tiger, crouched, with massive head rested on forepaws, the drawn-up hindquarters and slightly twitching tail showing that she meant mischief. She came at me in the most determined manner....She looked just like a huge cat that had been hunted by dogs—her fur all bedraggled and standing on end, eyes glaring with fury, and emitting the hoarse coughing roar of a charging tiger....jumping high above the grass at every bound—a really beautiful sight, with her very bright-coloured skin, hair erect, and tail streaming behind her.
>
> CAPT. JAMES FORSYTH, *The Highlands of Central India*

Interestingly enough, it was not the tiger that many of the forest tribes heeded the most. They reserved their respect for that other lord of the jungle, the wild elephant.

Before the 20th century brought his African cousin into greater prominence, it was the Asian, or Indian, elephant that was the more storied member of the clan. He was the caparisoned elephant of panoply and pageant, the war elephant that once faced Alexander the Great, the sacred elephant who lent his visage to the Hindu god Ganesha. And, of course, he was the elephant of the Indian fable, the one in which the blind men each grope a different part, mistaking it for the whole.

Tiger and prey, late 19th century

That was not the kind of mistake Charles Darwin often made. In one of the few places he ever mentions the elephant in his writings, it was not the trunk, nor the tail, nor the legs which interested him; it was the astonishing range of intelligence and emotion that he found captivating. Without needing to indulge in Kiplingesque anthropomorphism, Darwin recognized that those elephants captured and tamed to work teak plantations, carry maharajas, or storm into battle seemed to remember more than just mere commands. They might also recall—heartrendingly enough—happier days in their wild forest home:

The Indian elephant is known sometimes to weep. Sir E. Tennent, in describing these which he saw captured and bound in Ceylon, says, some "lay motionless on the ground, with no other indication of suffering than the tears which suffused their eyes and flowed incessantly." Speaking of another elephant he says, "When overpowered and made fast, his grief was most affecting; his violence sank to utter prostration, and he lay on the ground, uttering choking cries, with tears trickling down his cheeks." In the Zoological Gardens the keeper of the Indian elephants positively asserts that he has several times seen tears rolling down the face of the old female, when distressed by the removal of the young one....

CHARLES DARWIN, *The Expression of the Emotions in Man and Animals*

THE POISON TREE

THE EAST INDIES, FABLED FOR FRUITS AND FLOWERS AND SPICES, had once been a byword for the marvelous. Although cloves and nutmegs first drew European explorers and traders, it soon became apparent that much of the 3,000-mile arc of islands that we know today as Indonesia was blanketed by a rich and incredibly profuse tropical vegetation. With towering volcanoes looming over much of it, the Indies were the kind of place that might inspire imaginative, not to say fantastic, tales.

One such made its appearance in a 1783 article published in the *London Magazine.* Written by a Dutch doctor named Foersch, it told of his discovering in the highlands of Java a poisonous upas tree (*upas* being a Malay word for poison). This particular tree, the doctor claimed, emitted vapors so deadly it destroyed every living thing within a radius of dozens of miles. Javanese princes would even send condemned prisoners into this lethal vale in futile attempts to retrieve such an obviously useful substance. Only two in twenty would ever stagger back. It was this article, according to Robert Sears, author of the 19th-century *Wonders of the World*, that led to "an imposing fabric of fiction" being reared "on the simple groundwork of truth."

A continual exhalation (according to the few who returned) issued from the tree, and was seen to rise and spread in the air "like the putrid steam of a marshy cavern." Whatever this vapor or the miasmata from it touched, it killed; and as they had cursed that spot for centuries, not a tree, save the upas and its progeny—not a bush, nor a blade of grass, was found in the valley nor on the surrounding mountains, for a circuit of many miles. All animal life was equally extinct—there was not a bird of the air to be seen—not a rat, nor a mouse, nor even any of those reptiles that swarm in foul places. In the neighborhood of the tree the barren ground was covered with dead bodies and skeletons—the remains of preceding criminals. This was the only circumstance that showed animate beings had ever been there: and as the birds and beasts of prey and the consuming worms could not batten in that valley of death, those ghastly relics would long remain unconsumed to warn every new-comer of his all but inevitable fate.

ROBERT SEARS, *The Wonders of the World*

This story of the poisonous upas tree and its skeleton-strewn valley fired the imagination of Europe. Children were told it at bedtime; Byron and Pushkin immortalized it in verse. Meanwhile, naturalists were pushing through jungles from Ceylon to Celebes, arriving at the foot of stems the Malays had identified as upas trees. Gazing up the trunk and into the branches, the naturalists watched birds come and go without ill effect; they fingered the bark and did not drop on the spot. If they incised the bark of one such tree, the *antiar* of Java, a milky latex did exude, which was indeed extremely virulent, and used for the tipping of poison arrows. But by then, of course, the legend of the upas tree had run riot in Europe and America, becoming an unavoidable metaphor, indeed a cliché, for any person or institution that blasted everything within its influence.

Then, toward the close of the 19th century, its use withered and died, apparently of its own excess. At the same time it was finally admitted that nowhere on Java was found such a dismal valley with such a poisonous tree. Science had arrived in the fabulous Indies.

A Marvel of the East

THE DUTCH MAY HAVE BEEN THE OCCUPYING COLONIAL POWER, but it was an Englishman, Alfred Russel Wallace, who is now most associated with the golden age of science in those islands. In the eight years he spent wandering from shore to shore, Wallace collected 125,000 specimens and a harvest of observations he eventually turned into one of the classics of natural history, *The Malay Archipelago*. Even so, it was hard to avoid being hit—literally—by the marvelous.

In this land where famously luscious fruits—the mangosteen, the rambutan, the carambola—dropped from the forest trees each day of the year, it is suprising that the durian should be so highly esteemed that, according to Bernhard Paludanus, the native Malays "give it honourable titles, exalt it, and make verses on it." With an odor resembling rotten onions, garlic—or, in Alexander von Humboldt's overly exact description, "human Excrements"—it was a difficult fruit for Westerners to approach, much less to appreciate. Yet those who managed to do so, as did Wallace, discovered a taste without parallel:

> A rich butter-like custard highly flavoured with almonds gives the best general idea of it, but intermingled with it come wafts of flavour that call to mind cream-cheese, onion-sauce, brown sherry, and other incongruities. Then there is a rich glutinous smoothness in the pulp which nothing else possesses, but which adds to its delicacy.

The durian, Wallace concluded, was "worth a voyage to the East to experience." Yet it grew high up on a tree, in a shell like a cannonball, surrounded by sharp spines:

> The Durian is, however, sometimes dangerous. When the fruit begins to ripen it falls daily and almost hourly, and accidents not unfrequently happen to persons walking or working under the trees. When a Durian strikes a man in its fall, it produces a dreadful wound, the strong spines tearing open the flesh, while the blow itself is very heavy; but from this very circumstance death rarely ensues, the copious effusion of blood preventing the inflammation which might otherwise take place. A Dyak chief informed me that he had been struck down by a Durian falling on his head, which he thought would certainly have caused his death, yet he recovered in a very short time.
>
> Poets and moralists, judging from our English trees and fruits, have thought that small fruits always grew on lofty trees, so, that their fall should be harmless to man, while the large ones trailed on the ground. Two of the largest and heaviest fruits known, however, the Brazil-nut fruit (Bertholletia) and Durian, grow on lofty forest trees, from which they fall as soon as they are ripe, and often wound or kill the native inhabitants. From this we may learn two things: first, not to draw general conclusions from a very partial view of nature; and secondly, that trees and fruits, no less than the varied productions of the animal kingdom, do not appear to be organized with exclusive reference to the use and convenience of man.
>
> ALFRED RUSSEL WALLACE, *The Malay Archipelago*

No partial views for Wallace. As he roved the forests, dodging durians and hunting butterflies, he was grappling with fundamental questions about nature's workings. As the Reverend Charles Kingsley put them, these questions boiled down to: "Whether those crowded, struggling, competing shapes are stable or variable? Whether or not they are varying still?"

Pondering these things, Wallace often encountered certain trees that could either be admired for their fanciful and elegant fretwork, or denounced as "strangler figs," whose embrace spelled vegetable murder. But that kind of imaginative association, thought Wallace, was exactly the partial view of nature:

> The forests abound with gigantic trees with cylindrical, buttressed, or furrowed stems, while occasionally the traveller comes upon a wonderful fig-tree, whose trunk is itself a forest of stems and aërial roots. Still more rarely are found trees which appear to have begun growing in mid-air, and from the same point send out wide-spreading branches above and a complicated pyramid of roots descending for seventy or eighty feet to the ground below, and so spreading on every side, that one can stand in the very centre with the trunk of the tree immediately overhead. Trees of this character are found all over the Archipelago, and the illustration (taken from one which I often visited in the Aru Islands) will convey some idea of their general character. I believe that they originate as parasites, from seeds carried by birds and dropped in the fork of some lofty tree. Hence descend aerial roots, clasping and ultimately destroying the supporting tree, which is in time entirely replaced by the humble plant which was at first dependent upon it. Thus we have an actual struggle for life in the vegetable kingdom, not less fatal to the vanquished than the struggles among animals which we can so much more easily observe and understand.
>
> ALFRED RUSSEL WALLACE, *The Malay Archipelago*

A strangler fig does not "strangle," it merely struggles, groping blindly. Those crowded, struggling, competing shapes were indeed variable and necessarily opportunistic. Glimpses like these helped Wallace formulate something very like Darwin's "natural selection," and he is often credited with being a co-founder of the theory of evolution.

Such insights could still be unsettling. When in the remote Aru Islands, where he had observed and collected a specimen of the rare king bird of paradise, Wallace was troubled by the recognition that such magnificent creatures were not expressly created for man to gaze upon:

Twelve-wired bird of paradise, circa 1839

The remote island in which I found myself situated, in an almost unvisited sea, far from the tracks of merchant fleets and navies; the wild, luxuriant tropical forest, which stretched far away on every side; the rude, uncultured savages who gathered round me—all had their influence in determining the emotions with which I gazed upon this "thing of beauty." I thought of the long ages of the past, during which the successive generations of this little creature had run their course—year by year being born, and living and dying amid these dark and gloomy woods, with no intelligent eye to gaze upon their loveliness; to all appearance such a wanton waste of beauty. Such ideas excite a feeling of melancholy. It seems sad that on the one hand such exquisite creatures should live out their lives and exhibit their charms only in these wild inhospitable regions, doomed for ages yet to come to hopeless barbarism; while, on the other hand, should civilized man ever reach these distant lands, and bring moral, intellectual, and physical light into the recesses of these virgin forests, we may be sure that he will so disturb the nicely-balanced relations of organic and inorganic nature as to cause the disappearance, and finally the extinction, of these very beings whose wonderful structure and beauty he alone is fitted to appreciate and enjoy. This consideration must surely tell us that all living things were *not* made for man. Many of them have no relation to him. The cycle of their existence has gone on independently of his, and is disturbed or broken by every advance in man's intellectual development; and their happiness and enjoyments, their loves and hates, their struggles for existence, their vigorous life and early death, would seem to be immediately related to their own well-being and perpetuation alone, limited only by the equal well-being and perpetuation of the numberless other organisms with which each is more or less intimately connected.

ALFRED RUSSEL WALLACE, *The Malay Archipelago*

Man himself, it seems, is the poisonous upas tree.

THE RAVENING HORDE

YET THERE WERE SKELETON-STREWN TRAILS THROUGHOUT THE world's tropical forests. Only they were not evidence of poisonous exhalations but rather of the passage of the much-feared army ants. Though the skeletons might have been few and small, and the primary victims insects living in the leaf litter, the image of voracious and implacable legions annhilating all they encounter was a terrifying one. Henry Bates observed the dreaded columns—from a safe distance—in the Amazon. But his ants had their endearing moments. At times, "they seemed to have been all smitten with a sudden fit of laziness. Some were walking slowly about, others were brushing their antennae with their fore feet; but the drollest sight was their cleaning one another. Here and there an ant was seen stretching forth first one leg and then another, to be brushed or washed by one or more of its comrades, who performed the task by passing the limb between the jaws and the tongue, finishing by giving the antennae a friendly wipe."

That forest idyll is scarcely imaginable among the ants described by Paul Du Chaillu as ravaging the African jungle:

It is their habit to march through the forests in a long and regular line—a line about two inches broad and often several miles in length. All along this line are larger ants, who act as officers, stand outside the ranks, and keep this singular army in order. If they come to a place where there are no trees to shelter them from the sun, whose heat they cannot bear, they immediately construct underground tunnels, through which the whole army passes in columns to the forest beyond. These tunnels are four or five feet under ground, and are used only in the heat of the day or during a storm.

When they get hungry, the long file spreads itself through the forest in a front line, and devours all it overtakes with a fury which is quite irresistible. The elephant and gorilla fly before this attack. The black men run for their lives. Every animal that lives in their line of march is chased. They seem to understand and act upon the tactics of Napoleon, and concentrate with great speed their heaviest forces upon the point of attack. In an incredibly short space of time the mouse, or dog, or leopard, or deer, is overwhelmed, killed, eaten, and the bare skeleton only remains.

They seem to travel night and day. Many a time have I been awakened out of a sleep, and obliged to rush from the hut and into the water to save my life, and after all suffered intolerable agony from the bites

> *Many a time I have been awakened out of a sleep, and obliged to rush from the hut and into the water to save my life, and after all suffered intolerable agony from the bites of the advance guard, who had got into my clothes.*
>
> —PAUL DU CHAILLU

of the advance guard, who had got into my clothes. When they enter a house they clear it of all living things. Cockroaches are devoured in an instant. Rats and mice spring round the room in vain. An over whelming force of ants kills a strong rat in less than a minute, in spite of the most frantic struggles, and in less than another minute its bones are stripped. Every living thing in the house is devoured....

When on their march the insect-world flies before them, and I have often had the approach of a bashikouay army heralded to me by this means. Wherever they go they make a clean sweep, even ascending to the tops of the highest trees in pursuit of their prey....Their numbers are so great that one does not like to enter into calculations; but I have seen one continual line passing at good speed a particular place for twelve hours. The reader may imagine for himself how many millions on millions there may have been contained here."

PAUL DU CHAILLU, *Explorations and Adventures in Equatorial Africa*

That raised eyebrows even when first published in 1861. But then there were few who could dispute Du Chaillu's lurid accounts of African creatures, including the earliest description of the "ferocious" gorilla in print. Few explorers had penetrated the steaming, fever-plagued forests of the "Dark Continent," dark because unknown, and unknown because this was the original "white man's grave," whose malarial shore felled Europeans with sickening regularity. In 1856, however, young Du Chaillu had ventured alone into the mysterious interior of Gabon. He emerged four years later with valuable natural history collections and the sensational tales told in his best-selling book.

INSCRUTABLE AFRICA

BY 1890, WHEN JOSEPH CONRAD UNDERTOOK THE EVENTFUL journey up the Congo River that inspired him to write *Heart of Darkness,* Europeans were quaffing anti-malarial quinine in sufficient portions to embark on the colonial depredations that made much of the Congo a black man's grave as well. Set against this miasma of sickness, evil, and death, Conrad's story received much of its atmosphere from his impressions of the forest. As Marlow, Conrad's fictional alter ego, steams up the river toward his ultimate rendezvous with Kurtz, the renegade ivory trader, he sees in the numberless, looming trees crowding both banks a revelation of the primeval:

Going up that river was like travelling back to the earliest beginnings of the world, when vegetation rioted on the earth and the big trees were kings. An empty stream, a great silence, an impenetrable forest. The air was warm, thick, heavy, sluggish. There was no joy in the brilliance of sunshine. The long stretches of the waterway ran on, deserted, into the gloom of overshadowed distances. On silvery sandbanks hippos and alligators sunned themselves side by side. The broadening waters flowed through a mob of wooded islands; you lost your way on that river as you would in a desert, and butted all day long against shoals, trying to find the channel, till you thought yourself bewitched and cut off for ever from everything you had known once—somewhere—far away—in another existence perhaps. There were moments when one's past came back to one, as it will sometimes when you have not a moment to spare to yourself; but it came in the shape of an unrestful and noisy dream, remembered with wonder amongst the overwhelming realities of this strange world of plants, and water, and silence. And this stillness of life did not in the least resemble a peace. It was the stillness of an implacable force brooding over an inscrutable intention. It looked at you with a vengeful aspect....

Trees, trees, millions of trees, massive, immense, running up high; and at their foot, hugging the bank against the stream, crept the little begrimed steamboat, like a sluggish beetle crawling on the floor of a lofty portico. It made you feel very small, very lost, and yet it was not

Beetles in a flood, late 19th century

altogether depressing that feeling. After all, if you were small, the grimy beetle crawled on—which was just what you wanted it to do....

We were wanderers on a prehistoric earth, on an earth that wore the aspect of an unknown planet. We could have fancied ourselves the first of men taking possession of an accursed inheritance, to be subdued at the cost of profound anguish and of excessive toil...we were travelling in the night of first ages, of those ages that are gone, leaving hardly a sign—and no memories.

The earth seemed unearthly. We are accustomed to look upon the shackled form of a conquered monster, but there—there we could look at a thing monstrous and free. It was unearthly.

JOSEPH CONRAD, *Heart of Darkness*

Only 300 miles of that dense, deadly, disease-ridden, inscrutable forest separates the Congo basin from the Ogooué River to the north, which also snakes deep into the green interior. Yet only five years after Conrad made his memorable journey, 33-year-old Mary Kingsley steamed up the Ogooué. It might have been a different world:

This forest is beyond all my expectations of tropical luxuriance and beauty, and is a thing of another world to the forest of the Upper Calabar [in Nigeria], which, beautiful as it is, is a sad dowdy to this. There you certainly get a great sense of grimness and vastness; here you have an equal grimness and vastness with the addition of superb colour. This forest is a Cleopatra to which Calabar is but a Quaker. Not only does this forest depend on flowers for its illumination, for there are many kinds of trees having their young shoots, crimson, brown-pink, and creamy yellow: added to this there is also the relieving aspect of the prevailing fashion among West African trees, of wearing the trunk white with here and there upon it splashes of pale pink lichen, and vermilion-red fungus, which alone is sufficient to prevent the great mass of vegetation from being a monotony in green.

All day long we steam past ever-varying scenes of loveliness whose component parts are ever the same, yet the effect ever different. Doubtless it is wrong to call it a symphony, yet I know no other word to describe the scenery of the Ogowe...It is as full of life and beauty and passion as any symphony Beethoven ever wrote: the parts changing, interweaving, and returning. There are leit motifs here in it, too. See the papyrus ahead; and you know when you get abreast of it you will find the great forest sweeping away in a bay-like curve behind it against the dull gray sky, the splendid columns of its cotton and red woods looking like a façade of some limitless inchoate temple.

MARY KINGSLEY, *Travels in West Africa*

Mary Kingsley was not on the fever-inducing Oguooé for its aesthetics. Ostensibly she was there—alone—for "fish and fetish," collecting fish for the British Museum and studying fetish among the Fang, whose reputation as cannibals was not lessened by the way they sharpened their teeth. But she had clearly fallen under the spell of Africa. "Who would not come to its twin brother hell itself for all the beauty and charm of it," she wrote. Daft and imperturbable, she wore full-length Victorian skirts even while wading thigh deep in the black slime of swamps. She encountered leopards, crocodiles, pythons, and gorillas. As for insects: "You have no chance in a stand up fight with a thorough going African insect," she asserted, so one might as well get over it.

Late one night on an exceedingly beautiful, strangely melancholy, and vaguely menacing jungle lake, Kingsley climbed into her canoe. Out there something that is still unexplained was waiting:

It was a wonderfully lovely quiet night with no light save that from the stars. One immense planet shone pre-eminent in the purple sky, throwing a golden path down on to the still waters. Quantities of big fish sprung out of the water, their glistening silver-white scales flashing so that they look like slashing swords. Some bird was making a long, low boom-booming sound away on the forest shore. I paddled leisurely across the lake to the shore on the right, and seeing crawling on the ground some large glow-worms, drove the canoe on to the bank among some hippo grass, and got out to get them.

While engaged on this hunt I felt the earth quiver under my feet, and heard a soft big soughing sound, and looking round saw I had dropped in on a hippo banquet. I made out five of the immense brutes round me, so I softly returned to the canoe and shoved off, stealing along the bank, paddling under water, until I deemed it safe to run out across the lake for my island. I reached the other end of it to that on which the village is situated; and finding a miniature rocky bay with a soft patch of sand and no hippo grass, the incidents of the Fan hut suggested the advisability of a bath. Moreover, there was no china collection in that hut, and it would be a long time before I got another chance, so I go ashore again, and, carefully investigating the neighbourhood to make certain there was no human habitation near, I then indulged in a wash in peace. Drying one's self on one's cummerbund is not pure joy, but it can be done when you put your mind to it. While I was finishing my toilet I saw a strange thing happen. Down through the forest on the lake bank opposite came a violet ball the size of a small orange. When it reached the sand beach it hovered along it to and fro close to the ground. In a few minutes another ball of similarly colored light came towards it from behind one of the islets, and the two waver to and fro over the beach, sometimes circling round each other. I made off towards them in the canoe, thinking—as I still do—they were some brand new kind of luminous insect. When I got on to their beach one of them went off into the bushes and the other away over the water. I followed in the canoe, for the water here is very deep, and, when I almost thought I had got it, it went down into the water and I could see it glowing as it sunk until it vanished in the depths. I made my way back hastily, fearing my absence with the canoe might give rise, if discovered, to trouble, and by 3:30 I was back in the hut safe, but not so comfortable as I had been on the lake. A little before five my men are stirring and I get my tea. I do not state my escapade to them, but ask what those lights were. "Akom," said the Fan, and pointing to the shore of the lake where I had been during the night they said, "they came there, it was an 'Aku'"—or devil bush. More than ever did I regret not having secured one of those sort of two phenomena. What a joy a real devil, appropriately put up in raw alcohol, would have been to my scientific friends!

MARY KINGSLEY, *Travels in West Africa*

"I went to West Africa to die," Mary Kingsley later wrote. "West Africa amused me and was kind to me, and was scientifically interesting, and did not want to kill me just then." Instead, she might have added, it disclosed something luminous in its heart of darkness.

BURIED CITIES

FINALLY, THE PRIMEVAL FOREST MIGHT NOT BE SO PRIMEVAL, after all. Its roots might be sunk not in its mother soil but rather in the broken pavements of past civilizations. That is what John Lloyd Stephens discovered upon learning that ancient ruined cities, buried in jungle, could be found in Central America. Stephens, a New York lawyer turned best-selling travel writer, then persuaded the English topographical artist Frederick Catherwood to accompany him on a journey to these sites, which some people had fancifully claimed to be the work of ancient Egyptians, the Lost Tribes of Israel, or even refugees from vanished Atlantis. Nevertheless, having crossed one difficult range of mountains after another, it was "with the hope rather than the expectation of finding wonders" that, in November 1839, they followed a local guide into the ruins of Copán, the vast abandoned city in Honduras:

> With an interest perhaps stronger than we had ever felt in wandering among the ruins of Egypt, we followed our guide, who, sometimes missing his way, with a constant and vigorous use of his machete conducted us through the thick forest, among half-buried fragments, to fourteen more monuments of the same character and appearance, some with more elegant designs, and some in workmanship equal to finest monuments of the Egyptians. One, we found, had been displaced from its pedestal by enormous roots; another, locked in the close embrace of branches of trees, was almost lifted out of the earth; and still another had been hurled to the ground and bound down by huge vines and creepers. One with its altar before it stood in a grove of trees which grew around it, seemingly to shade and shroud it as a sacred thing; in the solemn stillness of the woods, it seemed a divinity mourning over a fallen people. The only sounds that disturbed the quiet of this buried city were the noise of monkeys moving among the tops of the trees and the cracking of dry branches broken by their weight. They moved over our heads in long and swift processions, forty or fifty at a time. Some with little ones wound in their long arms walked out to the end of boughs and, holding on with their hind feet or a curl of the

tail, sprang to a branch of the next tree; with a noise like a current of wind they passed on into the depths of the forest. It was the first time we had seen these mockeries of humanity and, amid these strange monuments, they seemed like wandering spirits of the departed race guarding the ruins of their former habitations.

We returned to the base of the pyramidal structure and ascended by regular stone steps, which in some places had been forced apart by bushes and saplings and in others thrown down by the growth of large trees. In parts they were ornamented with sculptured figures and rows of death's heads. Climbing over the ruined top, we reached a terrace overgrown with trees and, crossing it, descended by stone steps into an area so covered with trees that at first we could not make out its form. When the machete had cleared the way, we saw that it was a square with steps on all the sides almost as perfect as those of the Roman amphitheatre. The steps were ornamented with sculpture, and on the

Carved stela, Copán, by Frederick Catherwood, 1844

south side, about halfway up, forced out of its place by roots, was a colossal head, again evidently a portrait. We ascended these steps and reached a broad terrace a hundred feet high overlooking the river and supported by the wall which we had seen from the opposite bank. The whole terrace was covered with trees, and even at this height were two gigantic Ceibas, or wild cotton-trees of India, above twenty feet in circumference; their half-naked roots extended fifty or a hundred feet around, binding down the ruins and shading them with their wide-spreading branches.

We sat down on the very edge of the wall and strove in vain to penetrate the mystery by which we were surrounded. Who were the people that built this city? In the ruined cities of Egypt, even in the long-lost Petra, the stranger knows the story of the people whose vestiges he finds around him. America, say historians, was peopled by savages; but savages never reared these structures, savages never carved these stones. When we asked the Indians who had made them, their dull answer was "Quien sabe? (who knows?)"....

JOHN LLOYD STEPHENS, *Incidents of Travel in Central America, Chiapas, and Yucatan*

Altogether Stephens and Catherwood visited eight ruined cities—Copán, Quiriguá, Iximché, Utatlán, Zaculeu, Toniná, Palenque, and Uxmal—most of them submerged beneath a rolling sea of leaves. Seeking the jungle-shrouded remains of Palenque, for instance, they found that "the whole country for miles around is covered by a dense forest of gigantic trees, with a growth of bush and underwood impenetrable in any direction except by cutting a way with a machete. What lies buried in that forest it is impossible to say; without a guide, we might have gone within a hundred feet of all the buildings without discovering one of them." Camping in the ruined "palace" there, with night settling in and a thunderstorm drenching everything, the two explorers little thought that there might be a light in the wilderness for them, too:

At night we could not light a candle, but the darkness of the palace was lighted up by fireflies of extraordinary size and brilliancy, shooting through the corridors and stationary on the walls, forming a beautiful and striking spectacle. They were of the description with those we saw at Nopa, known by the name of shining beetles, and are mentioned by the early Spaniards, among the wonders of a world where all was new, "as showing the way to those who travel at night." The historian describes them as "somewhat smaller than Sparrows, having two stars close by their Eyes, and two more under their Wings, which gave so great a Light that by it they could spin, weave, write, and paint; and the Spaniards went by night to hunt the Utios or little Rabbits of that country; and a-fishing, carrying these Animals tied to their great Toes or Thumbs: and they called them Locuyos, being also of use to save them from the Gnats, which are there very troublesome. They took them in the Night with Firebrands, because they made to the Light, and came when called by their Name; and they are so unwieldy that when they fall they cannot rise again; and the Men stroaking their Faces and Hands with a sort of Moisture that is in those Stars, seemed to be afire as long as it lasted."...

It is with men as with fireflies: they come and they go. "In the romance of the world's history," Stephens concluded, "nothing ever impressed me more forcibly than the spectacle of this once great and lovely city, over-turned, desolate, and lost; discovered by accident, overgrown with trees for miles around, and without even a name to distinguish it. Apart from everything else, it was a mourning witness to the world's mutations."

And to the endless mutations of the forest as well: Jaguars might prowl the carved stairs, birds display in the empty courtyards, roots smother the palace gates. Insects might shrill and frogs grunt—*quack-quack, drum-drum, hoo-hoo*. For if the big trees ruled in the world's beginning, they might also reign at its end.

THE SUBLIME HARP

PEAKS AND CHASMS

"The adamant foundations of the earth have been wrought into a sublime harp..."
—JOHN WESLEY POWELL

MOUNTAINS AND GORGES, FELLS AND CLIFFS, TORRENTS and chasms and caves—to the orderly 17th century mind of the Reverend Thomas Burnet, such landscape features did not possess a wild romantic grandeur. They were, on the contrary, the "ruins of a broken world," a world that in its original perfection could only have been a perfect sphere. It is scarcely surprising that Burnet came from a "plain Country," from the level flats of eastern England.

But he had seen the Alps—and that really threw him:

[S]uppose a Man was carried asleep out of a plain Country amongst the Alps, and left there upon the Top of one of the highest Mountains, when he wak'd and look'd about him, he wou'd think himself in an inchanted Country, or carried into another World; every Thing wou'd appear to

OPPOSITE: *Sunrise over the Matterhorn, by Albert Bierstadt, 1875*

him so different to what he had ever seen or imagin'd before. To see on every Hand of him a Multitude of vast Bodies thrown together in Confusion, as those Mountains are; Rocks standing naked round about him; and the hollow Valleys gaping under him; and at his Feet, it may be, an Heap of Frozen Snow in the midst of summer. He would hear the Thunder come from below, and see the black Clouds hanging beneath him; upon such a Prospect it would not be easy to him to persuade himself that he was still upon the same Earth; but if he did, he would be convinc'd, at least, that there are some Regions of it strangely rude, and ruin-like, and very different from what he had ever thought of before.

Thomas Burnet, *Sacred Theory of the Earth*

Most of Burnet's contemporaries had never even seen a mountain. That didn't stop scholars like Robert Burton, author of *The Anatomy of Melancholy,* from sending the "long-winged hawk" of his imagination roving about the world, checking in on God passing the time by "painting butterflies' wings," and beholding fantastic mountains only to be found in books: not the real Olympus, Parnassus, Helicon, or Atlas, but those versions passed on to him by ancient authors. There was Aristotle's assertion, for instance, that the Caucasus Mountains were so tall that "the sun shines on its peaks for a third part of the night before sunrise and also after sunset"—which would make them anywhere from 50 to 290 miles high. And then there was Tenerife in the Canary Islands, which everyone knew was the tallest mountain in the world. "The pike of Teneriffe how high is it?" Burton asked rhetorically. "Seven miles, or 52, as Patricius holds, or 9, as Snellius demonstrates in his Eratosthenes?" Whatever the actual figure, it was so tall that, as Burton's contemporary the poet John Donne put it, "The floating Moone would shipwracke there, and sinke."

If mountains were not well understood in the 17th century, they were even less appreciated. One Welshman, who should have known better, could barely contain his disgust at traversing the Alps:

I am now got over the Alps and return'd to France; I had crossed and clambered up the Pyreneans to Spain before; they are not so high and hideous as the Alps; but for our mountains in Wales, as Eppint and Penwinmaur...they are but Molehills in comparison of these; they are but Pigmies compar'd to Giants, but Blisters to Imposthumes, or Pimples to Warts.

JAMES HOWELL, Familiar Letters

Attitudes, however, were about to change. Something was stirring in the European imagination. When in 1688 the English dramatist John Dennis crossed the Alps, the peaks and chasms only half filled him with revulsion. On the contrary, the "horrid Prospect...the dreadful Depth of the Precipice, and the Torrent that roar'd at the bottom, gave us such a view as was altogether new and amazing":

In the mean time we walk'd upon the very brink, in a literal sense, of Destruction; one Stumble, and both Life and Carcass had been at once destroy'd. The sense of all this produc'd different motions in me, viz., a delightful Horrour, a terrible Joy, and at the same time, that I was infinitely pleas'd, I trembled.

JOHN DENNIS, Miscellanies in Verse and Prose

He had discovered the sublime. Not the picturesque, not the beautiful—two categories it would stand against—but the sublime, which always invoked astonishment and amazement, delightful horrors, terrible joys, and pleasure in trembling. For the better part of the next two centuries the sublime was the characteristic mode of marveling at the stupendous and grand in natural scenery. It would be applied to mountains, cliffs, torrents, chasms, caves, glaciers, and the sea. And it always carried below its surface the intimation of mortality, the secret knowledge that with one misstep, you faced annihilation.

So fast did the cult of the sublime catch fire that by the mid-18th century the English poet Thomas Gray could urge mountains on everybody:

> I am returned from Scotland, charmed with my expedition; it is of the Highlands I speak; the Lowlands are worth seeing once, but the mountains are ecstatic, and ought to be visited in pilgrimage once a year. None but those monstrous creatures of God know how to join so much beauty with so much horror. A fig for your poets, painters, gardeners, and clergymen, that have not been among them; their imagination can be made up of nothing but bowling-greens, flowering shrubs, horse-ponds, Fleet ditches, shell grottoes, and Chinese rails.

Redpoll on thistle, 1858

THOMAS GRAY, *Works*

A century later, the revolution was complete. Far from being blisters and imposthumes, mountains were seen by the influential critic and writer John Ruskin as being no less than the "cathedrals of the earth, with their gates of rock, pavements of cloud, choirs of stream and stone, altars of snow, and vaults of purple traversed by the continual stars."

Here the poets were blazing the trail the explorers would follow. Setting out for that "inchanted country" of mountains and gorges, fells and cliffs, torrents and chasms and caves, the explorers carried not only their crampons and plane tables but also these attitudes toward natural scenery. Perhaps, as they did for Ruskin, these attitudes gave their step a little bounce:

[T]he slightest rise and fall in the road—a mossy bank at the side of a crag of chalk, with brambles at its brow, overhanging it,—a ripple over three or four stones in the stream by the bridge,—above all, a wild bit of ferny ground under a fir or two, looking as if, possibly, one might see a hill if one got to the other side of the trees, will instantly give me intense delight, because the shadow, or the hope, of the hills, is in them.

John Ruskin, Modern Painters

The Monarch of the Mountains

WHENEVER VICTOR FRANKENSTEIN NEEDED SOLACE AND SERENITY, we are told, he "sought the sight of the awful and majestic in nature." On at least one occasion that meant taking a carriage from his native Geneva up the winding valley of the River Arve to the mountain village of Chamonix, nestled under the enormous bulk of Mont Blanc, the highest mountain in Europe. The farther upriver the carriage climbed, the closer the precipices loomed:

The next day we pursued our journey upon mules; and as we ascended still higher, the valley assumed a more magnificent and astonishing character. Ruined castles hanging on the precipices of piny mountains; the impetuous Arve, and cottages every here and there peeping forth from among the trees, formed a scene of singular beauty. But it was augmented and rendered sublime by the mighty Alps, whose white and shining pyramids and domes towered above all, as belonging to another earth, the habitations of another race of beings...[Soon] immense glaciers approached the road; we heard the rumbling thunder of the falling avâlanche, and marked the smoke of its passage. Mont Blanc, the supreme and magnificent Mont Blanc, raised itself from the surrounding aiguilles, and its tremendous dome overlooked the valley.

Mary Shelley, Frankenstein

One might suppose Victor Frankenstein knew a thing or two about the awful and sublime. Certainly his creator did, as Mary Shelley based his journey on a similar one that she and her husband, Percy Bysshe Shelley, made in July 1816. On that occasion it was Percy, perhaps a model for Frankenstein, who was doing the marveling. "I never knew, I never imagined—what mountains were before," he wrote to a friend. "The immensity of these aerial summits excited, when they suddenly burst upon the sight, a sentiment of ecstatic wonder, not unallied to madness."

In fact, it is on the *Mer de Glace,* a famous glacier flowing off the slopes of Mont Blanc, that Frankenstein has a pivotal encounter with his monster, and where Percy seems to have had a pivotal encounter with a kind of monstrous being:

> This mass of ice has one general progress, which ceases neither day nor night; it breaks and bursts for ever: some undulations sink while others rise; it is never the same. The echo of rocks, or of the ice and snow which fall from their overhanging precipices, or roll from their aerial summits, scarcely ceases for one moment. One would think that Mont Blanc, like the god of the Stoics, was a vast animal, and that the frozen blood for ever circulated through his stony veins.
>
> PERCY BYSSHE SHELLEY,
"LETTER TO THOMAS LOVE PEACOCK, JULY 1816"

Shelley was neither the first nor the last to view Mont Blanc as more than a mere mountain. Horace-Bénédict de Saussure, who in 1786 had initiated the first expedition to reach the summit, waxed rhapsodic about its glories:

> These majestic glaciers, separated by great forests and crowned by granite crags of outstanding height cut in the form of great obelisks and

Saussure ascending Mont Blanc, 1787

mixed with snow and ice, present one of the noblest and most singular spectacles it is possible to imagine. The fresh and pure air ... the good cultivation of the soil...the pretty hamlets...give the impression of a new world, a sort of earthly paradise...

HORACE-BÉNÉDICT DE SAUSSURE, *Voyages dans les Alpes*

By the middle of the 19th century, the road up to Chamonix had become a well-traveled route. That was partly due to the unintentional efforts of Alexander von Humboldt, the great German geographer who in 1802 had attempted to climb Chimborazo, the Ecuadorian volcano then crowned the highest mountain in the world. Although turned back short of the top by altitude sickness, Humboldt had stood higher on this planet than any human being had done before him. By bringing science to the mountains, he had turned the page; thereafter mountains would be admired as stupendous marvels, and climbed.

The Andes were a world away, however; and so the first explorers of mountains had turned to the Alps. Before long there was not a wart or wen or imposthume of any note in the Alps that had not attracted its would-be climber. Yet Mont Blanc still reigned supreme—if only because, standing on its summit, you could cover with your mittened hand all the other famous peaks in the Alps. That's certainly how Leslie Stephen described it. "I profess myself to be a loyal adherent of the ancient Monarch of Mountains," the literary critic, climbing enthusiast, and father of novelist Virginia Woolf, freely admitted. "And, as such, I hold as a primary article of faith the doctrine that no Alpine summit is, as a whole, comparable in sublimity and beauty to Mont Blanc."

[W]ithin that single mass there is greater prodigality of the sublimest scenery than in whole mountain districts of inferior elevation. The sternest and most massive of cliffs, the wildest spires of distorted rock, bounding torrents of shattered ice, snowfields polished and even as a sea-shell, are combined into a whole of infinite variety and yet of artistic unity. One might wander for days, were such wandering made possible by other conditions, amongst his crowning snows, and every day would present new combinations of unsuspected grandeur.

LESLIE STEPHEN, *The Playground of Europe*

In one of Stephen's classic mountaineering essays, "Sunset on Mt. Blanc," he depicts a panorama of the Alps spread about the monarch like "a village of a hundred hovels grouped round a stupendous cathedral":

The ordinary view from Mont Blanc is not specially picturesque—and for a sufficient reason. The architect has concentrated his whole energies

OPPOSITE: *An Alpine gorge, circa 1890*

in producing a single impression. Everything has been so arranged as to intensify the sense of vast height and an illimitable horizon. In a good old guide-book I have read, on the authority (I think) of Pliny, that the highest mountain in the world is 300,000 feet above the sea; and one is apt to fancy, on ascending Mont Blanc, that the guess is not so far out....Fully to appreciate this effect requires a certain familiarity with Alpine scenery, for otherwise the effect produced is a dwarfing of the inferior mountains into pettiness instead of an exaltation of Mont Blanc into almost portentous magnificence. Grouped around you at unequal distances lie innumerable white patches, looking like the tented encampments of scattered army corps. Hold up a glove at arm's length, and it will cover the whole of such a group. On the boundless plain beneath (I say "plain," for the greatest mountain system of Europe appears to have subsided into a rather uneven plain), it is a mere spot, a trifling dent upon the huge shield on whose central boss you are placed. But you know, though at first you can hardly realise the knowledge, that insignificant discoloration represents a whole mountain district. One spot, for example, represents the clustered peaks of the Bernese Oberland; a block, as big as a pebble, is the soaring Jungfrau, the terrible mother of avalanches....One patch contains the main sources from which the Rhine descends to the German ocean, two or three more overlook the Italian plains and encircle the basin of the Po; from a more distant group flows the Danube, and from your feet the snows melt to supply the Rhone. You feel that you are in some sense looking down upon Europe from Rotterdam to Venice and from Varna to Marseilles.

And, not to be forgotten, there is the sunset:

The long series of western ranges melted into a uniform hue as the sun declined in their rear. Amidst their folds the Lake of Geneva became suddenly lighted up in a faint yellow gleam. To the east a blue gauze seemed to cover valley by valley as they sank into night and the intervening ridges rose with increasing distinctness, or rather it seemed that some fluid of exquisite delicacy of colour and substance was flooding all the lower country beneath the great mountains. Peak by peak the high snowfields caught the rosy glow and shone like signal-fires across the dim breadths of delicate twilight. Like Xerxes, we looked over the countless host sinking into rest, but with the rather different reflection, that a hundred years hence they would probably be doing much the same thing, whilst we should long have ceased to take any interest in the performance.

Leslie Stephen, The Playground of Europe

To which Mark Twain simply rolled his eyes and sent his alter ego, the protagonist of *A Tramp Abroad,* on his own journey to the top of Mont Blanc—by telescope, from a comfortable hotel terrace in Chamonix:

> I then said we would start immediately. I believe I said it calmly, though I was conscious of a shudder and of a paling cheek, in view of the nature of the exploit I was so unreflectingly engaging in. But the old daredevil spirit was upon me, and I said that as I had committed myself I would not back down; I would ascend Mont Blanc if it cost me my life. I told the man to slant his machine in the proper direction and let us be off.

Boldly the ascent by telescope proceeded. Glaciers and crevasses were crossed, crags and buttresses were skirted. Casting his eye about him on his way to the top, it seemed to Twain that "all I had ever seen before of sublimity and magnitude was small and insignificant compared to this":

> Presently we all stood together on the summit! What a view was spread out below! Away off under the northwestern horizon rolled the silent billows of the Farnese Oberland, their snowy crests glinting softly in the subdued lights of distance; in the north rose the giant form of the

Wobblehorn, draped from peak to shoulder in sable thunderclouds; beyond him, to the right, stretched the grand processional summits of the Cisalpine Cordillera, drowned in a sensuous haze; to the east loomed the colossal masses of the Yodelhorn, the Fuddlehorn and the Dinnerhorn, their cloudless summits flashing white and cold in the sun; beyond them shimmered the faint far line of the Ghauts of jubbelpore and the Aiguilles des Alleghenies; in the south towered the smoking peak of Popocatapetl and the unapproachable altitudes of the peerless Scrabblehorn; in the westsouthwest the stately range of the Himmalayas lay dreaming in a purple gloom; and thence all around the curving horizon the eye roved over a troubled sea of sun-kissed Alps, and noted, here and there, the noble proportions and soaring domes of the Bottlehorn, and the Saddlehorn, and the Shovelhorn, and the Powderhorn, all bathed in the glory of noon and mottled with softly gliding blots, the shadows flung from drifting clouds.

MARK TWAIN, *A Tramp Abroad*

It was a classic send-up of what had fast become an overworked genre. Nevertheless, in the same year—1880—that Twain published *A Tramp Abroad,* Edward Whymper, the conqueror of the Matterhorn, led the first team to reach the summit of Chimborazo, no longer the tallest mountain in the world but still nearly a mile higher than Mont Blanc. Whymper was the real thing, a climber's climber, and he saw things up there you couldn't spoof—simply because they had never been seen before:

We saw *a green sun,* and smears of colour something like verdigris green high up in the sky, which changed to equally extreme blood-reds, or to coarse brick-reds, and then passed in an instant to the colour of tarnished copper, or shining brass. No words can convey the faintest idea of the impressive appearance of these strange colours in the sky...resembling nothing to which they can properly be compared, and surpassing in vivid intensity the wildest effects of the most gorgeous sunsets.

The terms that I have employed to designate the colours which were seen are both inadequate and inexact. Their most striking features were their extraordinary strength, their extreme coarseness, and their dissimilarity from any tints or tones ever seen in the sky, even during sunrises or sunsets of exceptional brilliancy. They were unlike colors for which there are recognized terms...

EDWARD WHYMPER, *Travels Amongst the Great Andes of the Equator*

A few years later, in 1897, the soldier and mountaineer Edward Fitz Gerald led the first expedition to reach the summit of Aconcagua, the true monarch of the Andes, a half-mile higher than Chimborazo and so the highest mountain in the Western Hemisphere. And from that height, there is an unparalleled sunset:

The sun, a great ball of blood-red fire in a cloudless sky, was dipping into the waters of the Pacific. Rapidly it sank, and disappeared from view. Yet,

View of the Andes, circa 1840

as if still struggling for supremacy with the fast-approaching night, an after-glow of surpassing beauty spread over land and sea in a series of magnificent changes of colour. The mighty expanse of water from north to south, together with the sky above it, was suffused with a fiery red glow. While the red in the sky remained, the waters, through a variety of intermediate shades of colouring, turned slowly to purple and then to blue. And yet we were not in darkness, for with the sun's departure the risen moon declared itself with wondrous brightness, penetrating the thin atmosphere and flooding everything with its colder light. The effect produced by such a combination of brilliant moonlight and glorious sunset was beautiful beyond words. For during half an hour that wonderful glow rested on the horizon of the Pacific—a great red line of subdued fire suspended in mid-air, the darkness that had fallen like a pall on sea and land beneath severing its connection with the earth.

EDWARD ARTHUR FITZ GERALD, *The Highest Andes*

Yet they all came home in the end. When Edward Whymper, the climber's climber, died in 1911, he was buried in Chamonix, at the foot of Mont Blanc.

ABODE OF SNOW

FOR RUDYARD KIPLING, INDIA'S GRAND TRUNK ROAD WAS "SUCH A RIVER of life as nowhere else exists in the world." Yet the only way to escape the Wheel of Things was to leave that road and head for the Hills.

Above them, still enormously above them, earth towered away towards the snow-line, where from east to west across hundreds of miles, ruled as with a ruler, the last of the bold birches stopped. Above that, in scarps and blocks upheaved, the rocks strove to fight their heads above the white smother. Above these again, changeless since the world's beginning, but changing to every mood of sun and cloud, lay out the eternal snow.

RUDYARD KIPLING, Kim

Kipling's Kimball O'Hara was born and reared on the Indian plains. But he heads deep into the Himalaya, the "Abode of Snow," while assisting an old lama in seeking release from the "Wheel of Things" by perching "above the world, separated from delights, considering vast matters." Along the way, of course, Kim plays his part in the "Great Game," the cloak-and-dagger competition between the British and the Russians that spanned most of the 19th century and the whole breadth of Central Asia.

And in that young Kim reflected the host of soldiers, surveyors, explorers, and adventurers who were drawn to the "Roof of the World" to climb the highest mountains, hunt the *markhor* or *barasingh,* collect rare plants, consider vast matters, or just play their little role in the endless and endlessly fascinating Great Game.

> *No words can convey the faintest idea of the impressive appearance of these strange colours in the sky—seen one moment and gone the next—resembling nothing to which they can properly be compared, and surpassing in vivid intensity the wildest effects of the most gorgeous sunsets.*
>
> —EDWARD WHYMPER

Here they found mountains truly fit for the gods, with names to match: Nanga Parbat, Nanda Devi, Kanchenjunga, Annapurna. Mount Everest was one of the few exceptions—Peak XV, its original mapmaker's notation before the British named it for a mortal who happened to be a former director of the Survey of India—but then Everest was always exceptional, its untrodden snows destined to remain inviolate for some time to come. Everest, as George Mallory put it, still stood "vast in unchallenged and isolated supremacy."

Bharal, or Himalayan blue sheep, late 19th century

The high, uncharted world of the Himalaya was an undiscovered country for the Survey's mapmakers. Unnamed peaks were marked with a letter and a number; not gods' names to be sure, but sometimes grimly appropriate. There was, after all, K2, second highest mountain on Earth, a name that came to invoke the image of an icy dagger. That's certainly how Francis Younghusband saw it in 1887. The 24-year-old British Army subaltern had undertaken an epic journey from Manchuria across the Gobi Desert and into Tibet before crossing the Karakorums by the Mustagh Pass—a feat, never before accomplished by a European, that won him the Royal Geographical Society's gold medal:

...I chanced to look up rather suddenly, and a sight met my eyes which fairly staggered me. We had just turned a corner which brought into view, on the left hand, a peak of appalling height, which could be none other than K2, 28,278 feet in height, second only to Mount Everest. Viewed from this direction, it appeared to rise in an almost perfect cone, but to an inconceivable height. We were quite close under it —perhaps not a dozen miles from its summit—and here on the northern side, where it is literally clothed in glacier, there must have been from fourteen to sixteen thousand feet of solid ice. It was one of those sights which impress a man for ever, and produce a permanent effect upon the mind—a lasting sense of the greatness and grandeur of Nature's works—which he can never lose or forget.

Sir Francis Younghusband, *The Heart of a Continent*

The Roof of the World, the land of the gods, was never an easy place to visit. From the plains of India the giant ramparts of the Himalayas blocked passage. Eastern approaches were no better. Where India, China, and Burma met, some of Asia's greatest rivers—the Yangtze, the Salween, and the Mekong—roared through deep canyons in a geological jumble that the plant hunter Frank Kingdon-Ward called the "edge of the world":

[T]here is spread out before the traveller not so much a land of high mountains as a land of deep valleys; it is not this barrier beyond barrier, peak on peak which he sees in splendid array that impresses him, but these deep gloomy gorges into which none but the eagles wheeling far overhead can peer; gorges whose presence is realised rather than seen, with black shadows torn into every spur.

Frank Kingdon-Ward, *The Land of the Blue Poppy*

His colleague Reginald Farrer chose instead to call it the "eaves of the world," but he was the kind who carried a complete set of Jane Austen with him wherever he went in the field. Combing the Sino-Tibetan highlands for rare alpine plants, Farrer had ample opportunity to gaze out over that vast labyrinth of canyon and steep:

Gradually over the intervening hills unfolded high and jagged splendours of rock and ice and snow; one behind the other arose the huge ranges, surging like the frozen foam of an arising Aphrodite from the surf of lesser masses at their feet....It is like nothing I remember, at once much more episodic and much more regular than any effect in the European Alps. For these Tibetan ranges descend to China in so well-arranged a series of parallel sweeps that here, on the neck of one chain, you are looking far out across the intervening folds of hill and down and forest to another exactly opposite your own. And also, away to the left, one behind another, you see the successive links of the chain on which you yourself are standing, rising up in isolated masses, seen end-on, with the effect of a series of gigantic icebergs floating on a faintly rippled ocean that is the forested hill-country round their feet; with other masses behind it and behind it away to the left, till the eye loses itself in that archipelago of titanic ice-islands which is Eastern Tibet.

REGINALD FARRER, *On the Eaves of the World*

During the 1840s the adventurous French missionary Evariste Régis Huc, also known as Abbé Huc, struggled his way through that maze toward that crowning archipelago of ice. Crossing the upper reaches of the frozen Yangtze River, he observed "at a distance some black shapeless objects ranged in file" across the stream:

No change either in form or distinctness was apparent as we advanced, nor was it till we were quite close that we recognised in them a troop of wild oxen. There were more than fifty of them encrusted in the ice. No doubt they had tried to swim across at the moment of congelation, and had been unable to disengage themselves. Their beautiful heads, surmounted by huge horns, were still above the surface; but their bodies were held fast in the ice, which was so transparent that the position of the imprudent beasts was easily distinguishable; they looked as if still swimming, but the eagles and ravens had pecked out their eyes.

EVARISTE RÉGIS HUC, Recollections of a Journey through Tartary, Thibet, and China During the Years 1844, 1845, and 1846

While traveling with a Tibetan caravan, he encountered a man clearly freezing to death:

His face had the appearance of wax, his eyes were half open and glassy, and he had icicles suspended to his nostrils and the corners of his mouth. He just turned his eyes towards us with a terrible vacant expression; but he was quite frozen, and had been forsaken by his companions.

More than 40 men fell out this way before Lhasa was reached, and all were left behind for the circling eagles and ravens to finish.

Even at the turn of the 20th century, the American geographer Ellsworth Huntington, crossing the Karakorum Pass from India, counted one day "the remains of thirty-two horses, half eaten by wolves and ravens." On the following day it was "two hundred and twenty skeletons; and carcases of animals that must have died within the last two or three years." And a few days after that he "counted four hundred and seventy-four dead horses, not to mention numerous dismembered skeletons."

There were compensations—of sorts. At the same time that Huntington was crossing the Karakorum, the Swedish explorer Sven Hedin was departing the deserts of Central Asia and leading a small expedition through the seldom-traversed Kunlun Mountains, the northern ramparts of the Tibetan Plateau. Passing showers of clattering sleet were the only things to disturb the impression of total desolation, and only a man of Hedin's icy temperament could have found it sublime:

Although we led the lives of dogs in this country, which was as desolate as the moon is supposed to be, yet we reaped more than an equivalent reward in the discoveries and observations which we made from day to day. It was a delicious feeling, to know that we were the first human beings to tread those mountains, where there existed no path, where there never had been a path, and where there was not a footprint visible, except those made by the hoof of yak, antelope, or kulan. It was a no man's land; rivers, lakes, and mountains were all nameless; their shores, banks, and snow-fields had never been seen by any traveller's eyes but mine; they were mine own kingdom of a day. It was delightful—it was a great thing, to cruise, like a vessel that leaves no track behind her, amongst those upswellings of the world's "high sea," to make our way over those gigantic mountain waves. Only the waves which roll across the Tibetan highlands are petrified; and all distances and dimensions are cast on such a gigantic scale, that you may march for weeks at a time and still find the situation unchanged—still find yourself the centre of a universe of mountains....I felt like an atom of dust in the midst of the illimitable wastes, and fancied I could hear the swish of the planet as it rolled without rest, without cessation, along its everlasting orbit.

SVEN HEDIN, *Central Asia and Tibet*

Others chose more heartwarming consolations. In 1895, Col. Thomas Holdich returned to the high sparse world of the Pamirs, to Afghanistan's Wakhan Corridor, a buffer zone between British India and the Russian Empire that he had surveyed a decade before. Now a member of the Russo-British Pamir Boundary Commission, he was filling in the gaps in the exact place that Marco Polo once called "the highest place in the world":

The plain is called PAMIER, and you ride across it for twelve days together, finding nothing but a desert without habitations or any green thing, so that travellers are obliged to carry with them whatever they have need of. The region is so lofty and cold that you do not even see any birds flying. And I must notice also that because of this great cold, fire does not burn so brightly, nor give out so much heat as usual, nor does it cook food so effectually.

MARCO POLO, *The Travels of Marco Polo*

There the great Venetian was wrong. The Boundary Commission, having worked four months running transects across the steppes and glaciers, finished its work earlier than expected. Since there was no fuel in those tree-less wastes, they had packed in an enormous amount of firewood. On their last night in the field, with the September frosts descending, they decided to have a bonfire. Being proper officers, they issued invitations—for a dance:

Never, even in the viceregal halls of Simla, have I seen a dance go so well. The night was intensely cold, but clear, and the witchery of moonlight was over it all. It glinted off the ice coating of the lake, and sparkled in little scintillating shafts on the slopes of the snowdrifts that still lay about us. In the midst was the roaring, blazing bonfire, such a bonfire as the Pamirs had never seen before, and never will see again; and it shot its red glare through the camp where the akois stood around, making black shadows of the mixed multitude of great hairy camels who sat stolidly blinking in the background.

I felt like an atom of dust in the midst of the illimitable wastes, and fancied I could hear the swish of the planet as it rolled without rest, without cessation, along its everlasting orbit.

—SVEN HEDIN

Round about the fire either sat, or danced, the company, and they danced with a will; Cossacks and Kirghiz, men of Hunza and Kashmir,

Russians, English, French (there was one Frenchman, who was responsible for the grammar of the protocols) and Afghans—they were all well in it, and the music was as wild as the dance. "Orpheus" was the leader of the band. He played a pipe, the same pipe with which he usually enticed the sheep along the mountain paths as he drifted slowly ahead of them.... A Cossack supported him with a concertina, and there was a kerosine tin drum in addition. Nothing was wanting—certainly not refreshments. The grog was brewed in a vast Russian cauldron by my native cook and a Cossack orderly, and they warmed to their work as the night sped on.

Next morning we parted company, feeling assured that the Pamirs would remember us. The Russians packed their baggage on camels and trekked eastward, following the course of the Aksu. We stirred up our Kashmir ponies, and disappeared in the offing of the long plain to westward, and the Pamir wilderness was again left to the eternal silences and blackened fragments of the still smoking bonfire.

COL. SIR T. H. HOLDICH, *The Indian Borderland: 1880-1900*

Chinese takin, circa 1860-80

And sometimes the consolations consisted, lama-like, of considering vast matters. By the time he was 30 years old, Francis Younghusband was well on the way to embracing the mysticism that marked his later years. Yet whenever he recalled his youthful adventures in Central Asia, he always saw them framed by mountains:

> I see before me now the Tian-shan—the "Heavenly Mountains"—as I saw them from the Gobi Desert, their white summits forming part of heaven itself, and their base rooted in the broad bosom of the desert. I recall to my mind the sight of the Pamir Mountains, the outer wall of the "Roof of the World," viewed from the plains of Turkestan, and rising from them like one vast rampart. I think of the Mustagh—the "Ice Mountains"—rising tier upon tier before me, and the great peak K2, the second highest mountain in the world, soaring above all the rest. I remember the Nanga Parbat—the "Naked Mountain"—seen across the lovely vale of Kashmir, or, again, from the banks of the river Indus, above which it rises for twenty-three thousand feet in one continuous slope. All these scenes I recall, and many others with them—the Rakapushi Peak in Hunza, and the Tirich Mir in Chitral, each of them twenty-five thousand feet above sea-level; and I think of the first sight I ever had of high snow-mountains, when from the Juras I looked across to the Mont Blanc range, and could not at first believe that the snowy summits were not clouds, so high above this earth did they appear...
>
> SIR FRANCIS YOUNGHUSBAND, *The Heart of a Continent*

PLEASINGLY BEAUTIFUL, SUBLIMELY GRAND

DASHING AND ROARING AND SEETHING, THE RIVER CLYDE IN SCOTLAND tumbles through a wooded glen in a series of falls that in August 1803 had attracted the visiting English poet Samuel Taylor Coleridge. Casting about for the precise word to describe the spectacle—and the likely choices were "picturesque" (perhaps too dainty), "beautiful" (perhaps too lovely), and "sublime" (perhaps too grand)—he finally settled on "majestic":

> While I was still contemplating the scene, a gentleman and a lady came up, neither of whose faces bore much of the stamp of superior intelligence, and the first words the gentleman uttered were "It is very majestic." I was pleased to find such a confirmation of my opinion, and I complimented the spectator upon the choice of his epithet, saying that he had used the best word that could have been selected from our language. "Yes, sir," replied the gentleman, "I say it is very majestic: it is sublime, it is beautiful, it is grand, it is picturesque."—"Ay (added the lady), it is the prettiest thing I ever saw." I own that I was not a little disconcerted.
>
> SAMUEL TAYLOR COLERIDGE, *Collected Works*

That was not just a poet's partiality; accuracy of statement was an explorer's prejudice as well. In August 1750, two decades before Coleridge was even born, the Swedish botanist Peter Kalm was approaching what was reputed to be the greatest waterfall in the world. He was headed for Niagara because he suspected that the description written in 1697 by a French priest, Father Louis Hennepin, was a lie. The Frenchman had written that the spectacle was 600 feet high and that the waters tumbled "with an impetuosity that can be imagined in so high a fall, so prodigious, for its horrible mass of water. There are formed those thunders, those roarings, those fearful bounds and seethings, with that perpetual cloud rising above the cedars and spruces..."

Because he professed to be "not fond of the *Marvellous*," preferring to "see things as they are, and so to relate them," Kalm would provide an "exact description" of Niagara Falls. In the event, he duly corrected the good father—the water falls only about 170 feet—but even the hardened

Kalm, who had just been visiting Iroquois villages surrounded by palisades of human skulls, was soon swept away by the thundering marvel:

> When all this water comes to the very Fall, it throws itself down perpendicular! It is beyond all belief the surprise when you see this! I cannot with words express how amazing it is! You cannot see it without being quite terrified—to behold so vast a quantity of water falling headlong from a surprising height!
>
> PETER KALM, *The Gentleman's Quarterly*

English was not the Swede's primary language, but his description was accurate enough by anybody's standards:

> One could not gaze and contemplate without feelings of wonder and astonishment. The water seemed to flow gently and well-nigh lazily over the cliff at first; but the farther down it went the greater the speed... In its descent, near the bottom, the water strikes the rock in some places and there it foams and froths and roars in gigantic leaps, so that it gives the impression of a continuous firing of cannon, with a heavy, persistent and hastily appearing mist dashing forth.
>
> PETER KALM, *Travels in North America*

A century later, in November 1855, David Livingstone was being ferried down the Zambezi River in Africa when, still five miles upstream, he began hearing the roar and seeing the mist marking the presence of Mosioa-tunya, the "Smoke that Thunders." Skilled native canoe men brought him to an island in the middle of the stream, perched seemingly on the very edge of an abyss. "I believe that no one could perceive where the vast body of the water went. It seemed to lose itself in the earth, the opposite lip of the fissure into which it disappeared being only eighty feet distant":

At least I did not comprehend it till, creeping in awe to the verge, I peered down into a great rent which had been made from bank to bank, and saw that a stream a thousand yards broad leaped down a hundred feet, and then became suddenly compressed into a space of fifteen or twenty yards...In looking down into the fissure from the right side of the island, one sees nothing but a dense white cloud, which, at the time we visited the spot, had two bright rainbows on it. From this cloud rushed up a great jet of vapour exactly like steam, and it mounted two or three hundred feet high...On the left side the mass of vapour leaps quite clear of the rock, and forms a white unbroken fleece all the way down to the bottom. Its whiteness gives the idea of snow. As it breaks into (if I may use the term) pieces of water, all rushing in the same direction, each gives off several rays of foam, exactly as bits of steel when burnt in oxygen gas give off rays of sparks. The snow-white sheet seems like myriads of small comets rushing on in one direction, each of which leaves behind its nucleus rays of foam...

DAVID LIVINGSTONE, *Missionary Travels and Researches in Southern Africa*

Ever the proper 19th-century British explorer, Livingstone named Victoria Falls after his sovereign. Face to face with a stupendous marvel, the sober Scotsman had kept his emotions in check and his descriptions accurate but enthralling. Yet he made one mistake: Though born just downstream from the falls of the River Clyde, the great explorer described Victoria Falls, surely the most sublime waterfall in the world, as "this beautiful sight." Coleridge would have winced.

And so, perhaps, might have Meriwether Lewis, despite his rather idiosyncratic spelling. Less than two years after Coleridge's visit to the Falls of the Clyde, Lewis, his co-commander, William Clark, and the Corps of Discovery were exploring the uncharted reaches of the American West, advancing, in the early summer of 1805, into the very lee of the Rocky

OPPOSITE: *Niagara Falls, 1835*

Mountains. Climbing a hill on the afternoon of June 13, Lewis suddenly beheld the great falls of the Missouri River:

I hurryed down the hill which was about 200 feet high and difficult of access, to gaze on this sublimely grand spectacle. I took my position on the top of some rocks about 20 feet high opposite the center of the falls. This chain of rocks appear once to have formed a part of those over which the waters tumbled, but in the course of time has been seperated from it to the distance of 150 yards lying prarrallel to it and a butment against which the water after falling over the precipice beats with great fury....Immediately at the cascade the river is about 300 yds. wide; about ninty or a hundred yards of this next the lard. bluff is a smoth even sheet of water falling over a precipice of at least eighty feet. The remaining part of about 200 yards on my right formes the grandest sight I ever beheld...

I hurryed down the hill...to gaze on this sublimely grand spectacle....
From the reflection of the sun on the spray or mist...there is a beautifull rainbow produced which adds not a little to the beauty of this majestically grand senery.
—MERIWETHER LEWIS

In short the rocks seem to be most happily fixed to present a sheet of the whitest beaten froath for 200 yards in length and about 80 feet perpendicular. The water after decending strikes against the butment before mentioned or that on which I stand and seems to reverberate and being met by the more impetuous courant they roll and swell into half formed billows of great hight which rise and again disappear in an instant....

From the reflection of the sun on the spray or mist which arrises from these falls there is a beatifull rainbow produced which adds not a little to the beauty of this majestically grand senery.

MERIWETHER LEWIS, *The Journals of Lewis and Clark*

Yet, as he confided to his journal, the explorer was not happy with the imprecision of his own language:

> After weighting this imperfect description I again viewed the Falls and was so much disgusted with the imperfect idea which it conveyed of the scene that I determined to draw my pen across it and begin agin, but then reflected that I could not perhaps succeed better than pening the first impressions of the mind. I wished for the pencil of Salvator Rosa, a Titian, or the pen of Thomson that I might be enabled to give to the enlightened world some just idea of this truly magnificent and sublimely grand object, which has from the commencement of time been concealed from the view of civilized man. But this was fruitless and vain.

Next day Lewis explored farther upriver. There he discovered a second waterfall so breathtaking that he was momentarily confused over which spectacle impressed him more. Yet even beside a crackling campfire deep in the wilderness he could keep his categories straight:

> Nor could I for some time determine on which of those two great cataracts to bestoe the palm, on this or that when I had discovered yesterday; at length I determined between these two rivals for glory that this was pleasingly beautifull, while the other was sublimely grand.

Subterranean Cathedrals

In the late summer of 1772, the naturalist Joseph Banks undertook a voyage to Iceland, stopping along the way in Scotland's Inner Hebrides. Among those storm-lashed isles, he was told, was one he really ought to see. Staffa might be a small island, but it was a great marvel.

Banks had accompanied Captain Cook on his first circumnavigation of the globe, and been one of the first Europeans ever to set foot on the continent of Australia. But what he saw rearing out of the sea as he was rowed across the bay he could only describe as a "scene of magnificence which exceeded our expectations, though formed, as we thought, upon the most sanguine foundations." It looked like a palace from a fairy story, a palace built by giants:

> Compared to this what are the cathedrals or the palaces built by men! mere models or playthings, imitations as diminutive as his works will always be when compared to those of nature. Where is now the boast of the architect! regularity the only part in which he fancied himself to exceed his mistress, Nature, is here found in her possession, and here it has been for ages undescribed.
>
> Sir Joseph Banks, in Thomas Pennant's
A Tour in Scotland and Voyage to the Hebrides

What's more, proceeding along the shore, gazing at the forest of hexagonal basalt pillars upholding the island, Banks arrived at the mouth of a cave, "the most magnificent, I suppose, that has ever been described by travellers."

And that is the earliest mention of "Fingal's Cave," as Banks named it, honoring a mythological Celtic hero. But the effort to describe it would soon attract the creative energies of a parade of poets, painters, engravers, and musicians: Sir Walter Scott, J. M. W. Turner, Robert Louis Stevenson, Jules Verne, and Felix Mendelssohn, who was inspired to compose an overture that was long a standard in the symphonic repertory. One of the earliest such visitors was the poet John Keats, who in July 1818 tried to describe for his brother "this cathedral of the sea":

I am puzzled how to give yon an Idea of Staffa. It can only be represented by a first-rate drawing. One may compare the surface of the Island to a roof—this roof is supported by grand pillars of basalt standing together as thick as honeycombs. The finest thing is Fingal's cave—it is entirely a hollowing out of Basalt Pillars. Suppose now the Giants who rebelled against Jove had taken a whole Mass of black Columns and bound them together like bunches of matches—and then with immense axes had made a cavern in the body of these columns—Of course the roof and floor must be composed of the broken ends of the Columns—such is Fingal's cave, except that the Sea has done the work of excavations, and is continually dashing there—so that we walk along the sides of the cave on the pillars which are left as if for convenient stairs. The roof is arched somewhat gothic-wise, and the length of some of the entire side-pillars is 50 feet. About the island you might seat an army of Men each on a pillar….For solemnity and grandeur it far surpasses the finest Cathedral….But it is impossible to describe it.

JOHN KEATS, *The Letters of John Keats*

Fingal's Cave, Staffa, circa 1875

There already was a mode of description available, of course, for caves had joined mountains and waterfalls as fit subjects for the sublime. When E. F. Lee was exploring Kentucky's labyrinthine Mammoth Cave, he had recourse to it:

The Temple is an immense vault covering an area of two acres, and covered by a single dome of solid rock, one hundred and twenty feet high. It excels in size the Cave of Staffa; and rivals the celebrated vault in the Grotto of Antiparos [a cave in Greece], which is said to be the largest in the world. In passing through from one end to the other, the dome appears to follow like the sky in passing from place to place on the earth. In the middle of the dome there is a large mound of rocks rising on one side nearly to the top, very steep and forming what is called the Mountain. When first I ascended this mound from the cave below, I was struck with a feeling of awe more deep and intense, than any thing that I had ever before experienced....I knew that I was beneath the earth, and that this space, however large it might be, was actually bounded by solid walls....Every one has heard of the dome of the Mosque of St. Sophia, of St. Peter's and St. Paul's; they are never spoken of but in terms of admiration, as the

Rambling in Mammoth Cave, 1876.

chief works of architecture, and among the noblest and most stupendous examples of what man can do when aided by science; and yet when compared with the dome of this Temple, they sink into comparative insignificance. Such is the surpassing grandeur of Nature's works.

E. F. LEE, IN ALEXANDER CLARK BULLITT,
Rambles in the Mammoth Cave in the Year 1844

The sublime might be an appropriate response to such innately terrific, even terrifying, places, but as the 19th century progressed, sublime descriptions gave way to more picturesque, if not downright whimsical, ones. The subterranean cathedrals began resembling a cross between the Inferno and Alice in Wonderland, as in the fabulous caves at Adelsberg, or Postojna, in what was then Austria and is now Slovenia:

[E]verywhere the most wonderful varieties of stalactites and crystals met our admiring view. At one time we saw the guides lighting up some distant gallery far above our heads, which had all the appearance of verandahs adorned with Gothic tracery; at another, we came into what seemed the long-drawn isles of a Gothic cathedral, brilliantly illuminated. The whimsical variety of forms surpasses all the powers of description. Here was a butcher's shop, which seemed to be hung with joints of meat; and there, a throne with a magnificent canopy. There was the appearance of a statue with a bearded head, so perfect that you could have thought it the work of a sculptor; and further on, toward the end of our walk, the figure of a warrior with a helmet and coat-of-mail, and his arms crossed, of the illusion of which, with all my efforts, I could not possibly divest my mind....It is impossible for me to describe minutely all the wonderful varieties; the "Fountains," seeming, as they fall, to be frozen into stone; the "Graves," with weeping willows waving over them; the "Picture," the "Cannon," the "Pulpit," the "Sausage-maker's shop," and the "Prisons." I must not omit mentioning one part, which, though less grand than many others, is extremely curious. The *stalactites* have here formed themselves like folds of linen, and are so thin as to be transparent. Some are like shirt-ruffles, having a hem, and looking as if they were embroidered; and there is one, called the "Curtain," which hangs exactly in natural folds like a white and pendent sheet. Everywhere you hear the dripping as of a continual shower, showing that the mighty work is still going on, though the several stages of its progress are imperceptible.

Robert Sears, *The Wonders of the World*

Wherever in the world such show caves might be found, the tide of Western imagination inevitably seeped into them. Whatever the Australian Aborigines had made of the Jenolan Caves in the Blue Mountains west of Sydney, it surely bore little resemblance to this fantasia:

If an unfortunate wight were to trip, he might fall a distance of about 70 feet, and be shot without ceremony into the Devil's Coach-house. One remarkable stalagmite in the vicinity of this infernal shaft is shaped like a hat, and another is like a gigantic mushroom....Pointing upward is the gauntleted hand and forearm of a warrior of the olden time. There are representations of bewigged legal luminaries and bearded sages like Old Father Christmas or Santa Claus. Some of the columns which support the archway have tier upon tier of stalactites, drooping so as to counterfeit water flowing from a fountain, alternating with stalactite formation like boughs of weeping willow. One prominent stalagmite is like the back of a newly-shorn sheep, with shear-marks in the wool. On the western side is a figure like that of an orator in the act of exhortation. The forehead is bald, long white locks are flowing on to the shoulders, one arm is upraised, and the pose gives an idea of earnestness and force. In front, just below the bust, is a reading desk of stone, the outer edge of which is fringed with stalactites.

Samuel Cooke,
The Jenolan Caves: An Excursion in Australian Wonderland

If the caves weren't widely known, however, that overexuberant imagination might not find them. One such place, it seems, was the island of Qeshm, nestled against the southern coast of Iran at the apex of the Persian Gulf. Though sun blasted at the surface, Qeshm held hidden treasures underground, where for untold generations the abundant salt deposits had been mined. Col. Thomas Holdich and a fellow British officer heard about these caves and became the first Europeans, as far as they were aware, to visit them:

The stalactites have here formed themselves like folds of linen, and are so thin as to be transparent. Some are like shirt-ruffles, having a hem, and looking as if they were embroidered; and there is one, called the "Curtain," which hangs exactly in natural folds like a white and pendent sheet.

—ROBERT SEARS

In and about the irregularities of this marvellous excavation, where the salt had been split out, and small caves had been formed within the central dome, were wondrous side chapels filled in with salt tracery—the delicate lace-work which is formed by deliquescent salt in the moist steamy air of the Gulf in summer. I have looked down on a bamboo forest weighted and interlaced with snow; and I have seen the weird beauty of acres of wind-dried vegetation picked out with the delicate trinketry of frost, and gilt by the morning sun; but the smooth rounded grace of twisted salt pillars, and the fall of a salt lace curtain over folds of salt strata, is matchless amongst Nature's arts and handicrafts.

Wandering around in mute admiration, Holdich and his friend squeezed into an interior gallery, where they lit the equivalent of a ship's flare to see about them. In telling of what he then saw, there is so little of figurative abandon in Holdich's description that one is tempted to say that it was not a subterranean cathedral, purged of its pagan elements, that he beheld, but rather a kind of infernal mosque:

> With a splutter and fizz the ship's signal glared out into broad illumination. It lit up the gallery, and revealed a scene of such fantastic weirdness as no nightmare bred in the overworked brain of a master of pantomime could well have outmatched. We were in a long narrow disused salt gallery. Through it, here and there, moisture had either permeated, or else the humid Gulf atmosphere had first melted the salt and then twisted it into grotesque shapes and patterns, as it dripped and dropped slowly from the roof. A forest of twisted pillars covered with smooth round bosses of clear white salt efflorescence barred our way in an interminable crowd; the sides of the gallery were salt cascades, falling draperies of salt lace; the floor was frozen into a salt slide. In and out amongst the twisted and tortuous shafts of this crypt we made our way, whilst the intense blue glare of the light shimmered and broke into millions of quaint reflections. It was a dancing maze of blue lights, and jerking broken shadows; quite a typical home for all the goblins of Persia....
>
> COL. SIR T. H. HOLDICH, *The Indian Borderland: 1880-1900*

THE SUBLIME HARP

THOMAS JEFFERSON WAS UNDERSTANDABLY PROUD OF HIS NATIVE STATE. For one thing, tucked in the folds of the great Valley of Virginia, on a chunk of real estate he just happened to own, might be found what he called the "most sublime of Nature's works."

He was not alone in that opinion. Many visitors throughout the 18th and 19th centuries agreed that the Natural Bridge, a soaring limestone arch spanning a deep gorge, was worth the journey to see. A steady stream of artists and painters and poets arrived to marvel at the far-famed sight, ranked alongside Niagara as heading the list of America's most remarkable features. One taciturn observer described it simply as "God's greatest miracle in stone." Another more florid admirer found it impossible "to imagine anything more magnificently grand than this portentous and wondrous monument—of the gradual and insidious disintegrating power and might, in the long course of ages, of a stream of water!"

John Wesley Powell would have politely disagreed.

For three stomach-churning months in 1869 Powell and six companions had been the first men ever to run the 900-mile length of the roaring Colorado River. As they steered from one rapid to another, as they shot through the heart of soaring rocks and were driven between walls a mile high, he had glimpsed something inconceivably vaster, more magnificently grand, than the Natural Bridge. And having emerged on the other side, Powell, a geologist, began studying the marvel that could only be called the Grand Canyon. Having seen it from below, he now saw it from above. He examined its layered complexities; he mused on the processes that led to its formation. And when he finally came to describe it, what poured forth resembled the majestic finale to some great symphony, the grand all-encompassing crescendo of the sublime:

The Grand Canyon of the Colorado is a canyon composed of many canyons. It is a composite of thousands, of tens of thousands, of gorges. In like manner, each wall of the canyon is a composite structure, a wall composed of many walls, but never a repetition. Every one of these almost innumerable gorges is a world of beauty in itself. In the Grand Canyon there are thousands of gorges like that below Niagara Falls, and there are a thousand Yosemites. Yet all these canyons unite to form one grand canyon, the most sublime spectacle on the earth. Pluck up Mt. Washington by the roots to the level of the sea and drop it headfirst into the Grand

Canyon, and the dam will not force its waters over the walls. Pluck up the Blue Ridge and hurl it into the Grand Canyon, and it will not fill it.

The carving of the Grand Canyon is the work of rains and rivers. The vast labyrinth of canyon by which the plateau region drained by the Colorado is dissected is also the work of waters. Every river has excavated its own gorge and every creek has excavated its gorge. When a shower comes in this land, the rills carve canyons—but a little at each storm; and though storms are far apart and the heavens above are cloudless for most of the days of the year, still, years are plenty in the ages, and an intermittent rill called to life by a shower can do much in centuries of centuries....

Consider a rock 200,000 square miles in extent and more than a mile in thickness, against which the clouds have hurled their storms and beat it into sands and the rills have carried the sands into the creeks and the creeks have carried them into the rivers and the Colorado has carried them into the sea. We think of the mountains as forming clouds about their brows, but the clouds have formed the mountains. Great continental blocks are upheaved from beneath the sea by internal geologic forces that fashion the earth. Then the wandering clouds, the tempest-bearing clouds, the rainbow-decked clouds, with mighty power and with wonderful skill, carve out valleys and canyons and fashion hills and cliffs and mountains. The clouds are the artists sublime.

In winter some of the characteristics of the Grand Canyon are emphasized. The black gneiss below, the variegated quartzite, and the green or alcove sandstone form the foundation for the mighty red wall. The banded sandstone entablature is crowned by the tower limestone. In winter this is covered with snow. Seen from below, these changing elements seem to graduate into the heavens, and no plane of demarcation between wall and blue firmament can be seen. The heavens constitute a portion of the facade and mount into a vast dome from wall to

OPPOSITE: *John Wesley Powell's expedition in the Grand Canyon, 1869*

wall, spanning the Grand Canyon with empyrean blue. So the earth and the heavens are blended in one vast structure....

The wonders of the Grand Canyon cannot be adequately represented in symbols of speech, nor by speech itself. The resources of the graphic art are taxed beyond their powers in attempting to portray its features. Language and illustration combined must fail. The elements that unite to make the Grand Canyon the most sublime spectacle in nature are multifarious and exceedingly diverse. The Cyclopean forms which result from the sculpture of tempests through ages too long for man to compute, are wrought into endless details, to describe which would be a task equal in magnitude to that of describing the stars of the heavens or the multitudinous beauties of the forest with its traceries of foliage presented by oak and pine and poplar, by beech and linden and hawthorn, by tulip and lily and rose, by fern and moss and lichen. Besides the elements of form, there are elements of color, for here the colors of the heavens are rivaled by the colors of the rocks.

> *The carving of the Grand Canyon is the work of rains and rivers. The vast labyrinth of canyon by which the plateau region drained by the Colorado is dissected is also the work of waters. Every river has excavated its own gorge and every creek has excavated its gorge. When a shower comes in this land, the rills carve canyons.*
>
> —JOHN WESLEY POWELL

The rainbow is not more replete with hues. But form and color do not exhaust all the divine qualities of the Grand Canyon. It is the land of music. The river thunders in perpetual roar, swelling in floods of music when the storm gods play upon the rocks and fading away in soft and low murmurs when the infinite blue of heaven is unveiled. With the melody of the great tide rising and falling, swelling and vanishing forever, other melodies are heard in the gorges of the lateral canyons, while the waters plunge in the rapids among the rocks or leap in great cataracts. Thus the Grand Canyon is a land of song. Mountains of music swell in the rivers, hills of music billow in the creeks, and meadows of music murmur in the rills that ripple over the rocks. Altogether it is a symphony of multitudinous melodies. All this is the music of waters. The adamant foundations of the earth have been wrought into a sublime harp, upon which the clouds of the heavens play with mighty tempests or with gentle showers.

The glories and the beauties of form, color, and sound unite in the Grand Canyon—forms unrivaled even by the mountains, colors that vie with sunsets, and sounds that span the diapason from tempest to tinkling raindrop, from cataract to bubbling fountain. But more: it is a vast district of country. Were it a valley plain it would make a state. It can be seen only in parts from hour to hour and from day to day and from week to week and from month to month. A year scarcely suffices to see it all. It has infinite variety, and no part is ever duplicated. Its colors, though many and complex at any instant, change with the ascending and declining sun; lights and shadows appear and vanish with the passing clouds, and the changing seasons mark their passage in changing colors. You cannot see the Grand Canyon in one view, as if it were a changeless spectacle from which a curtain might be lifted, but to see it you have to toil from month to month through its labyrinths. It is a region more difficult to traverse than the Alps or the Himalayas, but if strength and courage are sufficient for the task, by a year's toil a concept of sublimity can be obtained never again to be equaled on the hither side of Paradise.

JOHN WESLEY POWELL, *The Canyons of the Colorado*

THE MYSTIC CIRCLES
THE POLES

*"Voyages of discovery have looked with deeper and deeper longings
toward the mystic circles of the polar regions."*
—MATTHEW FONTAINE MAURY

FEW EXPLORERS, HAVING SET FOOT UPON STRANGE NEW LANDS, had been met by quite such emissaries as James Murray was in 1907, when he arrived in Antarctica, perhaps the strangest land of all:

Emperors are very ceremonious in meeting other Emperors or men or dogs. They come up to a party of strangers in a straggling procession, some big important aldermanic fellow leading. At a respectful distance from the man or dog they halt, the old male waddles close up and bows gravely till his beak is almost touching his breast. Keeping his head bowed he makes a long speech, in a muttering manner, short sounds following in groups of four or five. Having finished the speech the head is still kept bowed a few seconds for politeness' sake, then it is raised and he describes with his bill as large a circle as the joints of his neck will allow, looking in your face at last to see if you have understood. If you have not comprehended, as is usually the case, he tries again. He is very patient with your

OPPOSITE: *Amundsen sets his sights on the South Pole, 1911*

stupidity, and feels sure that he will get it into your dull brain if he keeps at it long enough. By this time his followers are getting impatient. They are sure he is making a mess of it. Another male will waddle forward with dignity, elbow the first aside as if to say, "I'll show you how it ought to be done," and go through the whole business again. Their most solemn ceremonies were used towards the dogs, and three old fellows have been seen calmly bowing and speaking simultaneously to a dog, which for its part was yelping and straining at its chain in the effort to get at them.

JAMES MURRAY, IN ERNEST SHACKLETON, *The Heart of the Antarctic*

Murray, a 42-year-old Scottish biologist, had every right to marvel at his new friends. For they were as new to him as he was to them. Emperor penguins had been almost completely unknown, except for a few isolated specimens, until 1902, when a breeding colony was first discovered on Antarctica's Ross Ice Shelf.

Four centuries of determined effort lay behind that encounter. Ever since the dawn of the age of exploration, men had been probing the once inaccessible, once impenetrable zones surrounding the Poles, suspecting a secret behind the shielding icebergs and volcanoes, the ramparts of fire and ice:

Researches have been carried on from the bottom of the deepest pit to the top of the highest mountain, but these have not satisfied. Voyages of discovery, with their fascinations and their charms, have led many a noble champion both into the torrid and frigid zones; and notwithstanding the hardships, sufferings, and disasters to which many northern parties have found themselves exposed, seafaring men, as science has advanced, have looked with deeper and deeper longings toward the mystic circles of the polar regions. There icebergs are framed and glaciers launched. There the tides have their cradle, the whales their nursery. There the winds complete their circuits, and the currents of the sea their round in the wonderful system of oceanic circulation. There the Aurora Borealis is lighted up and the trembling needle brought to rest; and there too, in the mazes of that mystic circle, terrestrial forces of occult power and of vast influence upon the well-being of man are continually at play. Within the arctic circle is the pole of the winds and the poles of the cold, the pole of the earth and of the magnet. It is a circle of mysteries; and the desire to enter it, to explore its untrodden wastes and secret chambers, and to study its physical aspects, has grown into a longing. Noble daring has made Arctic ice and waters classic ground. It is no feverish excitement nor vain ambition that leads man there. It is a higher feeling, a holier motive—a desire to look into the works of creation, to comprehend the economy of our planet, and to grow wiser and better by the knowledge.

MATTHEW FONTAINE MAURY, *The Physical Geography of the Sea*

Quite likely both vain ambition and noble daring propelled men like Robert Falcon Scott to seek the ends of the Earth. Edwardian Britain's ideal of the dauntless polar explorer, Scott was the most recent in a long line that had included such names as Cabot, Hudson, Parry, Ross, and Franklin. Science was important to Scott, perhaps more so than to his predecessors, but when his British Antarctic Expedition arrived in Antarctica in 1911, the attainment of the South Pole was uppermost in his mind. The optimistic spirit of adventure seemed to be in the very air:

Such weather in such a place comes nearer to satisfying my ideal of perfection than any condition I have ever experienced. The warm glow of the sun with the keen invigorating cold of the air forms a combination which is inexpressibly health-giving and satisfying to me, whilst the golden light on this wonderful scene of mountain and ice satisfies every claim of scenic magnificence. No words of mine can convey the impressiveness of the wonderful panorama displayed to our eyes…

ROBERT FALCON SCOTT, *Scott's Last Expedition*

Scott might have been looking toward Discovery and Morning, those peaks in the Western Range he had named after the two ships that had served him so well on his first Antarctic expedition. Yet behind his camp still loomed the volcanoes Erebus and Terror, named for vessels from which Sir James Ross had originally charted that small slice of an immense and still unknown coastline. They were also the two vessels that Sir John Franklin, in the 1840s, would take into the icy mazes of the Arctic, seeking the Northwest Passage—and in those mazes they would be

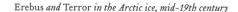

Erebus *and* Terror *in the Arctic ice, mid-19th century*

lost, Franklin and all of his men dying of disease, starvation, or exposure. Scott, too, would fall under that shadow of doom. "Great God! this is an awful place," he would write from the South Pole, shortly before he and his companions starved to death attempting to return.

Even the final "conquest" of the Poles would prove baffling. "The Pole at last. The prize of three centuries, my dream and goal for twenty years. Mine at last!" Robert E. Peary scrawled in April 1909, his unconvincing declaration that he of all his fellow contenders had finally achieved what many had once thought impossible, the attainment of the North Pole. Yet many people then and still today believe that he struck wide or fell short, and that he knew it. Even so, after beating Scott to the South Pole in 1911—an unquestioned and justly celebrated achievement—Roald Amundsen seemed, if anything, to be disappointed:

> The goal was reached, the journey ended. I cannot say—though I know it would sound much more effective—that the object of my life was attained. That would be romancing rather too barefacedly. I had better be honest and admit straight out that I have never known any man to be placed in such a diametrically opposite position to the goal of his desires as I was at that moment. The regions around the North Pole—well, yes, the North Pole itself—had attracted me from childhood, and here I was at the South Pole. Can anything more topsy-turvy be imagined?
> ROALD AMUNDSEN, *The South Pole*

The mystic circles would continually confound, and often destroy, those who sought to reveal their secrets. In 1914, the ship *Karluk* would be crushed in the Arctic ice, and biologist Murray would perish as a result. His friend the emperor penguin—"the very picture of a successful, self-satisfied, happy, unsuspicious countryman, gravely bowing like a Chinaman before a yelping dog"—perhaps fared no better. "I do not believe anybody on Earth has a worse time than an Emperor Penguin," wrote Apsley Cherry-Garrard, and he should know, for when a member of Scott's final expedition, he had survived the nightmarish midwinter journey—134 miles, on foot, the temperatures dipping to minus 60, the gales howling, the crevasses yawning, the darkness absolute—to the icy breeding grounds where the penguins huddled, just to collect an egg for science. His two companions would subsequently accompany Scott to the South Pole and die alongside him in the tent that proved their common shroud. "Cherry," his health broken, his teeth fractured by chattering, would live nearly a half century longer, writing what is often deemed the finest—and certainly the most moving—account of Polar exploration, *The Worst Journey in the World,* expiating an unwarranted sense of guilt that he should have done more to save his friends.

In this silent nature no events ever happen; all is shrouded in darkness; there is nothing in view save the twinkling stars, immeasurably far away in the freezing night, and the flickering sheen of the aurora borealis.

—FRIDTJOF NANSEN

Nevertheless, "years come and go unnoticed in this world of ice," wrote Amundsen's countryman, the Norwegian explorer Fridtjof Nansen. Having built what was then the sturdiest wooden vessel afloat, the *Fram,* Nansen in 1893 deliberately moored her in the Arctic icepack, hoping the drift would carry him over the North Pole. It carried him around rather than over, but it was still the closest human beings had come to that fabled spot until Peary's determined efforts a decade later. Still, it was a curiously passive way of actively exploring, and it afforded the reflective Nansen, deep one midwinter night, to consider just what kind of world it was that he had just entered:

In this silent nature no events ever happen; all is shrouded in darkness; there is nothing in view save the twinkling stars, immeasurably far away in the freezing night, and the flickering sheen of the aurora borealis. I can just discern close by the vague outline of the *Fram,* dimly standing out in the desolate gloom, with her rigging showing dark against the host of stars. Like an infinitesimal speck, the vessel seems lost amidst the boundless expanse of this realm of death. Nevertheless, under her deck there is a snug and cherished home for thirteen men undaunted by the majesty of this realm. In there, life is freely pulsating, while far away outside in the night there is nothing save death and silence, only broken now and then, at long intervals, by the violent pressure of the ice as it surges along in gigantic masses. It sounds most ominous in the great stillness, and one cannot help an uncanny feeling as if supernatural powers were at hand...

FRIDTJOF NANSEN, *Farthest North*

ALABASTER PALACES

WHEN HERMAN MELVILLE COMMENTED THAT Richard Henry Dana's descriptions of rounding Cape Horn must have been written with "an icicle," he may have recalled the episode in July 1836, when Dana, a Harvard man who had shipped as a common sailor, was summoned from belowdecks to gaze at the "finest sight" he might ever see:

And there lay, floating in the ocean, several miles off, an immense, irregular mass, its top and points covered with snow, and its centre of a deep indigo color. This was an iceberg, and of the largest size, as one of our men said who had been in the Northern ocean. As far as the eye could reach, the sea in every direction was of a deep blue color, the waves running high and fresh, and sparkling in the light, and in the midst lay this immense mountain-island, its cavities and valleys thrown into deep shade, and its points and pinnacles glittering in the sun. All hands were soon on deck, looking at it, and admiring in various ways its beauty and grandeur. But no description can give any idea of the strangeness, splendor, and, really, the sublimity, of the sight. Its great size;—for it must have been from two to three miles in circumference, and several hundred feet in height;—its slow motion, as its base rose and sank in the water, and its high points nodded against the clouds; the dashing of the waves upon it, which, breaking high with foam, lined its base with a white crust; and the thundering sound of the cracking of the mass, and the breaking and tumbling down of huge pieces; together with its nearness and approach, which added a slight element of fear—all combined to give to it the character of true sublimity. The main body of the mass was, as I have said, of an indigo color, its base crusted with frozen foam; and as it grew thin and transparent toward the edges and top, its color shaded off from a deep blue to the whiteness of snow.

Richard Henry Dana, *Two Years Before the Mast*

Few people, in an age before photography, had ever seen an iceberg. So when such literate seafarers as Dana encountered such sights they would, understandably, reach for their quills.

The particular iceberg that had so impressed Dana was an outrider of the Antarctic ice pack that had baffled all attempts to discover what lay at the South Pole. Captain James Cook had been the first to realize that in size and sheer numbers these bergs dwarfed anything found in the Arctic. On January 30, 1774, he had sailed *Resolution* farther south than any explorer had yet reached—and in doing so, had discovered the pack:

A little after 4 AM we precieved the Clowds to the South near the horizon to be of an unusual Snow white brightness which denounced our approach to field ice, soon after it was seen from the Mast-head and at 8 o'Clock we were close to the edge of it which extended East and West in a streight line far beyond our sight; as appear'd by the brightness of the horizon; in the Situation we were now in just the Southern half of the horizon was enlightned by the Reflected rays of the Ice to a considerable height. The Clowds near the horizon were of a perfect Snow whiteness and were difficult to be distinguished from the Ice hills whose lofty summits reached the Clowds. The outer or Northern edge of this immence Ice field was compose[d] of loose or broken ice so close packed together that nothing could enter it; about a Mile in began the firm ice, in one compact solid boddy and seemed to increase in height as you traced it to the South; In this field we counted Ninety Seven Ice Hills or Mountains, many of them vastly large. Such Ice Mountains as these are never seen in Greenland, so that we cannot draw a comparison between the Greenland Ice and this now before us...

JAMES COOK, *Journals*

Suspecting that the pack might extend all the way to the Pole itself, Cook prudently decided to turn the *Resolution* north and ease his way back out.

Subsequent explorers, however, would probe ever deeper into that icy labyrinth. The frequent fogs made it among the most hazardous passages on Earth, but when the sun broke through, this strange, glittering world might be rendered indescribably beautiful. Lt. Charles Wilkes, who as commander of the U.S. Exploring Expedition (1838–42) laid claim to having been the first ever to sight the Antarctic continent, crowned his purely scientific observations with a rare flash of imaginative exuberance:

Some of the bergs were of magnificent dimensions, one-third of a mile in length, and from one hundred and fifty to two hundred feet in height, with sides perfectly smooth, as though they had been chiselled. Others again exhibited lofty arches of many-coloured tints, leading into deep caverns, open to the swell of the sea, which rushing in, produced loud and distant thunderings. The flight of birds passing in and out of these caverns, recalled the recollection of ruined abbeys, castles, and caves, while here and there a bold projecting bluff, crowned with pinnacles and turrets, resembled some gothic keep. A little further onwards would be seen a vast fissure, as if some powerful force had rent in twain these mighty masses. Every noise on board, even our own voices, reverberated from the massive and pure white walls. These tabular bergs are like masses of beautiful alabaster; a verbal description of them can do little to convey the reality to the imagination of one who has not been among them. If an immense city of ruined alabaster palaces can be imagined, of every variety of shape and tint, and composed of huge piles of buildings grouped together, with long lanes or streets winding irregularly through them, some faint idea may be formed of the grandeur and beauty of the spectacle. The time and circumstances under which we were viewing them, threading our way through these vast bergs, we knew not to what

Wilkes Expedition visits an iceberg, 1840

end, left an impression upon me of these icy and desolate regions that can never be forgotten.

CHARLES WILKES, *Narrative of the U.S. Exploring Expedition*

When in late 1910 Robert Scott's British Antarctic Expedition wove its careful way through the pack—the *Terra Nova* was trapped in the ice for 20 days—the men were reminded not so much of alabaster palaces as they were of Edwardian London:

> We have had a marvellous day. The morning watch was cloudy, but it gradually cleared until the sky was a brilliant blue, fading on the horizon into green and pink. The floes were pink, floating in a deep blue sea, and all the shadows were mauve. We passed right under a monster berg, and all day have been threading lake after lake and lead after lead. "There is Regent Street," said somebody, and for some time we drove through great streets of perpendicular walls of ice. Many a time they were so straight that one imagined they had been cut off with a ruler some hundreds of yards in length.
>
> APSLEY CHERRY-GARRARD, *The Worst Journey in the World*

Frederick Cook was the surgeon onboard the *Belgica,* the vessel—carrying the members of the Belgian Antarctic Expedition—that was stopped short of its destination because trapped in the pack ice. There it remained throughout the long winter of 1898. To help dispel the sense of gloom caused by the growing darkness and the ceaseless groaning of the ice, the expedition members amused themselves by studying the array of icebergs continually arrayed before them. Science, as always, soon fell away as fancy prevailed, with Cook concluding that "the eye generally sees what the mind intends to picture"—whether it is the sublime or even, on occasion, the ridiculous:

Some five or six had the form of an easy chair, others that of a giant couch, still others assumed the forms of human faces....The Captain points to a berg, not particularly attractive to anyone, but he insists in describing upon it the face and the form of a beautiful woman, chiseled in walls of alabaster....but we see only dead white cliffs. There are some irregularities, a few delicate blue lines, some suggestive hummocks, and various dark cavities; but these we see in every berg, and with our different mental attitudes we fail to recognise the ascribed topography of a human figure....Upon a small tabular berg there is a shapeless mass of ice-blocks, and these blocks are so piled that one cannot help but notice them. To me the thing seemed like a marble statue of England's Prime Minister, Salisbury, raised upon a huge, rounded block of granite. I heard Arctowski suggest the Egyptian Sphinx, but Racovitza insisted upon the likeness of a polar bear...There was, however, one man with a glass. He looked intently for an hour at the thing without saying much. This was Michotte, the cook. After we had all finished our discussions, and had come to a general agreement about the bear, he shattered our allegory with a little giggle and followed it by the announcement that it was all a mistake;—"to me it looks like a pot of boiling soup."

Frederick Cook, Through the First Antarctic Night

Howlings and Thunderings

IN March 1915, with the *Endurance*, the ship carrying Ernest Shackleton's Imperial Trans-Antarctic Expedition, having been trapped in the pack ice since January, its captain, Frank Worsley, was paying close attention to the music of the floes:

Close to the berg the pressure makes all sorts of quaint noises. We heard tapping as from a hammer, grunts, groans and squeaks, electric trams running, birds singing, kettles boiling noisily, and an occasional swish as a large piece of ice, released from pressure, suddenly jumped or turned over. We noticed all sorts of quaint effects, such as huge bubbles or domes of ice, 40 ft. across and 4 or 5 ft. high. Large sinuous pancake sheets were spread over the floe in places, and in one spot we counted five such sheets, each about 2 1/2 in. thick, imbricated under one another. They look as though made of barley sugar and are very slippery.

FRANK WORSLEY, IN ERNEST SHACKLETON, *South*

Worsley concluded that the ship would probably be all right. He was wrong. Six months later the ice crushed the *Endurance,* and the expedition members, standing on the surrounding floes, watched their last connection to the outside world slip into the deep.

Everyone survived, of course, thanks to Shackleton's inspired leadership and Worsley's lifeboat seamanship, making the story of the *Endurance* one of the great sagas in the annals of polar exploration. The crew of the *Jeannette,* however, fared differently. In late 1879, Lt. George DeLong sailed that ship north through the Bering Strait, hoping to approach the Pole from an untried direction. Yet the vessel became trapped in the ice of the Chukchi Sea. In January 1880, deep in the midwinter night, that ice got restless, and it sounded not so much like poltergeists at work as like howling demons on the rise:

The Captain points to a berg.... [T]here are some irregularities, a few delicate blue lines, some suggestive hummocks, and various dark cavities; but these we see in every berg, and with our different mental attitudes we fail to recognise the ascribed topography of a human figure...

—FREDERICK COOK

The placid and almost level surface of ice suddenly heaved and swelled into great hills, buzzing and wheezing dolefully. Giant blocks pitched and rolled as though controlled by invisible hands, and the vast compressing bodies shrieked a shrill and horrible song that curdled the blood. On came the frozen waves, nearer and nearer. Seams ran and rattled across them with a thundering boom, while silent and awestruck we watched their terrible progress. Sunk in an amphitheatre, about five eighths of a mile in diameter, lay the ship, the great bank of moving ice, puffed in places to a height of fifty feet, gradually inclosing her on all sides. Preparations were made for her abandonment, but—what then? If the mighty circle continued to decrease, escape was hopeless, death inevitable. To think of scrambling up the slippery sides of the rolling mass would be of equal folly with an attempt to scale the falling waters of Niagara.

"The ice is approaching at the rate of one yard per minute. It is three hundred paces distant; so in three hundred minutes we shall pass over to the Great Beyond."

Thus one of the crew announced his computation of the time, distance, and calamity...

GEORGE MELVILLE, *In the Lena Delta*

On that occasion, the *Jeannette* was spared. Nearly two years after she was first trapped, however, the floes finally crushed and sank the vessel; over half the ship's complement, including DeLong, either died at sea or perished of starvation on the Siberian shore.

The dramatic story of the *Jeannette* gripped imaginations everywhere, including that of Fridtjof Nansen, who upon hearing that pieces of the doomed vessel had drifted counterclockwise around the Arctic was inspired to build the truly ice-defiant *Fram,* moor her in the pack, and perhaps drift over the Pole itself. Though the *Fram* might have been the strongest wooden ship ever constructed, there were times, during the nearly three

The Sea of Ice, by Caspar David Friedrich, 1824

years that she remained caught in the ice, when even Nansen, stalking among the midnight floes surrounding the vessel, might be terrified:

There are howlings and thunderings round you; you feel the ice tremble, and hear it rumbling under your feet; there is no peace anywhere. In the semi-darkness you can see it piling and tossing itself up into high ridges nearer and nearer you—floes ten, twelve, fifteen feet thick, broken, and flung on the top of each other as if they were feather-weights. They are quite near you now, and you jump away to save your life. But the ice splits in front of you, a black gulf opens, and water streams up. You turn in another direction, but there through the dark you can just see a new ridge of moving ice-blocks coming towards you. You try another direction, but there it is the same. All around there is thundering and roaring, as of some enormous waterfall, with explosions like cannon salvoes. Still nearer you it comes. The floe you are standing on gets smaller and smaller; water pours over it; there can be no escape except by scrambling over the rolling ice-blocks to get to the other side of the pack. But now the disturbance begins to calm down. The noise passes on, and is lost by degrees in the distance.

FRIDTJOF NANSEN, *Farthest North*

Even the knowledge that such terrific upheavals were caused by wave or tide roiling the icy surface could not lessen their awe-inspiring impact. And when seen in the gloom of an Antarctic twilight, as Louis Charles Bernacchi saw it on May 22, 1899, from the comparatively safe perch of Cape Adare, it made for an unforgettable spectacle. Bernacchi, the astronomer on Carsten Borchgrevink's Southern Cross Expedition, the first ever to overwinter on the Antarctic continent, had initially heard a "deep sonorous roar...like the din of a battle":

A moving mountain of ice had risen up...and was piling the ice on the shore. It extended for about eight hundred yards, and was on an average sixty feet high; the mass was moving the whole time and advancing upon the land. The grandeur of the spectacle was immense....Huge blocks of ice, thousands and thousands of tons in weight, were lifted up 70, 80, and 90 feet with irresistible force to the top of the mount. They would totter for a few seconds, and then come crashing down with a reverberating roar, sending up white clouds like steam into the air; not one, nor two, nor three blocks at a time, but thousands. At times great yawning gaps would appear in the mount, and the whole side would bulge out until with a fearful crash it would burst, and great blocks of ice fly into the air like so many straws.

LOUIS CHARLES BERNACCHI, *To the South Polar Regions*

Trained scientist though he was, Bernacchi was nevertheless swept away by the strange moaning wail he heard above the deafening tumult. It sounded, he later said, as if "spirits were shut up within and begging piteously to be released from their icy fetters."

Curious Beasts

IF HE CAN TELL A HORSE FROM A COW," SAMUEL JOHNSON ONCE REMARKED of his friend Oliver Goldsmith, "that's the extent of his knowledge of zoology."

Yet Goldsmith's *Animated Nature,* first published in 1774, went through edition after augmented edition well into the 19th century, even though the impecunious novelist, poet, and playwright had compiled the work by cribbing from other books, happily repeating every tall tale he encountered along the way:

> It often happens, that when a Greenlander and his wife are paddling out at sea, by coming too near an ice-float, a white bear unexpectedly jumps into their boat, and if he does not overset it, sits calmly where he first came down, and, like a passenger, suffers himself to be rowed along. It is probable the poor little Greenlander is not very fond of his new guest; however, he makes a virtue of necessity, and hospitably rows him to shore.
>
> OLIVER GOLDSMITH, *A History of the Earth and Animated Nature*

Goldsmith's fanciful polar bear, however, often hid a kernel of truth:

> [The polar bear], being unmolested in these desolate climates, and meeting no animal but what he can easily conquer, finding also a sufficient

supply of fishy provisions, grows to an enormous size; and as the lion is the tyrant of an African forest, so the bear remains undisputed master of the icy mountains in Spitzbergen and Greenland. When our mariners land upon those shores, in such parts as have not been frequented before, the white bears come down to view them with an awkward curiosity...

Though preferring the ice pack to mountains, and seals to fish, polar bears are curious beasts. And as explorers nudged their way into the icy world surrounding the Poles, not the least of their memorable encounters were with animals that had rarely if ever seen a human being; animals that not only appeared unusually curious, but sometimes preternaturally human as well.

In the mid-1850s, for instance, as he pushed ever farther up the frozen straits between Greenland and Canada's Ellesmere Island, the American explorer Elisha Kent Kane established food caches along the way. He labored to make them proof against the depredations of polar bears, but it didn't always work. "The final cache, which I relied so much upon, was entirely destroyed," he reported in his phenomenally popular *Arctic Explorations.* "It had been built with extreme care, of rocks which had been assembled by very heavy labor, and adjusted with much aid often from capstan-bars as levers. The entire construction was, so far as our means permitted, most effective and resisting":

Polar bear, 1846

Yet these tigers of the ice seemed hardly to have encountered an obstacle. Not a morsel of pemmican remained, except in the iron cases, which being round, with conical ends, defied both claws and teeth. They had rolled and pawed them in every direction, tossing them about like footballs, although over eighty pounds in weight. An alcohol can, strongly iron-bound, was dashed into small fragments, and a tin can of liquor smashed and twisted almost into a ball. The claws of the beast had perforated the metal and torn it up as with a chisel. They were too dainty for salt meats; ground coffee they had an evident relish for; old canvas was a favorite, for some reason or other; even our flag, which had been reared "to take possession" of the waste, was gnawed down to the very staff. They had made a regular frolic of it; rolling our bread-barrels over the ice; and, unable to masticate our heavy India-rubber cloth, they had tied it up in unimaginable hard knots.

A moving mountain of ice had risen up...and was piling the ice on the shore. It extended for about eight hundred yards, and was on an average sixty feet high....The grandeur of the spectacle was immense....Huge blocks of ice, thousands and thousands of tons in weight, were lifted up 70, 80, and 90 feet with irresistible force to the top of the mount.

—LOUIS CHARLES BERNACCHI

ELISHA KENT KANE, *Arctic Explorations*

At the other end of the Earth, Apsley Cherry-Garrard, all too familiar with the killer whales' habit of upending ice floes so as to spill seals into the water, found that working on those floes was a little unnerving. The "killers were too interested in us to be pleasant," he recalled, and though undoubtedly imputing to them a malevolence that was not there, he nevertheless did not like the look he thought he saw in that cetacean eye:

They had a habit of bobbing up and down perpendicularly, so as to see over the edge of a floe, in looking for seals. The huge black and yellow heads with sickening pig eyes only a few yards from us at times, and always around us, are among the most disconcerting recollections I have of that day. The immense fins were bad enough, but when they started a perpendicular dodge they were positively beastly.

At one point, things got a little too disconcerting:

"Good God, look at the whales," said some one, and there, in a pool of water behind the floe on which we were working, lay twelve great whales in perfect line facing the floe. And out in front of them, like the captain of a company of soldiers, was another. As we turned they dived as one whale, led by the big fellow in front, and we certainly expected that they would attack the floe on which we stood. Whether they never did so, or whether they tried and failed, for the floes here were fifteen or sixteen feet thick I do not know; we never saw them again.

APSLEY CHERRY-GARRARD, *The Worst Journey in the World*

A member of the Belgian Antarctic Expedition had a similar encounter with a fearsome leopard seal, one of the boldest predators in those waters. When the *Belgica* was trapped in the ice pack, the scientists had little choice but to work out on the surrounding floes:

A few nights past a sea leopard interviewed the meteorologist, Arctowski. The animal sprang suddenly from a new break in the ice onto the floe, upon which Arctowski had a number of delicate meteorological instruments, and without an introduction, or any signs of friendship,

OPPOSITE: *Bowhead whale menaced by orcas, late 19th century*

the animal crept rapidly over the snow and examined Arctowski and his paraphernalia with characteristic seal inquisitiveness. The meteorologist had nothing with which to defend himself, and he didn't appear to relish the teeth of the leopard as it advanced and separated its massive jaws with a bear-like snort. He walked around the floe, the leopard after him. The seal examined the instruments, but they were not to its liking, and as to Arctowski, it evidently did not regard him of sufficient interest to follow long, for after it had made two rounds the seal plunged into the waters, swam under the ice and around the floe, and then raised its head far out to get another glimpse of the meteorologist. Thinking that the creature contemplated another attack, Arctowski made warlike gestures, and uttered a volley of sulphureous Polish words, but the seal didn't mind that. It raised its head higher and higher out of the water, and displayed its teeth in the best possible manner. Now and then its lips moved, and there was audible a weird noise, with signs which we took to be the animal's manner of inviting its new acquaintance to a journey under the icy surface, where they might talk over the matter out of the cold blast of the wind, in the blue depths below.

FREDERICK COOK, *Through the First Antarctic Night*

One creature, however, seemed to have the corner on curiosity. "No one of us whose privilege it was to be there will forget our first sight of the penguins," recalled Cherry-Garrard. "Hardly had we reached the thick pack, which prevailed after the suburbs had been passed, when we saw the little Adélie penguins hurrying to meet us. Great Scott, they seemed to say, what's this, and soon we could hear the cry which we shall never forget. 'Aark, aark,' they said":

They are extraordinarily like children, these little people of the Antarctic world, either like children, or like old men, full of their own importance and late for dinner, in their black tail-coats and white shirt-fronts—and

A penguin colony, late 19th century

rather portly withal. We used to sing to them, as they to us, and you might often see "a group of explorers on the poop, singing 'She has rings on her fingers and bells on her toes, and she shall have music wherever she goes,' and so on at the top of their voices to an admiring group of Adélie penguins."

APSLEY CHERRY-GARRARD, *The Worst Journey in the World*

James Murray would have understood. "They are the civilised nations of these regions," the biologist observed of the emperor penguins, "and their civilisation, if much simpler than ours, is in some respects higher and more worthy of the name." Murray, the naturalist accompanying Ernest Shackleton's 1907–09 *Nimrod* expedition, really believed that the birds possessed an innate curiosity. "Having fed and got into good condition," he noted, "they leave the sea and go off in parties, apparently to see the country, and travel for days and weeks":

They were curious about any unusual object and would come a long way to see a motor-car [one was brought by the expedition] or a man. When out on these excursions the leader of a party keeps them together by a long shrill squawk....The first party to arrive inspected the boat, then crossed the lake to the camp. Soon they discovered the dogs, and thereafter all other interests were swallowed up in the interest excited by them. After the first discovery crowds came every day for a long time, and from the manner in which they went straight to the kennels one was tempted to believe that the fame of them had been noised abroad.

JAMES MURRAY, IN *The Heart of the Antarctic*

"Whatever a penguin does has individuality," Cherry-Garrard admitted, "and he lays bare his whole life for all to see":

He cannot fly away. And because he is quaint in all that he does, but still more because he is fighting against bigger odds than any other bird, and fighting always with the most gallant pluck, he comes to be considered as something apart from the ordinary bird—sometimes solemn, sometimes humorous, enterprising, chivalrous, cheeky—and always (unless you are driving a dog-team) a welcome and, in some ways, an almost human friend.

APSLEY CHERRY-GARRARD, *The Worst Journey in the World*

EXTRAORDINARY TWILIGHTS

ONE DAY—IF DAY IS THE RIGHT WORD FOR A PERIOD OF CLOCK TIME in the depths of the six-month Antarctic night—the men of the Belgian Antarctic Expedition, stranded aboard the *Belgica,* itself trapped in the pack ice, saw in the distance a very curious phenomenon:

Precisely at twelve o'clock a strange rectangular block of fire appeared in the east-south-east. Its size was that of a small tabular iceberg, but it had a dull crimson glow which made the scene at once weird and fascinating. Its base rested on the horizon and it seemed to rise, brighten, and move northerly. The sky here was a purple, thinly veiled by a light smoky haze, caused by icy crystals in the lower stratus of atmosphere, but there was not another speck of redness on this side of the heavens except the orange bow usually seen over the twilight zone. We watched this with considerable awe and amazement for ten minutes before we could determine its meaning. It passed through several stages of forms, finally it separated, and we discovered that it was the moon. It was in fact a sort of mirage of the moon, but the strange rectangular distortion, the fiery aspect, and its huge size, made a sight long to be remembered.

FREDERICK COOK, *Through the First Antarctic Night*

If anything recurs time and again in the literature of Polar exploration, it is the constant wonder at the strange atmospheric phenomena to be seen at the ends of the Earth. Mock suns, or parhelions; mock moons, or paraselenae; fog bows, lunar halos, ice blinks, water skies, and the refracted images of mountain and iceberg have as much as anything else made the mystic circles seem like another planet.

Color, for one thing, is often extraordinarily fine. Reports of red snow in the Arctic captivated 19th-century readers of exploration narratives. The "Crimson Cliffs" in north Greenland were described by Elisha Kent Kane in the 1850s as having a "fine deep rose hue…all the gorges and ravines in which the snows had lodged were deeply tinted with it." Those snows may have been stained by algal blooms, but that doesn't mean there wasn't colored snow to be found elsewhere:

[T]o visualize the Antarctic as a white land is a mistake, for, not only is there much rock projecting wherever mountains or rocky capes and islands rise, but the snow seldom looks white, and if carefully looked at will be found to be shaded with many colours, but chiefly with cobalt blue or rose-madder, and all the gradations of lilac and mauve which the mixture of these colours will produce. A White Day is so rare that I have recollections of going out from the hut or the tent and being impressed by the fact that the snow really looked white. When to the beautiful tints in the sky and the delicate shading on the snow are added perhaps the deep colours of the open sea, with reflections from the ice foot and ice-cliffs in it, all brilliant blues and emerald greens, then indeed a man may realize how beautiful this world can be, and how clean.

APSLEY CHERRY-GARRARD, The Worst Journey in the World

Expedition artists, such as Scott's Edward Wilson and Shackleton's George Marston, somehow managed to evoke that beauty, despite the harshest of conditions for doing so, with a remarkable fidelity:

Marston found, as other artists have found, that Nature's color-schemes in the Antarctic are remarkably crude, though often wondrously beautiful. Bright blues and greens are seen in violent contrast with brilliant reds, and an accurate record of the colours displayed in a sunset, as seen over broken ice, would suggest to many people an impressionistic poster of the kind seen in the London streets. Words fail one in an attempt to describe the wildly bizarre effects observed on days when the sky was fiery red and pale green, merging into a deep blue overhead, and the snow-fields and rocks showed violet, green and white under the light of the moon. Marston used to delight in the "grey days," when there was no direct sunlight and the snow all around showed the most subtle tones of grey; there would be no shadows anywhere, perhaps light drifts of snow would be blowing about, and the whole scene became like a frozen fairyland. The snow-bergs and snow-fields were white under direct light, but any hollows showed a vivid blue, deepening almost to black in the depths.

ERNEST SHACKLETON, The Heart of the Antarctic

Should the midnight sun be eclipsed momentarily by cloud or mountain, however, there would be a nearly instantaneous effect. The geologist Raymond Priestley observed the "sudden change from bright light to darkness in the tent, while outside the thin surface of ice covering the thaw-water round the rocks immediately contracts with reports like a succession of pistol-shots, and sometimes breaks up and flies about in all directions, making a noise like broken glass." That was simply the quick cooling of the ice "by the cold plateau wind immediately the sun's influence is withdrawn." It was like living on the moon.

More than one moon, by the way, might be seen in the polar sky. Refraction at high latitudes is such that mock suns and mock moons are common phenomena. The careful observation of such marvels was one of the stated objectives of the 1881–84 Lady Franklin Bay Expedition, which reached the northern parts of Ellesmere Island before falling victim to the usual Arctic horrors: several relief ships failed to arrive, and as a result, 14 of the 21 men starved to death. Its leader, however, Lt. Adolphus W. Greely, proved to be a careful celestial observer:

> The halo of the 24th was one of the most beautiful I have ever seen. It was a double halo, there being two perfect concentric half-circles, distant 23° and 46° from the sun, each half-circle having a contact arch of marked clearness. Six mock suns, two on either hand and two above the real sun, appeared during a part of the day, the prismatic colors in each case being as vivid and clear as in any rainbow. For the greater part of the forenoon the heavens were filled with such glory and wealth of color as surpassed any powers of description.
>
> ADOLPHUS W. GREELY, *Three Years of Arctic Service*

During the long periods of polar twilight, ice might glow as if made of gold, and scintillate as if layered with diamonds:

Red snow in Baffin Bay, circa 1890

The bergs had wholly lost their chilly aspect, and glittering in the blaze of the brilliant heavens, seemed in the distance like masses of burnished metal or solid flame. Nearer at hand they were huge blocks of Parian marble inlaid with mammoth gems of pearl and opal. One in particular exhibited the perfection of the grand. Its form was not unlike that of the Coliseum, and it lay so far away that half its height was buried beneath the line of blood-red waters. The sun, slowly rolling along the horizon, passed behind it, and it seemed as if the old Roman ruins had suddenly taken fire.

ISAAC ISRAEL HAYES, *The Open Polar Sea*

Yet it was refraction rather than reflection that sent the explorers reaching for those quill pens. Atmospheric refraction being especially pronounced at the ends of the Earth, the looming of objects from below the horizon and the subsequent play of mirage above it would prove to be continually captivating:

A most remarkable delusion of this kind was observed by Scoresby while sailing through the open ice, far from land. Suddenly an immense amphitheatre inclosed by high walls of basaltic ice, so like natural rock as to deceive one of his most experienced officers, rose around the ship. Sometimes the refraction produced on all sides a similar effect, but still more frequently remarkable contrasts. Single ice-blocks expanded into architectural figures of an extraordinary height, and sometimes the distant, deeply indented ice-border looked like a number of towers or minarets, or like a dense forest of naked trees. Scarcely had an object acquired a distinct form, when it began to dissolve into another.

GEORG HARTWIG, *The Polar World*

> *Nature's color-schemes in the Antarctic are...often wondrously beautiful. Words fail one in an attempt to describe the... effects observed on days when the sky was fiery red and pale green, merging into a deep blue overhead, and the snow-fields and rocks showed violet, green and white under the light of the moon.*
>
> —ERNEST SHACKLETON

Such architectural comparisons perhaps reached their dizzying height with Elisha Kent Kane. Looking into the distance one July night about 11 p.m., Kane saw the base of the hills assume a "columnar character, as marked as in the basalts of Staffa." After those hills were "elevated into Champagne bottles and mushrooms," however, his imagination snapped its scientific leash:

A strip of horizon, commencing about 8° to the east of the sun, and between it and the land, resembled an extended plain, covered with the debris of ruined cities. No effort of imagination was necessary for me to travel from the true watery horizon to the false one of refraction above it, and there to see huge structures lining an aerial ocean-margin. Some of rusty, Egyptian, rubbish-clogged propyla, and hypaethral courts—some tapering and columnar, like Palmyra and Baalbec—some with architrave and portico, like Telmessus or Athens, or else vague and grotto-like, such as dreamy memories recalled of Ellora and Carli....

But this thing of refraction is supernatural throughout. The wildest frolic of an opium-eater's revery is nothing to the phantasmagoria of the sky to-night. Karnaks of ice, turned upside down, were resting upon rainbow-colored pedestals: great needles, obelisks of pure whiteness, shot up above their false horizons, and, after an hour-glasslike contraction at their point of union with their duplicated images, lost themselves in the blue of the upper sky.

ELISHA KENT KANE,
The U.S. Grinnell Expedition in Search of Sir John Franklin

Even Ernest Shackleton was not immune to the architectural fancy—or his ghost writer was willing to embellish a bit—when describing the spring sky as seen from the *Endurance*, still trapped in the frozen grip of the Antarctic ice:

A wonderful mirage of the *fata Morgana* type was visible on August 20. The day was clear and bright, with a blue sky overhead and some rime aloft. The distant pack is thrown up into towering barrier-like cliffs, which are reflected in blue lakes and lanes of water at their base. Great white and golden cities of Oriental appearance at close intervals along these cliff tops indicate distant bergs, some not previously known to us. Floating above these are wavering violet and creamy lines of still more remote bergs and pack. The lines rise and fall, tremble, dissipate, and reappear in an endless transformation scene. The southern pack and bergs, catching the sun's rays, are golden, but to the north the ice masses are purple. Here the bergs assume changing forms, first a castle, then a balloon just clear of the horizon, that changes swiftly into an immense mushroom, a mosque, or a cathedral. The principal characteristic is the vertical lengthening of the object, a small pressure ridge being given the appearance of a line of battlements or towering cliffs...

ERNEST SHACKLETON, *South*

Frederick Cook was known to embellish a bit, too, notably his claims to have been the first to climb Mount McKinley and the first to reach the North Pole, both of which have long since been exploded. But his description of an Antarctic night—not night exactly, nor day exactly, but perhaps an extraordinary twilight—has the strange ring of truth:

Elisha Kent Kane, Arctic explorer, 1852

Outside the scene was beautiful, the sun was in the south, low on the horizon, spreading golden rays over thin stratus clouds to the zenith. In the north the moon was high, and though somewhat paled by the sun it was bright, and stood out in the cold, cloudless blue like a ball of lustreless silver. The endless sea of ice under us was ridged by a line of pressure, at right angles to the line of force, which was from south-west to north-east, and separated by inky lanes of water parallel to the lines. The entire ice was a mass of quivering blue. It was thus midnight and midsummer, and New Year's Day, and to this series of strange contradictions we owe the peculiar phenomenon of seeing both the sun and the moon at the same time, and that at a nocturnal scene.

FREDERICK COOK, *Through the First Antarctic Night*

ANOTHER WORLD

DEEP ONE SEPTEMBER NIGHT IN THE 1850S, CAPTAIN B. P. HOWES WAS conning the *Southern Cross* through a violent gale between Cape Horn and the Antarctic Peninsula. As the ship plunged through the furious seas, his attention was suddenly directed aloft:

The heavens were black as death: not a star was to be seen when the brilliant spectacle first appeared. I can not describe the awful grandeur of the scene; the heavens gradually changed from murky blackness till they became like livid fire, reflecting a lurid, glowing brilliancy over every thing. The ocean appeared like a sea of vermilion lashed into fury by the storm; the waves, dashing furiously over our sides, ever and anon rushed to leeward in crimson torrents. Our whole ship, sails, spars, and all, seemed to partake of the same ruddy hues. They were as if lighted up by some terrible conflagration...through which coruscations of auroral light would often shoot in spiral streaks and with meteoric brilliancy, altogether presented a scene of terrible grandeur.... Words fail to convey any just idea of the magnificence it presented. One must see it and feel it in order to realize it.

B. P. HOWES, QUOTED IN MATTHEW FONTAINE MAURY,
The Physical Geography of the Sea

Howes had seen that most marvelous and awe-inspiring of natural phenomena, the aurora—not only seen it, but was compelled to pen a description of it for the *Southern Cross*'s log. For the closer to the ends of the Earth one gets, the more amazing—indeed overpowering, if not overwhelming—does the aurora appear.

Sublime and splendid and majestic, mysterious and terrible and unearthly—however many the adjectives, the aurora has explanations to match. To Seneca, the heavens seemed to open and "vomit flames which before were hidden in its depths." To the anonymous author of the 13th-century *King's Mirror*, the celestial lights perhaps reflected the "fire which surrounds the seas of the north and of the south," or perhaps reflected the rays of the sun when it is below the horizon, or was "produced by the ice which radiates at night the light which it has absorbed by day." Those who believed that the Earth was hollow, with immense openings at both Poles, saw in the heavenly curtains of light the evidence of forest fires raging deep in the netherworld of the planet's interior. And those who study such things today assert that the aurora marks the trail of the solar wind through the charged particles of the ionosphere.

Yet as a phenomenon the aurora has always transcended its explanations. So many travelers to the Arctic and Antarctic marveled at its spectacle that the descriptions they have left us are as abundant and diverse as their temperaments were varied. The reactions of a great many, however, are probably encapsulated in the anecdote related by George Back, the English explorer who helped survey the Arctic coasts of Canada, which he heard from a fur trader he had met:

> He was travelling in a canoe in the English River, and had landed near the Kettle Fall, when the coruscations of the Aurora Borealis were so vivid and low that the voyageurs fell on their faces, and began praying and crying, fearing they should be killed; he himself threw away his gun and knife, that

they might not attract the flashes, for they were within two feet from the earth, flitting along with incredible swiftness, and moving parallel to its surface. They continued for upwards of five minutes, as near as he could judge, and made a loud rustling noise, like the waving of a flag in a strong breeze. After they had ceased, the sky became clear, with little wind.

Sir George Back, Narrative of the Arctic Land Expedition

Some observers kept a sense of humor in the face of the sublime. One night in April 1820, for instance, Captain William Scoresby watched the aurora lick about the constellation of the Great Bear. "Ursa Major," he reported, "was at one time encircled with such a characteristic blazonry of light, that the Bear seemed to spring into figure, and to be shaking his shaggy limbs, as if in contempt of the less distinguished constellations around him."

To Lt. William Hooper, standing on the shores of Canada's Great Bear Lake, the aurora was of course a "scene of sublime and awful magnificence"; but it also resembled at one moment a giant map, its rays converging like the "lines of longitude upon a globe," and at another moment, the surging waves of the sea:

> Around and about them are wreaths and scrolls, lines and curves, masses and skirmishers of the luminous fluid, never still for an instant, but waving, rolling, advancing and retiring, folding and unfolding, fast and changeful as thought can fly...others, again, seem mighty breakers, curling and turning under and about. There was one large mass, a perfect blaze of light, which seemed to be not twenty feet above me; others with less body appearing far, far away.
>
> William Hulme Hooper, Ten Months Among the Tents of the Tuski

Lieutenant Greely, leading the Lady Franklin Bay Expedition on Ellesmere Island, observed and described numerous auroras:

Aurora borealis, 1839

The aurora of January 21st was wonderful beyond description, and I have no words in which to convey any adequate idea of the beauty and splendor of the scene. It was a continuous change from arch to streamers, from streamers to patches and ribbons, and back again to arches, which covered the entire heavens for part of the time. It lasted for about twenty-two hours, during which at no moment were the phenomena other than vivid and remarkable. At one time there were three perfect arches, which spanned the southwestern sky from horizon to horizon.

Some auroras, however, manifested themselves in unique and sometimes whimsical form. One such resembled a colossal screw, or funnel; while another seemed like a kind of celestial volcano:

It first appeared in dim patches...which gradually brightened and took the shape of a regular cone, which lasted for five minutes or more, while from its well-defined summit ascended luminous auroral clouds with a whorling or curling motion. These clouds emanated apparently from the summit of the cone, in the form of sharply defined, spasmodic puffs, such as are seen at times issuing from the smoke-stack of a locomotive.

ADOLPHUS W. GREELY, *Three Years of Arctic Service*

To Fridtjof Nansen, the aurora glittered as well as shimmered; it was music made visible—"harp music, wild storming in the darkness":

Presently the aurora borealis shakes over the vault of heaven its veil of glittering silver—changing now to yellow, now to green, now to red. It spreads, it contracts again, in restless change; next it breaks into waving, many-folded bands of shining silver, over which shoot billows of glittering rays, and then the glory vanishes. Presently it shimmers in tongues of flame over the very zenith, and then again it shoots a bright ray right up from the horizon, until the whole melts away in the moonlight, and it is as though one heard the sigh of a departing spirit. Here and there are left a few waving streamers of light, vague as a foreboding—they are the dust from the aurora's glittering cloak. But now it is growing again; new lightnings shoot up, and the endless game begins afresh. And all the time this utter stillness, impressive as the symphony of infinitude.

FRIDTJOF NANSEN, *Farthest North*

George Kennan, in the Siberian Far East, watched a spectacular aurora, one of the grandest that had been observed there in half a century. "A broad arch of brilliant prismatic colours spanned the heavens from east to west like a gigantic rainbow," the awed Kennan wrote. "At intervals of one or two seconds, wide, luminous bands, parallel with the arch, rose suddenly out of the northern horizon and swept with a swift, steady majesty across the whole heavens, like long breakers of phosphorescent light rolling in from some limitless ocean of space."

Yet Kennan, who was in his early 20s at the time, must have had a copy of the Book of Revelation at hand, for he veers from exact description and is very soon swept up in apocalyptic raptures:

In a moment the great auroral rainbow, with all its wavering streamers, began to move slowly up toward the zenith, and a second arch of equal brilliancy formed directly under it, shooting up a long serried row of slender, coloured shooting lances toward the North Star, like a battalion of the celestial host presenting arms to its commanding angel. Every instant the display increased in unearthly grandeur. The luminous bands revolved swiftly, like the spokes of a great wheel of light, across the heavens; the streamers hurried back and forth with swift, tremulous motion from the ends of the arches to the centre, and now and then a great wave of crimson would surge up from the north and fairly deluge the whole sky with colour, tingeing the white snowy earth far and wide with its rosy reflection....I could not imagine any possible addition which even Almighty power could make to the grandeur of the aurora as it now appeared. The rapid alternations of crimson, blue, green, and yellow in the sky were reflected so vividly from the white surface of the snow, that the whole world seemed now steeped in blood, and then quivering in an atmosphere of pale, ghastly green, through which shone the unspeakable glories of the two mighty crimson and yellow arches. But the end was not yet. As we watched with upturned faces the swift ebb and flow of these great celestial tides of coloured light, the last seal of the glorious revelation was suddenly broken, and both arches were simultaneously shivered into a thousand parallel perpendicular bars, every one of which displayed in regular order, from top to bottom, the primary colours of the solar spectrum. From horizon to horizon there now stretched two vast curving bridges of coloured bars, across which we almost expected to see, passing and repassing, the bright inhabitants of another world.

GEORGE KENNAN, *Tent Life in Siberia*

Far off in Antarctica, Captain Robert Falcon Scott also glimpsed those otherworldly inhabitants. Awed by the auroras playing above him, he noted in his journal:

> There is infinite suggestion in this phenomenon, and in that lies its charm; the suggestion of life, form, colour, and movement never less than evanescent, mysterious,—no reality. It is the language of mystic signs and portents—the inspiration of the gods—wholly spiritual— divine signalling. Remindful of superstition, provocative of imagination. Might not the inhabitants of some other world (Mars) controlling mighty forces thus surround our globe with fiery symbols, a golden writing which we have not the key to decipher?
>
> ROBERT FALCON SCOTT, *Scott's Last Expedition*

Robert Scott died beneath that inscrutable canopy. Perhaps he never fully understood why he had ventured to the very end of the Earth, just as Apsley Cherry-Garrard, who returned to the busy haunts of men, never fully understood why it was that he must tell of it, tell of Erebus and Terror, Morning and Discovery, of how beautiful that world could be, and how alien.

Watching those fiery symbols shimmer high in the celestial spheres, Fridtjof Nansen once posed a philosophical question—one to which he, at least, could not entirely read the answer:

> I have never been able to grasp the fact that this earth will some day be spent and desolate and empty. To what end, in that case, all this beauty, with not a creature to rejoice in it? ...*This* is the coming earth—here are beauty and death. But to what purpose? Ah, what is the purpose of all these spheres? Read the answer if you can in the starry blue firmament.

OPPOSITE: *Northern lights, by Fridtjof Nansen, 1893*

ACKNOWLEDGMENTS

A BOOK SUCH AS THIS REPRESENTS BOTH A SOLITARY JOURNEY and a team effort. Since the team brings it to fruition, it is to the team members that I owe my primary thanks. Melissa Farris designed the cover and the book's overall look with customary style and panache. Sanaa Akkach executed that design with skillful judgment and a deft touch. For the "marvelous" illustrations we are all indebted to the savvy and levelheaded Christina Simms; and those illustrations have appeared in these pages thanks to the diligence of Rob Waymouth and Meredith Wilcox. Our sharp-eyed copyeditor, Judy Klein, pulled long hours ensuring that the "i"s were dotted and the "t"s were crossed. I am especially grateful to Susan Straight for so admirably steering this bark through the mazy channels of the publishing schedule, and to Lisa Thomas, once again, for floating an idea and then seeing it gets realized.

To my associates, Renee Braden and Cathy Hunter, I cannot express how much our years working together have meant to me. Your wisdom, humor, patience, and forbearing I shall never forget.

It is said that books are also good friends—and they had better be, for on a journey such as this they must be your constant companions. I was fortunate in having at hand the National Geographic Society's truly great library, and it was in its sanctum sanctorum, the Rare Book Room, that I always found a haven from the storms besetting our workaday lives. There reposed those classics in the literature of geography and exploration that spoke so eloquently of other havens and fiercer storms, and out of which so much of this volume has been drawn. May such infinite riches always abide in such a little room.

FURTHER READING

Amundsen, Roald. *The South Pole*. London: John Murray, 1913. Austin, Mary Hunter. *The Land of Little Rain*. New York: Houghton Mifflin, 1903. Back, Sir George. *Narrative of the Arctic Land Expedition*. London: John Murray, 1836.Bank, Joseph. See Hanksworth, John. *An Account of the Voyages*. Bates, Henry Walter. *The Naturalist on the River Amazons*. London: John Murray, 1863. Bell, Gertrude. *Syria: The Desert and the Sown*. London: William Heinemann, 1907. Bernacchi, Louis Charles. *To the South Polar Regions*. London: Hurst and Blackett, 1901. Bird, Isabella. *The Golden Chersonese*. London: John Murray, 1883. Brooke, Rupert. *Letters From America*. New York: Charles Scribner's Sons, 1916. Bruce, James. *Travels to Discover the Source of the Nile, in the Years 1768, 1769, 1770, 1771, 1772 and 1773*. Edinburgh: J. Ruthven, 1790. Bruce, James. *Travels in the Great Desert of Sahara*. Edinburgh: G. G. J. and J. Robinson, 1790. Bullen, Frank. *Denizens of the Deep*. New York: Flemings H. Revell, 1904. Bullitt, Alexander Clark. *Rambles in the Mammoth Cave During the Year 1844*. Louisville: Morton and Griswold, 1845. Burckhardt, Johann. *Travels in Nubia*. London: J. Murray, 1819. Burnet, Thomas. *The Sacred Theory of the Earth*. London: R. Norton, 1681. Burton, Richard Francis. *Personal Narrative of a Pilgrimage to Al-Madinah and Meccah*. London: Tylston and Edwards, 1893. de Castañeda, Pedro. *The Coronado Expedition, 1540-1542*. George Parker Winship, trans. and ed. (Extract from the 14th Annual Report of the Bureau of Ethnology, Washington: GPO, 1896; rpt., New York: AMS Press, 1973). Cather, Willa. *My Ántonia*. Boston and New York: Houghton Mifflin Company, 1918. Catlin, George. *Letters and Notes*. New York: Wiley and Putnam, 1841. Du Chaillu, Paul. *Explorations and Adventures in Equatorial Africa*. New York: Harper and Brothers, 1861. Chapman, Abel. *Savage Sudan*. New York: G. P. Putnam's Sons, 1921. Chardin, Sir John. *Voyages du chevalier Chardin en Perse, et autres lieux de l'Orient*. London: Printed for the Author, 1711. Cherry-Garrard, Apsley. *The Worst Journey in the World: A Tale of Loss and Courage in Antarctica*. London: Constable and Company, 1922. Coleridge, Samuel Taylor. *The Collected Works of S. T. Coleridge*. London: William Pickering, 1828. Conrad, Joseph. *Heart of Darkness.Blackwood's Edinburgh Magazine* February-April 1899. Conrad, Joseph. *The Mirror of the Sea*. New York: Doubleday, Page & Company, 1916. Cook, Frederick. *Through the First Antarctic Night*. New York: Doubleday and McClure Company, 1900. Cook, James. *Journals*. See Hanksworth, John. *An Account of the Voyages*. Cooke, Samuel. *The Jenolan Caves: An Excursion in Australian Wonderland*. London: Eyre and Spottiswoode, 1889. Cooper, James Fenimore. *Pathfinder*. Philadelphia: Lea and Blanchard, 1840. Curzon, George Nathaniel. *Persia and the Persians*. London: Longmans, Green and Company, 1892. Dana, Richard Henry. *Two Years Before the Mast*. London, Harper and Brothers, 1840. Darwin, Charles. *The Voyage of the Beagle* (original title: *Narrative of the Surveying Voyages of His Majesty's Ships Adventure and Beagle Between the Years 1826 and 1836*). London: Henry Colburn, 1839. Dennis, John. *Miscellanies in Verse and Prose*. London: James Knapton, 1693. Doughty, Charles. *Travels in Arabia Deserta*. Cambridge: Cambridge University Press, 1888. Drake, Sir Francis. *The World Encompassed*. London,: N. Bovrne, 1628. Farman, Elbert Eli. *Along the Nile with General Grant*. New York: Grafton Press, 1904. Farrer, Reginald. *On the Eaves of the World*. London: Edward Arnold, 1917. Faux, William. *Memorable Days in America*. London: W. Simpkin and R. Marshall, 1823. FitzGerald, Edward Arthur. *The Highest Andes*. London: Methuen, 1899. Forbes, Rosita. *The Secret of the Sahara: Kufara*. London: Cassell and Company, 1921. Frazer, Sir James. *The Golden Bough*, 2nd ed. London: MacMillan and Company, 1900. Gray, Thomas. *The Works of Thomas Gray*. London: J. Mawman, 1816. Greely, Adolphus W. *Three Years of Arctic Service*. New York: Charles Scribner's Sons, 1894. Gregg, Josiah. *Commerce of the Prairies*. New York: Henry G. Langley, 1844. Goldsmith, Oliver. *An History of the Earth and Animated Nature*. London: J. Nourse, 1774. Hack, Maria. *Tales of Travellers for Winter Evenings*. London: Darton and Harvey, 1818. Hanksworth, John. *An Account of the Voyages*. London: Longmans, Green, and Company, 1869. Hartwig, Georg. *The Polar World*. London: Longmans, Green, and Company, 1869. Hartwig, Georg. *The Polar and Tropical Worlds*. Chicago: Hugh Heron, 1877. Hayes, Isaac Israel. *The Open Polar Sea*. New York: Hurd and Houghton, 1867. Haywood, Captain A. H. W. *Through Timbuctu and Across the Great Sahara*. London: Seely, Service and Company, 1912. Hedin Sven. *Central Asia and Tibet*. London: Hurst and Blackett, 1903. Hedin, Sven. *Through Asia*. London: Methuen and Company, 1898. Herodotus. *The Histories (Herodoti Halicarnassei historiarum libri ix)*. Oxford: Gaisford, 1840. Holdich, Colonel T. H. *The Indian Borderland, 1880-1900*. London: Methuen and Company,1901. Hooper, William Hulme. *Ten Months Among the Tents of the Tuski*. London: John Murray, 1853. Howell, James. *Familiar Letters*. London: Humphrey Moseley, 1645. Hubbard, G.E. *From the Gulf to Ararat*. New York: E.P. Dutton & Company, 1917. Huc, Evariste Régis. *Recollections of a Journey through Tartary, Thibet, and China During the Years 1844, 1845 and 1846*. New York: D. Appleton and Company, 1803. Hudson, W.H. *The Naturalist in La Plata*. London: Chapman and Hall, LD, 1892. Hudson, W.H. *Far Away and Long Ago*. New York: E.P. Dutton & Company, 1918. Hugo, Victor. *The Toilers of the Sea*. George Routledge and Sons, Limited, 1896. Humboldt, Alexander von. *Aspects of Nature*. London: Longman and Company, 1849 (Translation). Huntington, Ellsworth. *The Pulse of Asia*. Boston: Houghton, Mifflin and Company, 1907. Johnson, Willard. "Cloud Scenery of the High Plains," *National Geographic* (December 1898). Jones, Frederic Wood. *Coral and atolls*. London: Lovell Reeve and

Company, 1912. Kalm, Pehr (Peter). *Travels into North America.* Warrington, U.K.: William Eyres, 1770. Kane, Elisha Kent. *The U.S. Grinnell Expedition in Search of Sir John Franklin.* New York: Harper and Brothers Publishers, 1854. Kane, Elisha Kent. *Arctic Explorations.* Philadelphia: Childs and Peterson, 1857. Keats, John. *The Complete Poetical Works and Letters of John Keats.* Boston: Riverside Press, 1899. Kennan, George. *Tent Life in Siberia.* New York: G. P. Putnam and Sons, 1870. Kingdon-Ward, Frank. *The Land of the Blue Poppy.* Cambridge: Cambridge University Press, 1913. Kinglake, A. W. *Eothen.* London: John Ollivier, 1844. Kingsley, Mary H. *Travels in West Africa.* London: Macmillan, 1897. Kipling, Rudyard. *Kim.* London: Macmillan, 1901. Lepsius, Dr. Richard. *Letters from Egypt, Ethiopia, and the Peninsula of Sinai:* London: Henry G. Bohn, 1853. Lewis, Meriwether, and William Clark, Paul Allen, Nicholas Biddle. *History of the Expedition Under the Command of Captains Lewis and Clark.* Philadelphia: Bradford and Inskeep, 1814. Livingstone, David. *Missionary Travels and Researches in Southern Africa.* London: John Murray, 1857. Loti, Pierre. *Egypt: The Death of Philae.* London: T. Werner Laurie, 1908. Madden, R. R. *Travels in Turkey, Egypt, Nubia, and Palestine:* London: Henry Colburn, 1829. Maury, Matthew Fontaine. *The Physical Geography of the Sea:* New York: Harper and Brothers, 1855. Melville, George. *In the Lena Delta.* Boston: Houghton, Mifflin and Company, 1892. Melville, Herman. *The Encantadas* in Putnam's Magazine. New York: G. P. Putman's *Sons, 1854.* Melville, Herman. *Moby Dick.* London: Richard Bentley, 1851. Mommsen, Theodor. *Res Gestae Divi Augusti.* Berlin: Weidmann, 1883. Moseley, Henry. *Notes by a Naturalist on the Challenger.* London: Macmillan and Company, 1879. Nansen, Fridtjof. *Farthest North.* New York: Harper and Brothers Publishers, 1898. Napier, Captain John. *Edinburgh Philosophical Journal (1821-22).* Nicolson, Marjorie Hope. *Mountain Gloom and Mountain Glory: The Development of the Aesthetics of the Infinite:* New York: Cornell University Press, 1959. Palmer, Edward Henry. *The Desert of the Exodus.* New York: Harper and Brothers, 1872. Park, Mungo. *Travels in the Interior Districts of Africa.* London: John Murray, 1815. Parkman, Francis. *The Oregon Trail.* Boston: Little, Brown and Company, 1892. Pease, Sir Alfred. *The Book of the Lion.* New York: Charles Scribner's Sons, 1914. Pennant, Thomas. *A Tour in Scotland and Voyage to the Hebrides: 1772.* London: Benjamin White, 1776. Piddington, Henry. *Sailor's Horn Book for the Law of Storms.* 1844. Pigafetta, Antonio. *The First Voyage Round the World.* London: The Hakluyt Society, 1774. Poe, Edgar Allan. *A Descent into the Maelstrom. Graham's Lady's and Gentleman's Magazine* (May 1841). Polo, MarCompany *The Travels of Marco Polo.* John Frampton, 1579. Powell, John Wesley. *The Canyons of the Colorado.* Meadville, Pennsylvania: Flood and Vincent, 1895. Purdy, John *The New Sailing Directory for the Ethiopic or Southern Atlantic Ocean.* London: Richard Holmes Laurie, 1855. Richardson, James. *Travels in the Great Desert of Sahara in the Years of 1845 & 1846.* London: Richard Bentley, 1848. Ruskin, John. *Modern Painters.* New York: Charles E. Merrill and Company, 1891. de Santa-Anna Nery, Baron. *The Land of the Amazons.* New York: E. P. Dutton and Company, 1901. de Saussure, Horace-Bénédict. *Voyages dans les Alpes. 1779-1796.* Paris-Geneva: Champion-Slatkine, 1796. Scidmore, Eliza. *Java, Garden of the East.* New York: The Century Company, 1907. Scott, Robert Falcon. *Scott's Last Expedition.* New York: Dood, Mead and Company, 1913. Sears, Robert. *Wonders of the World, in Nature, Art and Mind.* New York: Robert Sears, J. S. Redfield, Clinton Hall, 1856. Selous, Frederick. *African Nature Notes and Reminiscences.* London: Macmillan and Company, 1908. Shackleton, Ernest. *The Heart of the Antarctic.* London, William Heinemann., 1909. Shackleton, Ernest. *South.* London: Heinemann, 1919. Shelley, Mary. *Frankenstein.* London: Henry Colburn, 1826. Shelley, Percy Bysshe. *Selected Letters of Percy Bysshe.* London: K. Paul, Trench, and Company, 1884. Stephen, Leslie. *Playground of Europe.* London: Longmans, Green and Company,1871. Stephens, John Lloyd. *Travels in Egypt, Arabia Petraea, and the Holy Land.* London: Harper and Brothers, 1837. Stephens, John Lloyd. *Incidents of Travel in Central America, Chiapas, and Yucatan.* London: John Murray, 1841. Stevenson, Robert Louis. *In the South Seas.* New York: Charles Scribner's Sons, 1891. Stevenson, Robert Louis. *Across the Plains with Other Memories and Essays.* London: Chatto and Windus, 1892. Synge, John Millington. *The Aran Islands.* Dublin: Maunsel and Company,1907. Thomson, Joseph. *Through Masai Land.* London: Sampson Low, Marston, Searle and Rivington, 1885. Thoreau, Henry David. *The Maine Woods.* Boston: Ticknor and Fields, 1864. Thoreau, Henry David. *Cape Cod.* Boston: Ticknor and Fields, 1865. Tomlinson, H.M. *The Sea and the Jungle.* New York, E. P. Dutton and Company, 1920. Treloar, W. P. *The Prince of Palms.* London: Sampson Low and Company, 1884. Twain, Mark. *The Innocents Abroad.* San Francisco, California and Hartford, Connecticut: H. H. Bancroft and Company, 1869. Twain, Mark. *A Tramp Abroad.* Hartford, Connecticut: American Publishing Company, 1880. Van Dyke, John. *The Desert.* New York: Charles Scribner's Sons, 1901. Wallace, Alfred Russel. *A Narrative of Travels on the Amazon and Rio Negro.* 1853. Wallace, Alfred Russel. *The Malay Archipelago: the Land of the Orang-utan, and the Bird of Paradise; A narrative of Travel, with Studies of Man and Nature, in 1869.* London: Macmillan Company, 1869. Warburton, Peter Edgerton. *Journey across the Western Interior of Australia.* London, 1875. Ward, John. *Pyramids and Progress.* London: Eyre and Spottiswoode, 1900. Weigall, Arthur. *Travels in the Upper Egyptian Deserts.* Edinburgh and London: William Blackwood and Sons, 1909. Whymper, Edward. *Travels Amongst the Great Andes of the Equator.* London: John Murray, 1892. Wilkes, Charles. *Narrative of the United States Exploring Expedition.* Philadelphia: Lea and Blanchard, 1845. Wilson, Alexander. *American Ornithology.* Philadelphia: Bradford and Inskeep, 1808-1814. Younghusband, Sir Francis. *Heart of a Continent.* London: John Murray, 1896. Yule, Sir Henry. *The Travels of Marco Polo.* New York: Scribner, 1903.

AUTHORS LIST

ILLUSTRATIONS CREDITS